Mastering VIEW, ViewSheet and ViewStore

Clive Williamson

Sigma Press, Wilmslow

© C. Williamson, 1987.

All Rights Reserved. No part of this publication may be reproduced, stored in a retrieval system, or transmitted in any form or by any means, electronic, mechanical, photocopying, recording or otherwise, without prior written permission.

First published in 1987 by

Sigma Press
98a Water Lane, Wilmslow, SK9 5BB, England.

ISBN 1 85058 051 0

Printed in Malta by Interprint Limited

British Library Cataloguing in Publication Data

```
Williamson, Clive
   Mastering VIEW, ViewSheet and ViewStore
   1. VIEW (Word Processing Program)
   I. Title
   652'.5'028553      Z52.5.V5
   ISBN 1-85058-051-0
```

Distributed by

John Wiley & Sons Ltd., Baffins Lane, Chichester, West Sussex, England.

Acknowledgments

Cover photograph and screen shots by Clive Williamson.

The graphics were drawn by the author on a BBC Micro using Robocom's Bitstik 2 CAD system with the aid of the Robo Graphics library discs. Unless otherwise stated, the examples in the book were printed on an Epson LQ800 fitted with the ESC/P Identity Module and Sans Serif alternative Font Module.

Throughout this book the abbreviation 'BBC' refers to the British Broadcasting Corporation.

For Marita in New Zealand

Preface

This book is a guide to using Acorn's VIEW family of business software, beginning with the setting up of a suitable system from scratch, then rapidly taking the user through many of the features and possibilities offered by the BBC Micro with the VIEW word processor, its companion spreadsheet ViewSheet, and the ViewStore database. The complete set of View software represents a very cost-effective way of turning the BBC Microcomputer system into a stimulating and time-saving tool in the home, classroom or office. All three products have very professional facilities, and the idea behind this book is to take the user through each program in turn, first examining its general use, then moving on to more advanced operations.

After each of the products has been mastered, the usefulness of the system can be enhanced by learning how to pass information between the separate packages. In many applications, the software's versatility is greatly increased by relatively simple techniques for transporting text and/or figures from one program's files to another. This is invaluable in the production of things like comprehensive financial reports, or standard letters and printed labels for mailshots. The linking or 'exchange' of data is the key to making full use of the software, as it transforms the useful single product into part of a very powerful system, often saving time and money as a result. The techniques involved in this information exchange are examined in the latter part of the book. The book also covers the use of other members of the VIEW family: the utilities associated with checking the spelling of documents (ViewSpell), printing them out (View Printer Drivers, and the Printer Driver Generator), and making graphical representations of data contained in, or worked out by, ViewSheet and ViewStore (ViewPlot).

VIEW Version 3

This book was written using the current VIEW version 3, which is available as an upgrade from Acorn for users of the earlier VIEW 1.4, 2.1, and HI-VIEW. Acorn now see 3.0 as the 'standard', and recommend that everyone should try to upgrade to it, as it contains a number of useful new features and has generally been tidied up a great deal, making its operation even smoother. Having used VIEW at all three stages of its development, the author definitely advises an upgrade if you can afford it, and can bear to be without your chip for a few days! VIEW 3 is fitted as standard to the Acorn/BBC Master Series 128 and Master Compact, (the ViewSheet spreadsheet is also in the Master 128), and this book is especially intended for those starting with these machines.

v

I would like to extend my thanks to the following, who have helped either directly or indirectly with the preparation of this book: Robert Macmillan, Paul Hudson and David Bell at Acorn; Clive King at Robocom; Epson UK Ltd for the use of their LX80 and LQ800 printers; and Philips Electronics for the loan of a monochrome BM7502 word processing monitor. Thanks are also due to Robin Mudge for continued inspiration, to Brian Whitehead for his graphic design ideas, and to Dave, Fenella, June, and Angie for encouragement during the project. Special thanks go to Nicki for her invaluable advice and support when it was most needed. The book was written using the VIEW word processor (version 3.0) running on a BBC Model B fitted with a 6502 Second Processor and the Sidewise ROM board.

Clive Williamson Kew, 1986

CONTENTS

CHAPTER ONE: Introduction 1
The VIEW Family 1
The Word Processor 4
The Spreadsheet 5
The Database 6
Integrating All Three programs 7
The Rest of the VIEW Family 7

CHAPTER TWO: Setting Up the System 9
The BBC Micro 9
Shadow RAM 9
6502 Second Processor 9
The Acorn Electron 10
Fitting the Software 10
The Screen 11
    Working in Colour 12
    Changing Colours on the BBC Micro 12
    Working Conditions 13
Printers 13
    Dot Matrix 13
    Daisywheel 14
    Friction and Tractor Feeds 15
    Controlling the Printer 15
    The Printer Buffer 17
The Filing System 22
    Disc Versus Cassette 22
    Using Disc Drives with the BBC Micro 22
    Types of Disc Drive 23
    Loading and Saving Files 24
    The Advanced Disc Filing System 25
    Using ADFS 25

Section One: The Word Processor

CHAPTER THREE: Word Processing with VIEW 31
The Word Processor 31
What Can a Word Processor Do? 32
A Word Processor's Facilities 32
Starting with VIEW 34
Altering Your Text 38
Reformatting the Text 39
Turning Off Justification 39
Pressing BREAK by Mistake 40
Screen Modes 41
Saving and Loading Your Text 44
Printing Out Your Text 45
VIEW'S Page Layout 46
SHEETS 46

CHAPTER FOUR: Improving the Page Layout 47
Laying Out the Text 47
Making Up Your Own Rulers 49
    Using TABs 49
Stored Commands 50
    Page Length (PL) 52
    Left Margin (LM) 52
    Page Eject (PE) 53
    Line Spacing (LS) 53
    Top, Bottom, Header and Footer Margins 54
    Headers and Footers 55
    Setting Registers (SR) 56
    Creating a 'Start' File 57
Line Layout 58
Creating a Help Page 59

CHAPTER FIVE: Printing from the VIEW Family 61
Using a Pre-Made Driver 61
Microspacing 64
Making Your Own Driver 64
Printing Several Files at Once 66
Printing Several Identical Copies 67
Printing Problems 67

CHAPTER SIX: Common VIEW Problems 69
Running Out of Memory 69
Using Separate Files 70

Continuous Processing 71
Can I Save a Section of Text? 74
Dealing with Error Messages 74
Problems with VIEW 1.4 75
Problems with VIEW 2.1 76

CHAPTER SEVEN: Advanced Techniques 81
Speeding Up Your Work 81
Speeding Up the Cursor 81
Using Markers 83
Writing with a Scratch Pad 83
Saving and Loading Portions of Text 84
Finding Words in the Text 85
Copying Sections of Text 90
Using Function Keys 90
Printing Books and Reports 94
Standard Letters 96
Address Labels 100
ViewSpell 102
ViewIndex 103

Section Two: The Spreadsheet

CHAPTER EIGHT: ViewSheet 107
About Spreadsheet Software 107
What to Look For in a Spreadsheet 109
ViewSheet 110
Starting a Simple Spreadsheet 111
Improving the Look of the Example Sheet 116
The Numerical Format 116
Protecting Your Work 117
Deleting Unwanted Rows and Columns 118
Printing Out the Sheet 119

CHAPTER NINE: Spreadsheet Applications 121
The Spreadsheet as a Calculator 121
Tables and Price-Lists 124
The Spreadsheet as Database 129
An Insurance List 129
ViewSheet's Mathematical Operators and Functions 132

CHAPTER TEN: Advanced use of ViewSheet 137
ViewSheet's Windows 137
The Window Parameters 138
Printer Windows 140

ix

Saving the Window Definitions 140
Designing Spreadsheets 141
Problems Using ViewSheet 142
Complex Examples on ViewSheet 142
Expanding the Sheet Further 147
Tying the Sheets Together 147

Section Three: The Database

CHAPTER ELEVEN: Introduction to ViewStore 157
What is a Database? 157
ViewStore 158
Starting a Simple Database 160
Designing the Database 161
Running ViewStore 162
Defining the Database Format 164
Moving the Cursor 166
Saving the Details So Far 170
Entering Data 170
Searching the Data 171
More Advanced Searches 171
Making Complex Selections 174
Making a Select File 174
Obtaining Reports 175
Complex Reporting 175
Generating Mailing List Labels 179

CHAPTER TWELVE: ViewStore Examples 181
Mailshot and Standard Letters Database 181
Accounting 188
Office Administration 190
Library (Stock and Issues) 197

CHAPTER THIRTEEN: ViewStore Hints and Tips 203
Running Out of Room Using the Report Utility 203
Rebuilding Indexes after using Convert 203
Indexes on Entering Data 204
Scrolling Fields 204
Database Drive 204
Backing Up Your Work 204
The Difference between Alphanumeric and Textual Field Types 204
F. Report 204
Selecting on Blank Fields 205
Using Wildcard Characters 205
Sort memory 205

x

Printer Drivers 205
BASIC Utilities 206
Editing Report Format Files 206
Importing Corrupt Databases 207
Final Report Editing 207
Case Sensitivity in Non-standard DFS 207
File Sizes and Utilities 207
Bytes to Reserve - Load Time Tradeoff 207
Writing Utilities 207
Label Utility 208
Entering Records 208
Report Format File Prefix 208
Minimal space after using the Setup Utility 208

Section Four: Integration

CHAPTER FOURTEEN: Integration 211
Linking the VIEW Products 211
Simple Exchange Using *SPOOL 213
Reading Files into VIEW 217
From ViewStore to VIEW: Alternative Methods 217
    Macros 217
Reading Entire Database Files 218
From ViewSheet to ViewStore 220
From ViewStore to ViewSheet 225
Links from the REPORT Utility 225
VIEWPLOT 231
OVERVIEW 233

CHAPTER ONE

Introduction

The rapid development of the personal computer has prompted a radical change in the way people use words and numbers at home, at school, and in the office. Today it is possible to manipulate this 'data' - the term used for information held in a computer - in ways which would have seemed remarkable a few years ago. For a relatively small outlay it is now easy to set up a computer system that can relieve the drudgery of typing, process lots of facts and figures in various ways, and dramatically increase the efficiency and versatility of a single person in a range of different environments. If the microcomputer is sensibly applied it is capable of giving exciting results in four major areas - word processing, data processing, spreadsheet analysis and telecommunications - and this book deals extensively with the first three, using Acorn's VIEW range of software. Telecommunications is also covered to a small extent in the context of dealing with text to be sent or received text over electronic mail systems via a BBC micro.

The VIEW Family

It is difficult to categorise the VIEW 'family': it could simply be called 'business' software, on the grounds that it emulates (and occasionally improves on) many of the features found in costly commercial packages of word processor, spreadsheet and database programs. The VIEW products can also legitimately be described as 'home' software, since they can find many uses in a home of the '80s, where several members of a family use one personal computer to perform similar, or widely differing, functions. The pricing of the main VIEW programs is certainly more in line with home computer software than that of a typical business package! The VIEW range can also be seen as a useful educational tool, giving pupils the option of writing and revising text, entering and processing data, and performing complex scientific or business-style predictions and calculations.

Ultimately, the best way to look at the VIEW family is as a very cost-effective way of extending the use of the BBC Micro system. The same micro that is used to play games or control a robot can be converted instantly into a word processor, a spreadsheet, or a database. Thus VIEW is one way of transforming the BBC Micro into a functional tool, whether it be for business, home or educational use. The BBC Micro, and to some extent the Acorn Electron, can be tailored to suit individual needs. A typical system consisting of a BBC Micro, a TV or monitor, a printer, some sort of storage device (e.g. a cassette recorder, or preferably one or more disc drives) and one of the VIEW software products, is the starting point for a whole range of business-type activities.

In addition to the micro's capacity to help in business when used on its own - as a 'stand-alone' device - there is the possibility of linking it up with the outside world. Once a body of text has been entered into the computer, it is a simple matter to send that text from one computer to another by exchanging discs, or through a local area network of similar computers, or more dramatically, by means of an Electronic Mail or Telex system using the telephone. The trend towards the uniting of computer technology and telecommunications is growing rapidly. Now that communications hardware is so cheap and easy to use, there is already the potential for every micro owner to send and receive text electronically all over the world. It seems likely that Electronic Mail will become much more widespread in the future, with instant telephone line access to magazines and databases held on computers. The VIEW range of software offers a way of preparing for, and responding to, the Information Age - through the medium of the BBC Micro.

Two major products are associated with the VIEW word processor - the ViewSheet spreadsheet, and ViewStore, a database which requires discs for storing its information - both are quite complex, and need some commitment to get the best results. This book aims to help users through the initial stages of working with each one, and moves on to give specific examples of their use.

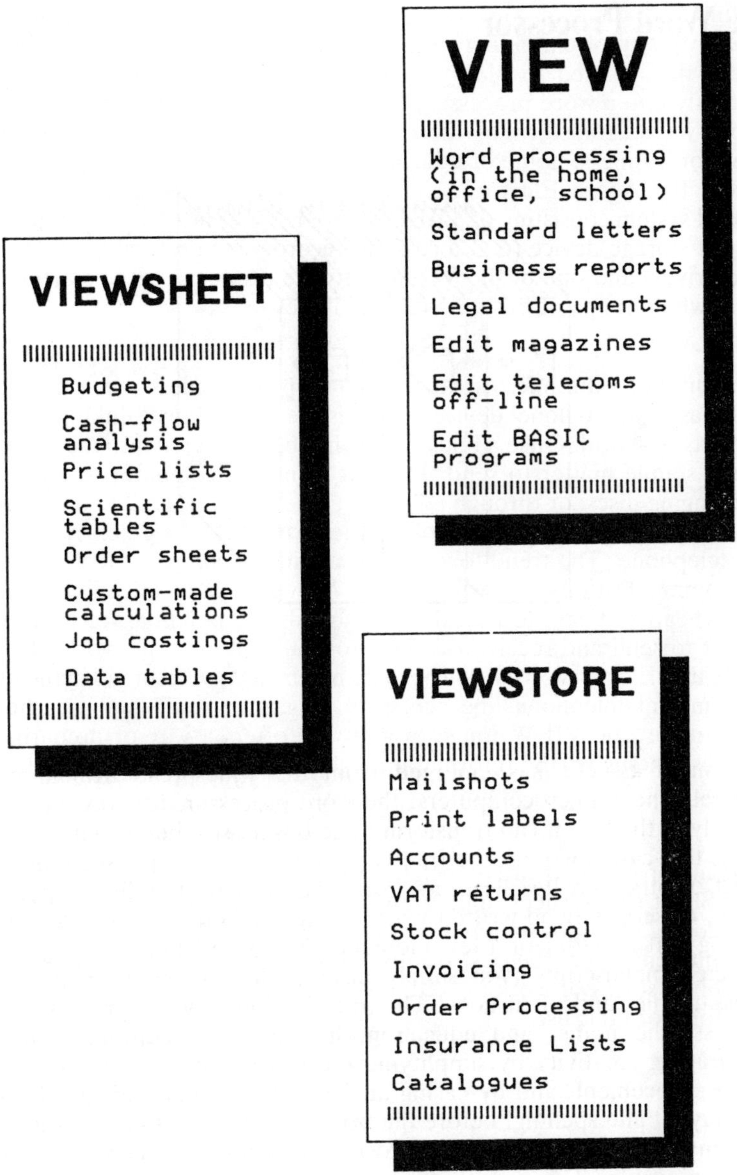

VIEWSHEET

Budgeting

Cash-flow analysis

Price lists

Scientific tables

Order sheets

Custom-made calculations

Job costings

Data tables

VIEW

Word processing (in the home, office, school)

Standard letters

Business reports

Legal documents

Edit magazines

Edit telecoms off-line

Edit BASIC programs

VIEWSTORE

Mailshots

Print labels

Accounts

VAT returns

Stock control

Invoicing

Order Processing

Insurance Lists

Catalogues

Figure 1.1 Typical uses for the three main VIEW products

The Word Processor

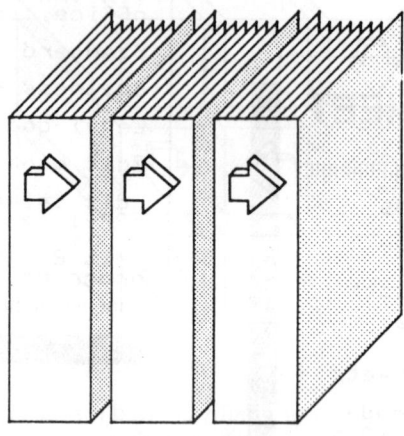

One major benefit has emerged from the widespread availability of relatively cheap microcomputers: the word processor. It is revolutionary, not only in the way it can transform large businesses, but also in its ability to free the 'casual writer', the free-lance journalist, the club secretary, and a host of other small-scale users, from the burden of endless repetitious typing, or scruffy hand-written work. It has made the task of editing and revising text a matter of a few moments. No more laborious re-typing of corrected manuscripts: you simply instruct the computer to 'print' the necessary file, and off it goes! The introduction of word processing into business, the home, and education, has had the additional effect of encouraging creativity by simplifying the process of moving text around within a document, and by easing analysis of the work and the checking of its layout and spelling, before the printing out stage. Once the chore of re-typing is removed, the whole process of writing can become freer and more enjoyable. The results can read better, and can also look more professional! Anyone with a word processor can produce impeccably finished work. The only variable is the quality given by the final output device - the printer - and here it is a case of choosing something that will suit your requirements and your pocket!

The Spreadsheet

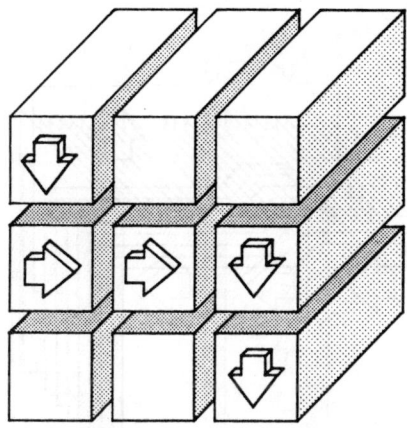

This innovative concept was originally created for the Apple II by Visicorp, and was instantly recognised and taken up by businesses as a valuable asset. The spreadsheet allows 'what if?' predictive analysis of cash-flow, the development of financial, statistical and scientific tables, and generally enables large numbers of interrelated calculations to be performed and neatly presented by a computer with the minimum of fuss. Text can readily be included in a spreadsheet, in the form of headings, instructions and comments.

A complete spreadsheet calculation is known as a 'model', and since a host of different models can be created, saved onto disc and updated at any time, the same original program can be used to handle many different types of calculations. The beauty of the spreadsheet is that it is usually set up from scratch, and hence can be tailored to all sorts of different uses. This type of software is by no means limited to the office, however, as it can be turned readily to less demanding tasks such as home budgeting, setting up calculation tables to check on mortgage repayments, and even small-scale accounting. In schools the spreadsheet can present experimental results in tabular form, or as graphs using extra plotter software, and is excellent for working out exam mark averages and totals. Acorn's spreadsheet program, ViewSheet, offers advanced facilities which allow different parts of a large-scale model to be seen on the screen at the same time, using adjustable 'windows' onto the sheet; it also allows the results from one sheet to update another. The output of ViewSheet can either be sent directly to a printer, or used as part of a report on the VIEW word processor.

The Database

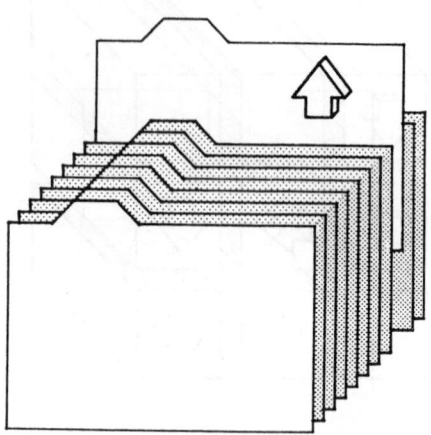

The database is the computer version of any filing system from a card index to a filing cabinet. The amount of information that can be filed is usually limited by the capacity of the disc drive or drives used to store the data. Properly used, a database such as ViewStore can be a great asset to a business or club, and can also do useful work in the home environment. The job of a club secretary provides a good example: if a database is kept of members names and addresses and their subscription renewal date, monthly mail shots can be produced automatically by the computer the month before the subscriptions fall due, consisting of reminder letters and address labels to go with them. Given more data about individual members, the database could also be interrogated to find those living in the same area, or of similar age or interests.

It is usually possible to examine the data held in the database in various ways, sorting it alphabetically or numerically, selecting individual records that conform to a specified range of values, and performing calculations on its numerical contents. Often a database has to be configured in a set format before it can be used to store data, so a degree of thought is necessary in the initial stages to get the best results from the system. Thus the database can be incredibly powerful - it also tends to be the most complex and demanding business software to set up satisfactorily.

Integrating All Three Programs

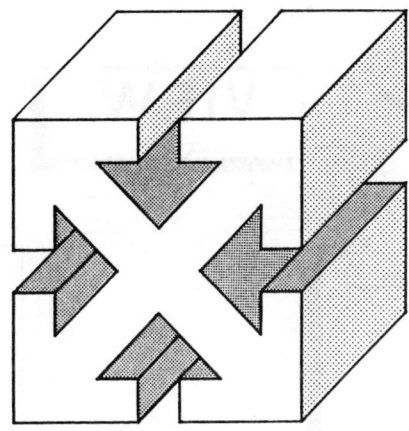

The individual VIEW products can all be run quite happily on their own - there is no need to buy all three - but their usefulness increases by leaps and bounds when they are used in combination. Provision has been made to pass information from both ViewSheet and ViewStore into the VIEW word processor, and this powerful feature means that very complex reports can be created using two or more of the packages. In addition, special links can be made between the spreadsheet and database, so that reports generated on ViewStore automatically update ViewSheet's files. This can be particularly useful in things like accounting, budgeting and stock control, where advanced mathematical treatments need to be performed on information best handled initially in database form.

The Rest of the VIEW Family

Other members of the VIEW family add still more to the versatility of the system. ViewSpell is a program accompanied by 70,000 word dictionary, which provides automatic checking of the spelling in VIEW documents. ViewIndex allows the preparation of indexes, helping in the production of complete books on the BBC system. It is also possible to obtain a graphical representation of numerical data from ViewSheet and ViewStore on the screen. The graphs obtained from ViewPlot can either be used as on-screen illustrations, printed out as part of a report, or photographed to be included in slide shows or overhead transparency presentations.

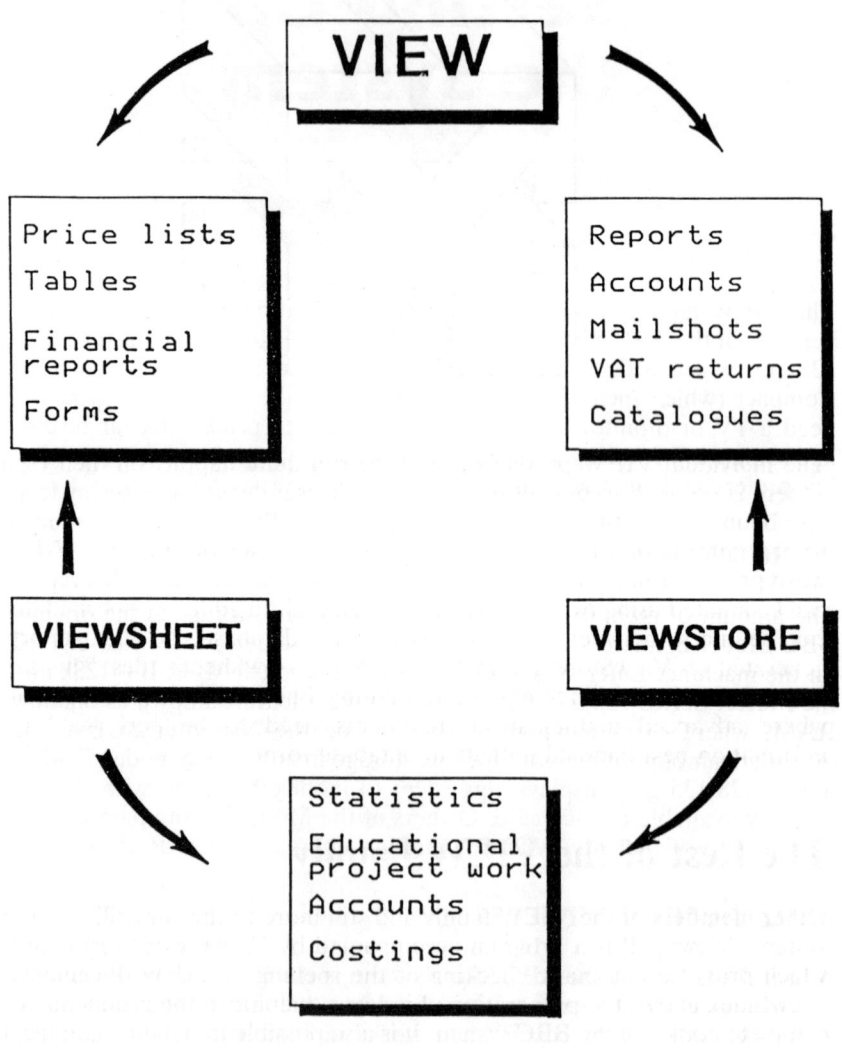

Figure 1.2 Links between VIEW, ViewSheet and ViewStore.

CHAPTER TWO

Setting Up the System

The BBC Micro

The VIEW family of business software is compatible with all the current versions of the BBC Micro: the Model B; B+; B+ 128k; the Master Series 128 (on which VIEW and ViewSheet are fitted as standard); and the Compact (which includes VIEW). Apart from the micro itself, you will need a TV or monitor of some kind, a printer to print out your results, and some way of storing your data. You can get by with a cassette recorder, but preferably you should use one or more disc drives.

Shadow RAM

The amount of memory available for text and data storage in the original BBC Model B micro was dependent on which screen mode was selected on the machine. Later versions of the BBC Micro (the B+, B+ 128k and the Master Series 128 and Compact) all have a feature known as Shadow RAM, where extra memory is fitted inside the computer to give the maximum amount of memory for text storage in any screen mode. Shadow modes 128-135 give displays equivalent to modes 0 - 7, but with the full memory available in each case. Owners of the Model B can upgrade their machines to this facility by buying and installing a Shadow RAM board.

6502 Second Processor

A useful addition to the BBC Micro system is the 6502 Second Processor, which connects to the main machine by way of the 'Tube' interface socket. This 64k RAM 'co-processor' then works in conjunction with the BBC Micro to give greater memory capacity to the system, and faster processing time. The main machine handles all the screen display, input and output and keyboard routines, leaving the co-processor to get on with running the program in question. The two processors together run software roughly half as fast again as the ordinary BBC B or B+, making actions like searching or scrolling through VIEW text significantly faster. Disc-handling routines are also speeded up. This add-on is particularly useful to users of the Model B, as it makes the amount of memory available for storage independent of screen mode, with approximately 30k bytes of RAM free when using the early versions of VIEW, or the current ViewSheet and ViewStore. A bonus for VIEW users is the increase in available memory when using Version 3.0, which automatically re-locates in the Second Processor to give about 47k of text storage (or roughly 8000 words). (Acorn make a 65C12 Turbo co-processor board, which is specially designed to be fitted inside the Master machine, and gives similar features to that of the Second Processor described above, but with a slight increase in speed over the original design.)

The Acorn Electron

An Electron fitted with the **PLUS 1** interface can run both VIEW and ViewSheet software, in the form of plug-in ROM cartridges. The Electron is essentially a cut-down version of the BBC Micro, running the same BASIC language, and having compatible cassette storage. It is a viable alternative to the Beeb where cost is an important consideration, although the addition of a PLUS 3 disc system and the PLUS 1 expansion combination to the Electron reduces the price advantage to some extent.

Acorn have a policy of continual development, so upgrades may be made to the specification of the machines mentioned above, or new models may be released which offer different facilites and features. Generally though, any upgrades are likely to be compatible with the existing range of VIEW software.

Fitting the Software

VIEW, ViewSheet and ViewStore are usually supplied in the form of plug-in ROM chips, which is a great bonus, as the software lies dormant inside the micro ready to be called up instantly, rather than needing to be loaded in from cassette or disc each time.

Software supplied in ROM form must be installed inside the micro in one of its spare sideways ROM sockets. This can normally be done by your dealer at the time of purchase, but in the event of having to do it yourself, precise details are included with all the VIEW language ROMs. Before you fit a ROM, you must decide whether you want the language in it to override the BASIC chip when the BBC Micro is switched on so that the machine comes on automatically running one of the VIEW programs instead of BASIC. This is governed by the order in which the chips are placed inside the micro. The highest-numbered socket (i.e. the socket to the right on a Model B, or to the back of the machine on later models) takes precedence when the machine is switched on (or when it is completely reset by pressing the Control (**CTRL**) and **BREAK** keys together).

If BASIC is given precedence, and VIEW or one of the other VIEW programs is placed in a lower-numbered socket, then the word processor can be switched on by entering:

*WORD <RETURN>

Similarly, ViewSheet and ViewStore are switched on by typing:

*SHEET <RETURN>

and

*STORE <RETURN>

respectively. To get back to the BASIC language, the same form of command is required:

*BASIC <RETURN>

Pressing the **BREAK** key will reset the machine to the currently selected language ROM, whereas a 'hard reset' (pressing **CTRL** and **BREAK** together) will restore whatever language is placed in the highest-numbered socket. In the case of the Master Series 128, the 'Control Panel' program in the introductory software can be used to configure the micro to run any of the language ROMs fitted inside as soon as it is switched on or given a hard reset.

The Screen

Most domestic BBC Micro users connect the machine's UHF output to a standard television set. This produces a reasonable display, but in applications where prolonged use is anticipated, the slightly blurred image obtained on a domestic television can be extremely tiring to watch. A sharp picture is particularly important when using the 80 character per line display. As family users will probably end up buying a second set of some sort anyway - if only to put an end to the fights for the TV set - the solution could be to obtain a high-definition colour monitor. This could handle the fine detail created by the BBC Micro, making it equally suited to games, educational and business use. Purely business users will probably select a very sharp monochrome monitor with a green or orange screen. In all, the BBC Micro is equipped with three different sorts of outputs for driving visual displays, and is hence capable of feeding a wide variety of televisions and monitors.

Working in Colour

You can readily obtain different coloured text using VIEW (and the other VIEW family software) so if you are using a colour monitor, you may prefer to change the normal display from white text on black to something a little less hard on the eye. Good combinations are green, yellow or pale blue on black, or white on dark blue. If you are using a low resolution colour monitor in an 80 column mode, it is often best to go for the green text colour, as this is easy to read, and only uses one colour 'gun' in the monitor's tube, so it can often give sharper results as there are no registration problems.

Changing Colours on the BBC Micro

To change the screen colour, you need to go into your selected mode, then enter a series of characters in the Command mode: for green text, you should hold down the **CTRL** key, then press the following key sequence:

S A B @ @ @

The text colour will change to green as soon as you press the last '@' character, and you can then let go of the **CTRL** key. (If you are familiar with BBC BASIC, you will realise that this is the equivalent of using a VDU 19 command, but if you aren't, never mind!) Note that this only works in modes 0 - 6; not Mode 7.
The sequences for other useful colours are as follows:

For yellow: **S A C** @ @ @

For cyan (pale blue): **S A F** @ @ @

and to restore the normal white text: **S A G** @ @ @

To keep the foreground white, but change the background colour to dark blue, enter:

S @ D @ @ @

again, keeping the **CTRL** key pressed the whole time. To restore the black background, use:

S @ @ @ @ @

Working Conditions

It is not a good idea to work with a monitor under fluorescent lights because the lighting can interfere with the display on some sets and give rise to imperceptible but disturbing 'strobing' effects (i.e. rapid changes in the brightness of the screen image). Using a long-persistance orange or P39 green screen monochrome monitor will give the best results under these conditions, but note that the latter is unsuitable for fast-moving graphics displays, as they will appear blurred. Some people are adversely affected by the static electricity given off by colour TV tubes, and if you are, it is a good idea to have a humidifier or ioniser nearby to neutralize the effects of the set. Failing that, at least try to establish a flow of fresh air in the room! To avoid the possibility of eye strain, it is best to work at the micro in relatively short bursts if you can, with rest periods or different activities in between.

Printers

A printer is often the first major add-on bought for a computer system, whether it be for examining and correcting listings of a BASIC program under development, simple word processing, or to produce pictures by making dot-for-dot representations of the micro's screen graphic images (known as 'screen-dumps'). A printer is certainly an important part of any business set-up, as the quality of printed output is the thing most seen by others, and ultimately affects the business's image. The BBC Micro supports a wide variety of printers as it is fitted with two connections (or 'interfaces') for them: the Centronics parallel and the RS423 Serial types. The latter is compatible with the more common RS232 interface, and most printers are fitted either with this, or a Centronics interface, or both. The printers most often used for word processing and business use are the dot matrix and daisywheel types.

Dot Matrix

These are the most popular, being relatively cheap, fast and capable of producing both textual and graphic output. The printing is achieved by a vertical line of tiny pins mounted in a print head, which moves across the paper, printing by impact through an inked ribbon as it goes. Each character is made up of a matrix of tiny dots produced by the pins, and the quality and shape is determined by the number of dots used.

```
Example Printout from the Epson LX80
Example Printout from the Epson LX80
Example Printout from the Epson LX80
Example Printout from the Epson LX80
Example Printout
Example Printout from the Epson LX80
Example Printout from the Epson LX80
```
Example Printout from the Epson LX80

Figure 2.1 Print styles from a dot matrix printer (the Epson LX80).

Print speeds are relatively fast, and are usually quoted as being around 80-160 characters per second. The noise levels from dot matrix printers are quite high, but new designs are improving on this problem. In the past, the print quality from a dot matrix printer was not quite up to letter standard, but recent improvements have brought the output of many models pretty close to it! A large number are now available with Near Letter Quality (NLQ) modes, and these can give extremely good results, albeit at a lower print speed than the normal 'draft' mode. It is usually possible to obtain a large number of other print styles (such as condensed, double width and bold typefaces) by sending 'control codes' to the printer.

Daisywheel

Daisywheel printers produce a 'typewriter' style of output using a plastic or metal wheel with characters on spokes round a central hub. The wheel is spun to position the correct character and a typewriter impact action makes it strike the paper through a ribbon. This sort of printer is usually much slower than the dot matrix variety (giving only 10-20 characters per second on the inexpensive versions), but its output is of correspondence quality, making it eminently suited to business and professional use. Carbon ribbons give a crisper result than the traditional inked variety. This sort of printer is usually very noisy in operation, and is generally more expensive than dot matrix models.

```
Typical text quality from
a daisywheel printer.
ABCDEFGHIJklmnop123456789
```

Figure 2.2 Print style from a typical daisywheel printer.

Friction and Tractor feeds

Apart from choosing the type of printer and interface, another important option when buying a printer is whether to use paper supplied in 'fan-fold' form or separate sheets. Some printers can cope with both sorts of paper, others need extra parts to convert them to one or other type of feed. Fan-fold paper has sprocket holes down both sides, which allow it to be pulled through the printer on cogs positioned on both sides of the paper path. The system is known as tractor feed, and sticky address labels are often supplied on backing paper for use in this way. A range of printing paper is supplied in this form, including good quality cartridge, and the sprocket holes are punched on perforated strips which can be torn off to leave a perfectly straight edge. It is even possible to have individual sheets of headed note paper set into a fan-fold for use in this way.

In the case of separate sheets, or continuous rolls without sprocket holes, a friction feed is needed. This works on the same lines as a typewriter, using contact with a rubber roller to pull the paper through. You may have to feed each sheet in by hand (a very tedious process) or buy a relatively expensive optional cut-sheet feeder which does the job automatically.

Often printers come with either fricton or tractor feed as standard, and you have to pay extra to get the other option fitted, so it is important to check that the printer you buy can use the right sort of paper for your needs. On some tractor-fed printers the sprockets can be adjusted to take different widths of paper or labels, and some of the more expensive printers can take paper up to 15 inches wide, making them highly suitable for producing things like legal documents or complex spreadsheet printouts.

Controlling the Printer

Normally the BBC Micro needs a command to turn the printer on and off, but this is not necessary when printing from the VIEW range as the software takes care of the switching automatically. No extra commands are needed if the interface you are using is the Centronics type since this uses the computer's default setting, but things aren't so easy if you use the RS423 interface or an Econet network. In either case an *FX call must be issued to change the interface the printer output is sent to:

> *FX 5,2 selects the serial output (for RS423). *FX 5,4 selects printing on the Econet network. *FX 5,1 reselects the Centronics parallel printer output.

Information is normally sent to the RS423 interface at a specific rate of 9600 baud (meaning 9600 bytes per second), but not every serial printer can accept this rate, so you may have to use another ***FX** command (in this case ***FX** 8) to set a new transmission rate to match your printer. The following is a complete list of the options in the BBC Micro:

*FX8,1	75 baud
*FX8,2	150 baud
*FX8,3	300 baud
*FX8,4	1200 baud
*FX8,5	2400 baud
*FX8,6	4800 baud
*FX8,7	9600 baud
*FX8,8	19200 baud

While some printers need to be sent data at a specific rate, others can be switched to work with different rates, in which case try a fairly high rate, such as 9600 first, and reduce this if you experience any difficulty with the system. As 9600 is the default setting at the BBC Micro end, there is no need to use ***FX** 8,7 if your printer works when set to this rate. (The fastest 19200 rate is unusual, and not actually guaranteed to work by Acorn.)

Another **FX** call, ***FX**6, can be used to prevent certain characters from reaching the printer. The BBC Micro suppresses character 10 by default (the line feed character) so that extra gaps do not occur between lines of print on a printer that performs its own 'carriage return' automatically at the end of each line.

The exact codes required to control features such as print style and density on dot matrix printers vary from one machine to another, but in general a stream of VDU commands can be used from BASIC, separated by commas. The manual supplied with your printer should give precise details of all the control codes, but your dealer - or the printer manufacturer - may be able to help if you have any problems making the machines do what you want! It is possible to buy plug-in ROMs for the BBC Micro that can give full control of your printer's features, and the VIEW Printer Drivers can be used to send different control sequences to your printer, so that sections of text marked with Highlight characters 1 and 2 (**SHIFT** *f4* and **SHIFT** *f5*) at the writing stage can automatically appear underlined or bold when the text is printed out (see Chapter Five).

At the printer end there is one key thing that must be set up. There are usually some tiny sets of switches - known as 'DIP' switches - somewhere inside, and by consulting the printer's manual it should be possible to find which one of these switches governs a feature called 'auto line feed'. This should be set on, otherwise you will get all the printed output on one line of the paper! Auto line feed advances the paper automatically each time your software sends a return character at the end of a line to be printed.

The Printer Buffer

Once you begin printing from the VIEW software, your micro will be 'tied up' until it has been able to send all the data to the printer. The time taken to do this depends on the size of the internal memory in the printer (known as the 'buffer') - the larger the buffer, the sooner your micro will be free to do something else. A 2K buffer is quite normal now, but with RAM chips getting cheaper all the time, this figure is starting to increase. If the hold-ups caused by printing are a real problem, you may consider purchasing an external printer buffer as an add-on for your computer system. The BBC Master Series Turbo comes with software to make some of the machine's internal RAM act as a printer buffer.

A Menu Program to Switch Epson Printer Functions

As you are likely to need to set up your printer quite often, here is a printer menu program for use with Epson dot matrix printers. The program is suitable in its given form for the LX80 and LQ800 models, but most of the selections will work with the rest of the Epson range. If you own a different make of dot matrix printer you may be able to adapt the listing to your own needs with careful study of your printer manual. Some of the available typefaces are shown in Figure 2.4.

```
   10 MODE7: REM (c) CLIVE WILLIAMSON 1986
   20 DIM menu$(9)
   30 DIM choice(9)
   40 PROCinit
   50 PROCpage
   60 PROCprinton
   70 PROCselect
   80 END
   90 :
  100 DEFPROCpage
  110 VDU23,1,0;0;0;0;
  120 VDU 28,3,31,39,5
  130 FOR A%= 0 TO 3:PRINT TAB(0,A%);white$;ground$
  140    NEXT
  150 PRINTTAB(9,1);CHR$(141);blue$;T$
  160 PRINTTAB(9,2);CHR$(141);blue$;T$
  170 FOR B%= 4 TO 23
  180    PRINT TAB(0,B%);blue$;ground$
```

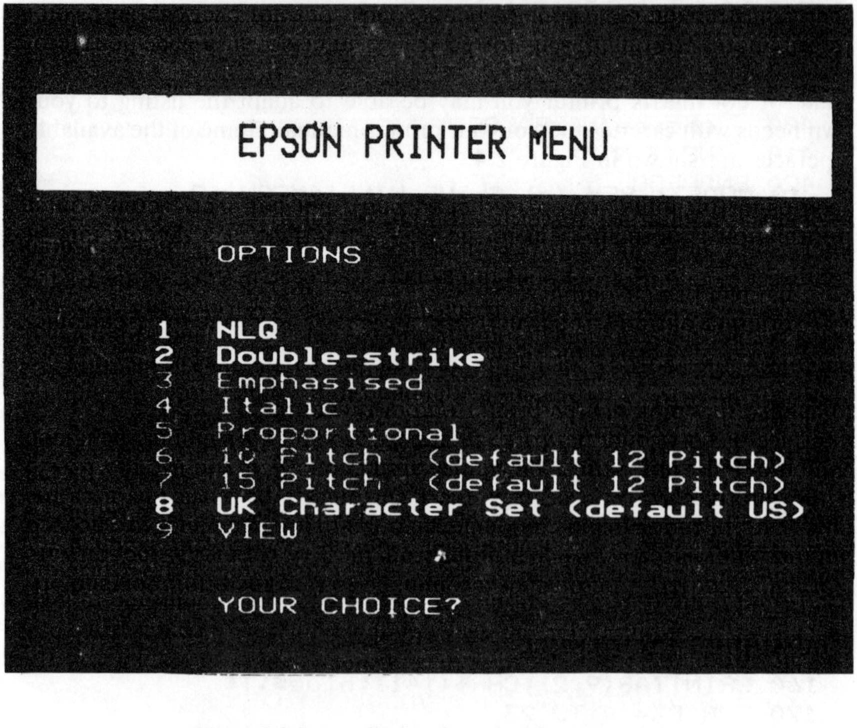

Figure 2.3 Screen displays from the Menu program.

```
  190    PRINT TAB(3,B%);cyan$
  200    NEXT
  210 ENDPROC
  220 :
  230 DEFPROCprinton
  240 PRINT TAB(12,7);"TURN PRINTER ON"
  250 PRINT TAB(7,9);"(then press the SP
ACE BAR)"
  260 input=GET
  270 REPEAT UNTIL input=32
  280 PRINT TAB(12,7);SPC(15)
  290 PRINT TAB(7,9);SPC(26)
  300 VDU2,1,27,1,64,3: REM initialises
the printer
  310 ENDPROC
  320 :
  330 DEFPROCinit
  340 T$="EPSON PRINTER MENU"
  350 white$=CHR$(135)
  360 blue$=CHR$(132)
  370 cyan$=CHR$(134)
  380 ground$=CHR$(157)
  390 FOR N=1 TO 9
  400    choice(N)=FALSE
  410    NEXT N
  420 ENDPROC
  430 :
  440 DEFPROCselect
  450 PRINTTAB(10,6);"OPTIONS"
  460 FOR C%=1 TO 9
  470    READ menu$(C%)
  480    z=8
  490    y=z+C%
  500    x=6
  510    PRINTTAB(x,y);cyan$;C%;"   ";menu
$(C%)
  520    NEXT
  530 DATA NLQ,Double-strike,Emphasised,
Italic,Proportional
  540 DATA 10 Pitch   (default 12 Pitch),
15 Pitch   (default 12 Pitch),UK Characte
r Set (default US),VIEW
  550 REPEAT
  560    PRINTTAB(10,20);"YOUR CHOICE?";
  570    input=GET
```

19

```
  580    IF input<49 OR input>57 PROCbeep
:GOTO 570
  590    input=input-48
  600    ON input GOTO 620,640,660,680,70
0,720,740,760,780
  610    UNTIL FALSE
  620 IF choice(input)=FALSE THEN PROCon
(120,1) ELSE PROCoff(120,0)
  630 GOTO 560
  640 IF choice(input)=FALSE THEN PROCon
1(71) ELSE PROCoff1(72)
  650 GOTO560
  660 IF choice(input)=FALSE THEN PROCon
1(69) ELSE PROCoff1(70)
  670 GOTO560
  680 IF choice(input)=FALSE THEN PROCon
1(52) ELSE PROCoff1(53)
  690 GOTO560
  700 IF choice(input)=FALSE THEN PROCon
(112,1) ELSE PROCoff(112,0)
  710 GOTO560
  720 IF choice(input)=FALSE THEN PROCon
1(80) ELSE PROCoff1(77)
  730 PRINTTAB(6,9+input);cyan$:choice(i
nput+1)=FALSE:GOTO560
  740 IF choice(input)=FALSE THEN PROCon
1(103) ELSE PROCoff1(77)
  750 PRINTTAB(6,7+input);cyan$:choice(i
nput-1)=FALSE:GOTO560
  760 IF choice(input)=FALSE THEN PROCon
(82,3) ELSE PROCoff(82,0)
  770 GOTO560
  780 PROCreset:*WORD   :REM could *EXEC
a file instead
  790 ENDPROC
  800 :
  810 DEFPROCbeep
  820 SOUND 1,-12,50,8
  830 ENDPROC
  840 :
  850 DEFPROCon(X,Y)
  860 PRINTTAB(6,8+input);white$
  870 VDU2,1,27,1,X,1,Y,3
  880 choice(input)=TRUE
  890 ENDPROC
```

```
 900 :
 910 DEFPROCoff(X,Y)
 920 PRINTTAB(6,8+input);cyan$
 930 VDU2,1,27,1,X,1,Y,3
 940 choice(input)=FALSE
 950 ENDPROC
 960 :
 970 DEFPROCon1(X)
 980 PRINTTAB(6,8+input);white$
 990 VDU2,1,27,1,X,3
1000 choice(input)=TRUE
1010 ENDPROC
1020 :
1030 DEFPROCoff1(X)
1040 PRINTTAB(6,8+input);cyan$
1050 VDU2,1,27,1,X,3
1060 choice(input)=FALSE
1070 ENDPROC
1080 :
1090 DEFPROCreset
1100 VDU23,1,1;0;0;0;
1110 VDU26
1120 ENDPROC
```

To enter the listing, you should be in BASIC, and you will probably find the **AUTO** facility and the **COPY** key particularly useful. Leave out line 780 until the program is fully developed, because you will lose all your work if the micro changes to the VIEW language. Make at least two copies of the program on different discs. After studying your printer manual, you may decide to enter your own values inside the brackets associated with each PROCon and PROCoff, in order to adapt the program for your own needs, or different models of printer.

Example Printout from the Epson LQ800
Example Printout from the Epson LQ800
Example Printout from the Epson LQ800
Example Printout from the Epson LQ800
Example Printout from the Epson LQ800
Example Printout from the Epson LQ800
Example Printout from the Epson LQ800

Figure 2.4 Range of typefaces possible using the Menu program with the Epson LQ800 printer.

FX users may like to replace the NLQ option with a condensed print style. Use PROCon1(15) and Procoff1(33) in line 620.

OPTIONS	LQ800	LX80	FX Range	RX Range	MX Range
NLQ	X	X	–	–	–
Double Strike	X	X	X	X	X
Emphasised	X	X	X	X	X
Italic	X	X	X	–	–
Proportional	X	–	X	–	–
10 Pitch	X	X	X	X	–
15 Pitch	X	X	–	–	–
US/UK	X	X	X	X	X

Table 2.5 Compatibility Chart for Menu programme with Epson printers.

The Filing System

Disc Versus Cassette

As the programs and documents you write and use become more complex, so the time it takes to load and save them on cassette increases. There comes a point where a faster storage medium is needed, with a bigger capacity, and the usual answer to the problem is to use floppy discs. While a program or file of information might take several minutes to load from a cassette, the typical time taken to find the data and load it in from disc might be a couple of seconds. The disc drive has 'random access' to the disc surface and this gives disc software the potential of being more versatile and powerful than that written for a cassette-based system. In addition, storage on disc is rather more reliable than using cassette tapes, which can suffer from 'drop-outs' and poor tape head alignment. It is advisable to upgrade as soon as possible, especially if you intend to use your BBC Micro for business applications.

Using Disc Drives with the BBC Micro

Disc drives offer a fast, and on the whole convenient, method of storing data from the VIEW range of business software. They are consistently more reliable than cassette data recorders, much faster in operation, and they have now fallen sufficiently in price to make them quite competitive with cassette recorders. Disc drives can be run with either Acorn's standard Disc Filing System (**DFS**), or their Advanced Disc Filing System (**ADFS**), depending on the type of BBC Micro and disc interface you are using. The **DFS** and **ADFS** are fundamentally different in the way they store data on the discs, and so they are not directly compatible with each other.

In addition to Acorn's 'official' disc filing systems there are a large number of non-standard **DFS** kits available for the BBC Micro from independent sources, some of which are not compatible with either Acorn system. This book deals only with the standard Acorn products, although many of the commands are identical on systems developed and sold by other manufacturers.

Types of Disc Drive

Disc drives can be bought in a number of different formats, each offering varying amounts of data storage. The capacity of your disc system depends on four things:

1. The number of disc drives
2. Whether they are single or double sided
3. How many tracks they have (usually 40 or 80 per side)
4. The type of disc interface fitted to your micro

Table 2.6 shows some of the options available on the BBC Micro system, and the number of bytes of information they can hold. (A single byte is needed to store each character, so a page of A4 text is roughly 5600 bytes.)

Disc Drive	DFS	ADFS
40 TRACK		
Single sided	100k	160k
Double sided	200k	320k
80 TRACK		
Single sided	200k	320k
Double sided	400k	640k

Table 2.6

You can see that a typical 80 track dual disc drive system having double sided drives is capable of handling 800k of data with the **DFS**, and 1280k using the **ADFS**. This configuration is the most efficient in business terms, both because of reliability (you effectively have an operational spare) and speed of data handling when copying and backing-up files. This level of storage also may be essential if you are using ViewStore to hold large quantities of information. As an alternative to normal disc drives, the **ADFS** can also be used in conjunction with Winchester hard discs, and these can typically hold 10 or 20 Megabytes of data. Some 80 track disc drives can be switched to read 40 track discs, which can be very useful if you already have 40 track software, but would rather go for the higher capacity of 80 track drives. (This switching can sometimes be done using software.)

Loading and Saving Files

When you have written some text you may well want to keep it, either to work on again later, to use as a starting point for new work, or as a reference. You can use the **SAVE** instruction to preserve your data as a file in the current filing system. **SAVE** is common to VIEW and ViewSheet (but not to ViewStore) and is very simple to use. In order to save your text, you will need to give it a 'filename' by which you (and the disc system) can identify it. In the case of the **DFS**, this name can be up to seven characters long in upper or lower case, but should ideally not include the characters:

: . *

as these have special meanings in the filing system (see your manual for details). Having chosen a name, let's say ERIC, you should press **ESCAPE** to get to the Command Mode and enter:

SAVE ERIC <RETURN>

You can check that a file has been correctly saved by **SCREEN**ing its contents. This is described fully in Chapter Three. When a file is saved, VIEW also saves a block of spare space at the end of the file in case you need to extend and resave the text. (Note: if at some later stage you tidy up your discs using *****COMPACT**, this space will be deleted.)

It is a good idea to get into the habit of saving your text regularly as you work - say every 10 or 15 minutes - just in case you hit a wrong key, the micro develops a fault, or someone unplugs the equipment by mistake to plug in a kettle. If you have a recent copy of the work on disc, you can always begin again with the bulk of the work intact. If you are using VIEW 3 or ViewSheet, the **SAVE** routine can be speeded up considerably by using the **NAME** command. This lets you allocate a specific name to the file in memory, so that if you just enter SAVE <RETURN> from the command page, the work will be saved under the name you have allocated. To **NAME** your file, simply enter:

NAME ERIC <RETURN>

from the Command screen, and you will see the name (ERIC) appear on the second status line.

Once you have begun saving files on disc, you will naturally want to retrieve them! This is done with the **LOAD** command. If you decide to load a file into memory, you should first ensure that the micro does not contain any text that you want to keep, as the act of loading a file clears out anything that was there before. To retrieve the previously saved file go to the Command screen and enter:

LOAD ERIC <RETURN>

If you now press **ESCAPE** to return to the Text mode, you will see that the new file is in memory, ready to be examined, printed out, or worked on. (Note that this method of saving and loading applies only to the VIEW software: if you are saving or loading a BASIC program you must enclose the file name in double quotes.)

The Advanced Disc Filing System

The BBC Master Series comes fitted with an alternative disc filing system - the **ADFS** or Advanced Disc Filing System - and this is also available as a plug-in **ROM** to upgrade the BBC B+ and B+128 machines. (In the case of the Model B an extra upgrade is needed first, replacing the disc controller chip with the necessary later version.) The **ADFS** is essential if you intend to use a Winchester disc drive.

Using the ADFS

The **LOAD** and **SAVE** procedures described earlier in this chapter are slightly more complicated if you chose to use the **ADFS** instead of the original **DFS**. This is because the discs are capable of taking a virtually unlimited number of file names in a 'hierarchical' directory structure, rather than the 31 files per drive supported by the **DFS**. As a result, a set-up procedure must be carried out, and the file names themselves must be accurately specified.

The structure of data storage under the **ADFS** is known as a hierarchical structure because the system begins with one major 'root' directory (the '$' directory), and this can contain up to 47 files or more directories, and each of the directories can contain 47 more files or directories, and so on. The theoretical picture of all this is rather like the branches of a tree, and the complete path to your file through each directory must be quoted, so that the **ADFS** can find the right program.

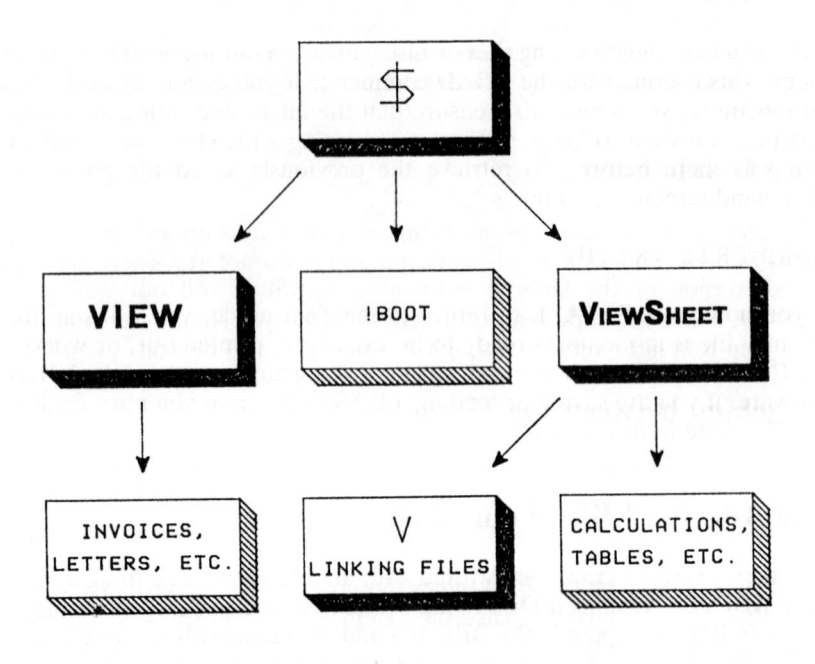

Figure 2.7 Diagram of tree structure of files for VIEW

The resulting file names can sometimes get very long, so it is handy to get used to using the *DIR command to give you fast access to a particular directory, or else the inconvenience of typing long file names each time could outweigh the advantages of the extra storage on the disc surfaces and the unlimited file names and directories. By setting the current directory, and also the filename (using the NAME command in VIEW 3 or ViewSheet) you will probably only have to enter the details once, and you can then save the data simply by entering SAVE, or even the SA abbreviation each time. It is also worth giving careful consideration to the way you organise your disc storage, so that you do not end up with too many long routes through to the files you want to get at frequently. The ability to use up to 10 characters to name the files in the **ADFS** certainly helps you to identify the file's contents more clearly than the seven allowed by the **DFS**.

Disc Developments

The Disc Filing System from Acorn is under a continual process of improvement, and as a result some programs do not run correctly with earlier version of the **DFS**. In particular, ViewStore will not work with **DFS** 0.9, and if you experience difficulty with this you should upgrade your **DFS** chip to a later version through Acorn, or a local dealer.

Switching between the Filing Systems

If you have a BBC Micro with more than one filing system fitted, you may find it necessary to enter an operating system command to switch to another system. The range of commands includes:

*TAPE	or *TAPE12 gives the normal cassette system.
*TAPE3	gives the cassette system with slower speed loading and saving.
*NET	gives the ECONET network filing system.
*TELESOFT	gives the telesoftware filing system.
*ROM	gives the ROM or ROM cartridge filing system.
*ADFS	gives the Advanced Disc Filing System.
*DISC	or *DISK gives the Disc Filing System (DFS).

SECTION ONE

The Word Processor

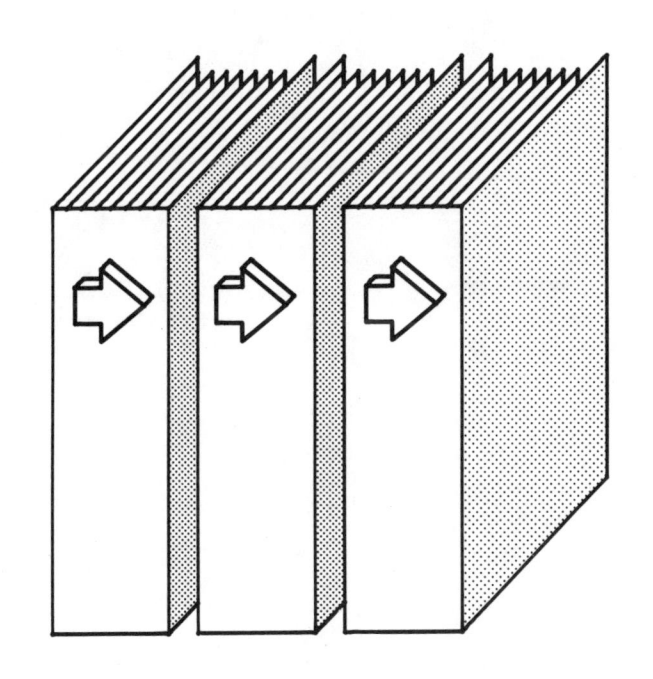

VIEW

CHAPTER THREE

Word Processing with VIEW

The Word Processor

Word processing software - running on a microcomputer with a printer attached - is the ideal replacement for the traditional typewriter in many instances. The word processor is essentially a means of storing text electronically inside the computer's memory and displaying it on a screen, rather than typing or printing it directly onto paper. This 'indirect' approach has three main advantages.

1. Nothing is final - work can be printed out at any stage, corrected in the computer's memory and then re-printed, with remarkable ease. This is a marvellous concept for anyone who has to make constant revisions, or whose typing or spelling are poor.

2. Work that is repetitious, and involves re-typing many times over, can be made far more efficient by a word processor. New material can be created from existing 'building blocks' of stored text. The same basic framework can be used to produce many different finished articles or reports, and a standard letter can be re-addressed many times without the need to re-type the main body of the text. (The computer's power can often be harnessed to do this automatically.)

3. Once text is in the word processor, electronic means can be used to transfer it: it can be sent as a telex, or as electronic mail over the telephone using a modem, without the need for re-typing. Conversely, incoming text from either electronic mail or the telex system can be read by the word processor, and used immediately in reports, or sent on to other destinations. It can even be sent directly to publishing and printing equipment over the telephone. Text can be prepared offline in advance using the word processor, then sent with the minimum cost, as all the errors have been corrected before connecting up to the telephone.

Other advantages become clear once the word processor is linked with extra software, as data from one type of program such as a spreadsheet or a database can usually be used by the word processor to create complex reports or letters.

What Can a Word Processor Do?

Using a word processor, writers can revise their text many times with the minimum of effort, and some publishers* can now type-set directly from word-processed files on disc. Club secretaries can produce standard letters, companies can prepare their own in-house magazines, and small businesses can run more efficiently by cutting down on the time taken to deal with invoicing or letter writing. The word processor is by no means restricted to the office. Thanks to modern technology and the widespread availability of micros it is now in use in classrooms and the home as well. Once people have tried a word processor, they usually wonder how on earth they managed without one. And children in schools can be encouraged to take an active interest in creative writing by virtue of the word processor's ability to accept unlimited alterations to text.

Any letter, form or invoice can be held on file, loaded into the micro and used as the basis for a new document, drastically cutting down the time spent on re-typing, and in laying out text. Gone is the need to use correcting fluid on mistakes - the offending letters or passages can be overtyped on the screen, or deleted from the computer's memory at the touch of a key.

A word processor can be connected to a variety of different printers, so the final print quality is governed by the choice of printer, not the word processor itself. A cheap dot matrix printer is a good option on a budget, while a Near Letter Quality (NLQ) dot matrix is a versatile but slightly more expensive option, and daisywheel or laser printers give the ultimate in quality, but at a price. Hence anyone starting a word processor system on a budget has a useful upgrade path in terms of printer quality - you can always change your printer later. Neat, repeatable results can certainly be obtained for a relatively small outlay.

A Word Processor's Facilities

Some major facilities you would expect to find on a word processor are:

1. Automatic word-wrap. When you reach the end of one line of typing, the next word is automatically placed on the next line.

*Including Sigma Press

2. Search and replace. Finding a specified word, or words, within the text, with the option of replacing them with an alternative.

3. Right-hand justification. Alignment of all, or selected, text with the right-hand margin, giving newspaper-style straight edges to both sides of the text.

4. Move and copy. Marked sections of text can be moved from one place in a document to another, or left where they are but copied to a new position.

5. Automatic page numbering and headings. These can be added throughout the text, or in specific sections.

6. Standard letters. Ability to support standard letters, on its own, or when linked to a database.

7. Read text files. The word processor should be able to read text from other sources, such as a spreadsheet, or electronic mail, so that it can be included in your documents if required.

8. Printer control. This should enable the production of different print styles when used with a variety of printers, giving features such as bold or underlined text.

9. Spelling checker. The word processor should be able to link with extra software to check the spelling of the document's contents.

10. Indexer. It is sometimes useful if an index can be made from the contents of the text automatically.

11. Preview facility. Some way of telling what the final text will look like when printed. Some word processors work in a 'What You See Is What You Get' fashion (WYSIWYG), while others have some way of previewing the text complete with headings, pagination, and so on.

12. Several text windows. It is often useful to be able to look at, or work on, two or more documents at once, and to transfer text from one file to another, by splitting the screen display.

Features numbered 1 to 11 are all found in the VIEW word processor, as are the ability to read one document into another to create a new work, and to set the layout of areas of text, then alter it if necessary.

Note: This book is based on VIEW version 3.0. Where possible, comments are included which relate to using earlier versions. Upgrades to VIEW 3 are available direct from Acorn Computers.

Starting with VIEW

First, turn all the equipment on, making sure that if you have a Second Processor, it is turned on before the BBC Micro itself. It is quite a good idea to turn all the peripheral equipment on first, then the BBC Micro, in order to minimise the effect of mains interference. To begin word processing with VIEW, first fit the function key strip in the holder above the keyboard, then enter the command.

```
*WORD<RETURN>
```

You will see an almost blank screen, with some information in the top left-hand corner. This is VIEW's Command screen, and beneath the information you should see a flashing cursor immediately following the VIEW prompt (=>) as in Figure 3.1.

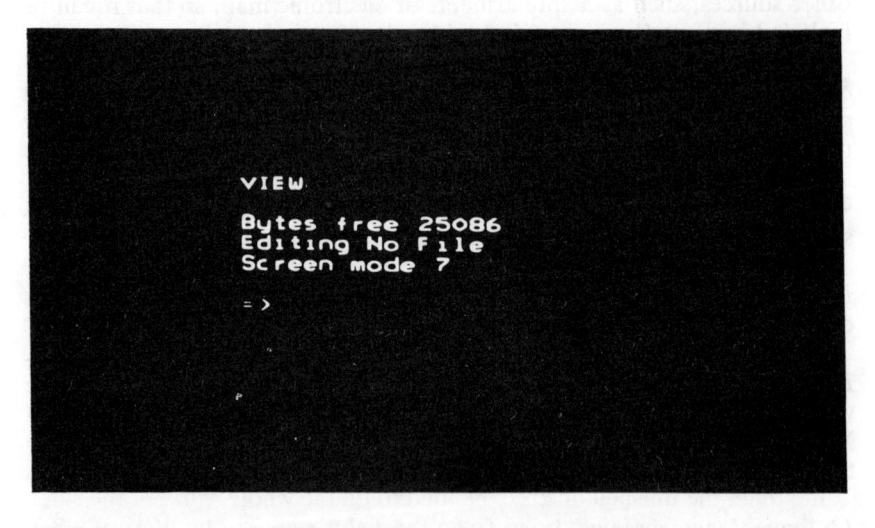

```
VIEW
Bytes free 25086
Editing No File
Screen mode 7
=>
```

Figure 3.1 The VIEW Command screen.

The top line of information on this screen shows how much memory is available to store text (in this case 28296 bytes). This figure will vary according to screen mode on the BBC B and the Electron, and depending on whether or not a second processor is fitted and running. We will assume that the micro's display is in the 40 character Mode 7 (Mode 6 on the Electron). Whilst in the Command mode, VIEW is expecting to be given instructions relating to loading or saving, formatting, searching, or printing the text. When you are starting afresh, there will be no text file to load, so you will want to get into the text entry mode as soon as possible. You do this simply by pressing the **ESCAPE** key, which acts as a 'toggle' or switch between the Command mode and Text mode.

(Users of VIEW 1.4 and 2.1 will need to enter:

NEW <RETURN>

before they can go to Text mode and begin work.)

Once **ESCAPE** is pressed, you will see the screen change to a line of full stops and stars, with another line of stars beneath it. The former is known as the text 'ruler', which indicates the length of the text line, while the latter, the row of stars, shows the end of text in memory. The flashing cursor is on a blank line between the two. You are now ready to enter some text. Note that BBC Micros other than the Master Series normally switch on with the 'Caps Lock' operative, indicated by the middle red light being lit at the left of the keyboard. All the the text you enter will be in upper case until you press the **CAPS LOCK** key to cancel the effect and allow text entry in upper or lower case. Holding one of the **SHIFT** keys down then gives upper case, just as on an ordinary typewriter. Once caps lock is cancelled, the indicator light will go out, and you can start typing. If you happen to make a mistake, you can press the **DELETE** key at the bottom right of the keyboard to remove the character immediately to the left of the flashing cursor, then re-type the character.

Notice that when you fill one line with text, any word that crosses the end of the line is automatically placed at the start of the next line, and at the same time, the finished line is expanded to fill the whole width of the ruler, so that there is a straight edge down the right-hand margin of your work. This effect is known as right justification, and works by adding extra spaces between the words to make the line the same length as the text ruler above it. Don't worry if you do not like this effect - it can be turned off quite simply, as you will see later.

Type in a few lines of text, so that you can see how easy it is to move the cursor around your 'document' using the arrowed cursor keys at the top right of the keyboard. Pressing ← or → will move the cursor one character to the left or right on the screen, while pressing ↑ or ↓ will move the cursor up or down by one line of text at a time (see Figure 3.2). If you keep any of the keys pressed, they will start to repeat after a short interval, and you will find the cursor moving fluidly to the left, right, up or down through the block of text.

One line up

[↑]

One character left [←]   [→] One character right

[↓]

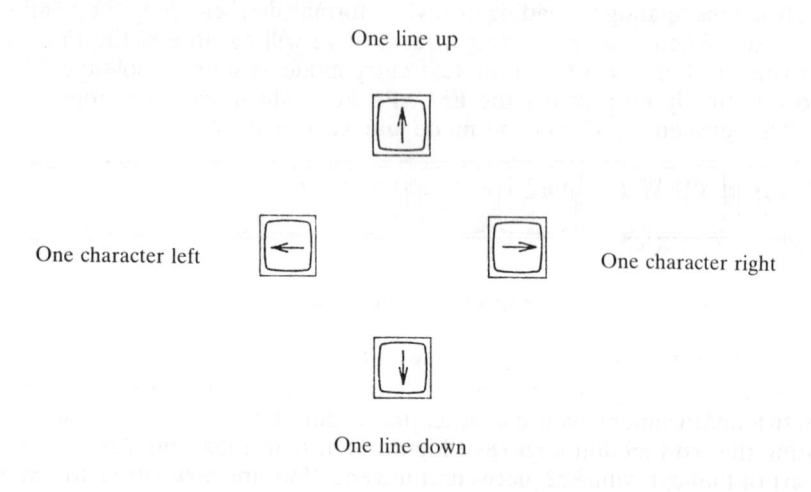

One line down

Figure 3.2 Cursor movement using the cursor keys.

Faster cursor movement can be achieved in a number of different ways. Holding the **SHIFT** key down while pressing one of the cursor keys has the effects shown in Figure 3.3.

Move up by one screenful of text

[SHIFT] + [↑]

[SHIFT] + [←]   [SHIFT] + [→]

One word left   One word right

[SHIFT] + [↓]

Move down by one screenful of text

Figure 3.3 Cursor movement using the **SHIFT** and cursor keys.

If your document does not fill more than one entire screenful of text, the latter two commands have the effect of moving the cursor to the beginning or end of the text.

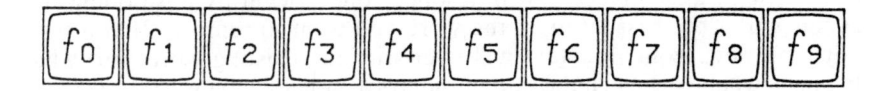

```
[f0] [f1] [f2] [f3] [f4] [f5] [f6] [f7] [f8] [f9]
```

Figure 3.4 VIEW function key strip.

In a long document, you can reach the beginning and end of the text by using the red function keys (See Figure 3.4). *f1* will take the cursor to the start of the text, while *f2* places it at the end. Two more function keys give useful cursor movements: *f4*.to the beginning of the current line, *f5* to the end of the line; but take care not to hit *f3* 'Delete end of line' by mistake. This immediately removes all the text following the cursor on that line! If you are using VIEW 3, you can obtain the same effects as function keys *f1*, *f2*, *f4*, and *f5* by holding down the **CTRL** key, and pressing one of the cursor keys as in Figure 3.5.

Beginning of text
[CTRL] + [↑]

[CTRL] + [←]   [CTRL] + [→]
Beginning of line   End of line

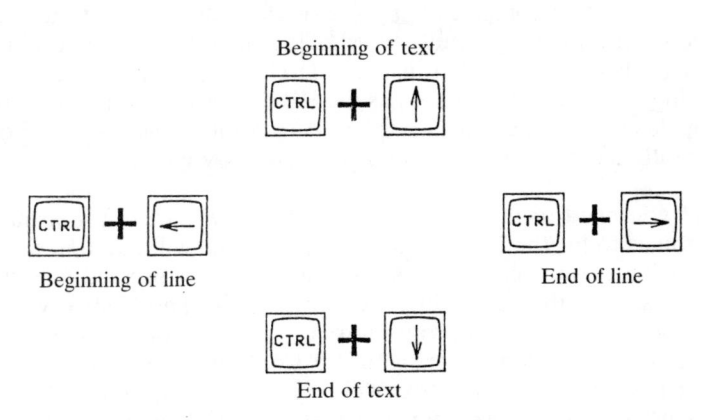

[CTRL] + [↓]
End of text

Figure 3.5 Cursor movement using the **CTRL** and cursor keys.

You will notice that these moves are similar in effect to those obtained when holding down the **SHIFT** key - only increased in scale - hence the key presses needed to move around the text are quite logical, and easily mastered after a short time using VIEW.

Altering Your Text

The **DELETE** key is fine for quickly removing the last character you typed, but what happens if you want to get rid of an entire word near the start of your text, and replace it with a longer one? Begin by positioning the cursor under the first letter of the word you want to remove. If you type anything now, your new text will overwrite the existing word, but what happens when you reach the end of the word and need to insert some extra characters? This can easily be done with the Insert Character function key (*f8*): simply add the necessary number of spaces on the line, and type in the rest of the new word. In the long term, there is an easier solution to editing the text in this way. Again, positioning the cursor under the first character of the offending word, remove it by pressing the Delete Character function key (*f9*) until all the letters are gone. Each time you press *f9*, the letter over the cursor will be erased, and the rest of the text will move backwards to fill in the space. You can make use of the auto-repeat here, and simply hold the key down until all the letters are gone. Then you will need to make use of VIEW's 'insert' facility, by pressing the **CTRL** key and function key *f4*, labelled Insert Mode. (You will see the letter I (for insert) appear at the top left of the screen when you do this.) New text will now be inserted on the line, rather than going over what is already there! So VIEW effectively offers two options for correcting text. Many people prefer to work in the insert mode, although overtype is given as the first option.

If you need to delete a complete line of text, the quick way is to use the Delete Line function key (*f7*), but a word of warning here. As VIEW is a little slower at deleting lines than it is single characters, it is best not to keep your finger pressed on this key, as the BBC Micro will remember the auto-repeats faster than it can act on them. As a result it easy to overshoot and accidentally delete more lines than you originally intended.

Likewise, if you need to make a gap to insert a new paragraph, a quick way to do this is to hit the Insert Line key (*f6*), which will add a new line in the text at the cursor's current position each time it is pressed, and will automatically shuffle the remaining text downwards. The best way is to insert three new lines at the appropriate point, so that you can leave one spare line above and below where you are working in the text. As you type in your new paragraph, the text will begin to wrap round at the end of the line as usual, forcing the old text down by a line each time as it does so.

Reformatting the Text

As a consequence of making any change to your document, you may find that the previously neat appearance of the right-hand margin has gone. Some lines may be shorter than the others, while others are now so long that words, or parts of words, are hidden off the edge of the display, having been shuffled along to the right. You will need to make VIEW re-format any sections or 'blocks' of text where changes have been made to regain a tidy-looking appearance. You can do this simply by placing the cursor somewhere on the first line of the block in question, and pressing the Format Block function key (*f0*). The formatting will then take place, leaving the text in a neat condition again, with an even right-hand margin, and all the words visible on the screen. The program will re-justify the text where necessary, and will continue formatting until it comes to a blank line, or one that starts with a blank space. You can repeat this procedure for every block you have changed, or go into the Command mode and enter:

FORMAT <RETURN>

and the entire text will be re-formatted. This can save a lot of time, but can also lead to complications with the precise layout of your text, when things on consecutive lines, such a heading and its dashed underline, can be run together. For example:

TITLE
=====

will become:

TITLE=====

If this happens using the **FORMAT** command, you can split the lines again using function key **CTRL** *f6*, (Split Line).

Turning Off Justification

Not everyone wants their text justified to the right! Adding spaces to the text can make it more difficult to read, especially if there are relatively few characters on a line, so it might be useful to try turning the justification off and re-formatting the text to see how it looks. This is done with another combination of control and function keys - **CTRL** *f3* - which switches the justification on and off. The letter J at the top left of the text screen shows that justification is selected, but when you press **CTRL** *f3*, you will see it disappear. Now try placing the cursor under the first word in a paragraph and pressing the *f0* Format Block key. VIEW will now format the paragraph without justifying it. The effect is less 'tidy', but definitely easier on the eye as it scans better without the random extra spaces, and this mode of operation may be preferred by some for normal text entry.

```
F I......*.......*.......*.......*.<
.. .....*.......*.......*.......*.<
Not   everyone  wants  their  text
justified  to  the  right!  Adding
spaces  to  the  text  can  make  it
more difficult to read, especially
if  there   are   relatively   few
characters on a line, so it might
be  useful  to   try  turning  the
justification       off       and
re-formatting  the text to see how
it looks.
       ....*.......*.......*.......*.<
Not everyone wants their text
justified to the right! Adding
spaces to the text can make it
more difficult to read, especially
if there are relatively few
characters on a line, so it might
be useful to try turning the
justification off and
re-formatting the text to see how
it looks._
```

The above comparison between justified and unjustified text is a little unfair, because the ruler width is so narrow, but it does serve to illustrate how hard it can be to read the justified version!

Pressing BREAK by Mistake

By now, you will find that you are using the function keys quite a lot, which brings us to the possibility that you might press the **BREAK** key by mistake while you are using the keyboard. On the earlier VIEW 1.4 and 2.1 this is potentially disastrous if you haven't saved your text onto disc or tape, since the VIEW Command screen reappears in the start-up mode indicating a completely blank memory! All your text has vanished into thin air. But all is not lost, thank goodness, as it is possible to retrieve the previous contents of the micro's memory by entering the **OLD** command from the Command screen before you type anything else, i.e:

```
OLD <RETURN>
```

The memory status should then show that there is something in memory once more, and you can then re-enter all the necessary set-up conditions (bar typing in **NEW**, of course, which will clear out the memory again!) VIEW 3 has no **OLD** command as such, but preserves the text in memory automatically if **BREAK** is pressed.

Screen Modes

```
F I........*.......*......*......*.<
    6502 Second Processor
    --------------------
    A useful addition to the BBC Micro
    system is the 6502 Second
    Processor, which connects to the
    main machine by way of the 'Tube'
    interface socket. This 64k RAM
    'co-processor' then works in
    conjunction with the BBC Micro to
    give greater memory capacity to
    the system, and faster processing
    time. The main machine handles
    all the screen display, input and
    output and keyboard routines,
    leaving the co-processor to get on
    with running the program in
    question. The two processors
    together run software roughly half
    as fast again as the ordinary BBC
    B or B+, making actions like
    searching or scrolling through
    VIEW text significantly faster.
    Disc-handling routines are also
    speeded up. This add-on is
```

VIEW's screen display using Mode 7.

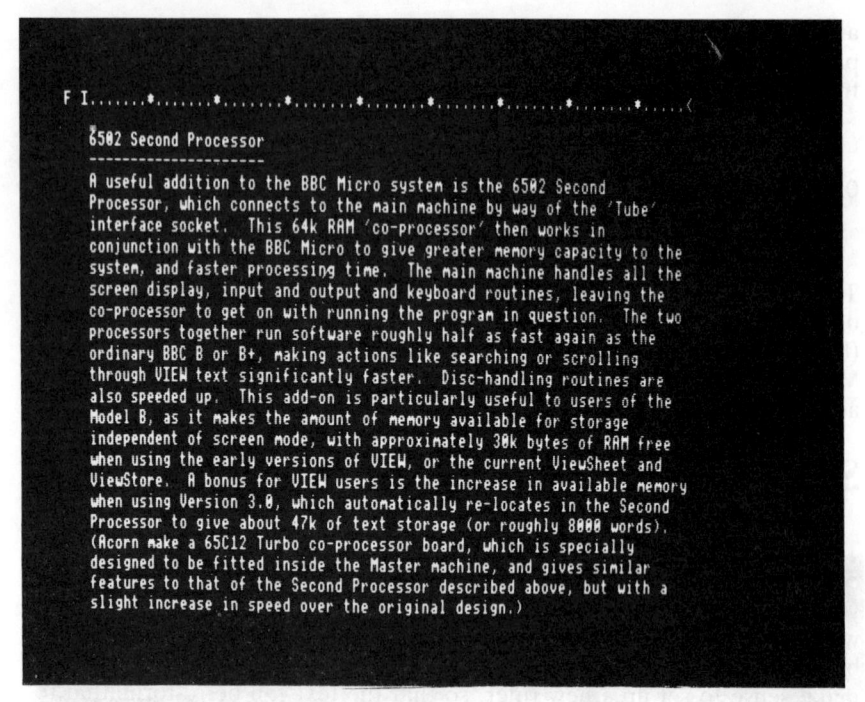

```
F I......*......*......*......*......*......*......*......*.....(
6502 Second Processor
---------------------
A useful addition to the BBC Micro system is the 6502 Second
Processor, which connects to the main machine by way of the 'Tube'
interface socket. This 64k RAM 'co-processor' then works in
conjunction with the BBC Micro to give greater memory capacity to the
system, and faster processing time. The main machine handles all the
screen display, input and output and keyboard routines, leaving the
co-processor to get on with running the program in question. The two
processors together run software roughly half as fast again as the
ordinary BBC B or B+, making actions like searching or scrolling
through VIEW text significantly faster. Disc-handling routines are
also speeded up. This add-on is particularly useful to users of the
Model B, as it makes the amount of memory available for storage
independent of screen mode, with approximately 30k bytes of RAM free
when using the early versions of VIEW, or the current ViewSheet and
ViewStore. A bonus for VIEW users is the increase in available memory
when using Version 3.0, which automatically re-locates in the Second
Processor to give about 47k of text storage (or roughly 8000 words).
(Acorn make a 65C12 Turbo co-processor board, which is specially
designed to be fitted inside the Master machine, and gives similar
features to that of the Second Processor described above, but with a
slight increase in speed over the original design.)
```

The 80 column display using Mode 3.

Up to now, you have probably been working in Mode 7 - the BBC Micro's teletext display - this is the screen mode that the BBC machine is in when it is first switched on. Mode 7 was chosen as the 'default' mode because is the most legible form of screen display on most television sets, as the letters are fairly large, and appear to be well-shaped. If you are using a good quality monitor, you may have no problem reading the smaller text available in the 80 character per line modes (0 and 3), but you may be annoyed by the fact that the text appears to jiggle up and down. This is because of the 'interlace' effect. The video image is made up from two separate parts, or frames, which interlace at slightly different positions on the screen to produce one picture. This system improves the legibility of text on an ordinary TV, but is very off-putting on a high resolution monitor. Typing:

*TV 0,1

before changing mode will switch off the interlace in all the graphics modes (Modes 0-6) producing a rock-steady image on the monitor.

Before you can change modes, you must get back to the VIEW Command screen. This is simply done by pressing the **ESCAPE** key. The screen will immediately change back to the original VIEW display. The text is quite safe when you do this! If you press **ESCAPE** again you will see it once more - try it now. So the **ESCAPE** key definitely swaps between the Text and Command screens! On the Command screen, you will see the VIEW prompt (=>), meaning that the machine is ready for instructions. If you are using a high definition monitor, either monochrome or colour, don't forget to enter *TV 0,1 at this stage. Apparently, nothing happens when you do, but the machine remembers that it must switch off the picture interlace the next time it changes mode, and this will give a steady screen image in any screen mode except Mode 7. Table 3.6 shows the screen modes and memory free using VIEW on a variety of different machines. You might want to see the 80 character display, in which case try Mode 3 by entering:

MODE 3 <RETURN>

The screen will change to give smaller text, and if you entered the *TV command the annoying flicker should have gone. If you now press **ESCAPE**, you will see your text displayed in the new screen mode. The ruler which was in operation in Mode 7 is still in operation now, so the text will only be 34 characters wide. As you can display 74 characters in Mode 3, it would make sense to set up a new ruler, so that the text can be re-formatted to the full width of the screen. The easiest way of doing this is to place the cursor under the first line of text. If you are using VIEW version 1.4 you will have to insert a line for the ruler, or it will overwrite your text. All later versions of VIEW shift the text down by a line to make room when you press the **CTRL** and *f5* keys (Default Ruler). The default length is the maximum number of characters that can comfortably be seen in any particular mode, in this case 74. In practice, rulers can be any length up to 132 characters in any screen mode, but if the ruler goes off the screen to the right, VIEW has to scroll sideways as you work, and this is less comfortable in use than a fixed screen with the text only moving up and down. For the time being, we will keep the ruler to the width of the screen.

Now you are in the new screen mode with a longer ruler, try re-formatting your text by placing the cursor under the first character and using *f0* again. You will see that the text is totally rearranged to fit the new, wider ruler. On the earlier BBC B Micro, it is preferable to use Mode 3 rather than Mode 0 for your 80 column display as it uses up less memory, hence leaving much more room for text storage. On a system based on the BBC B+ or the Master Series, there is no difference between the modes as far as memory is concerned, so it depends whether you prefer to see 24 lines well spaced out with a broad flashing cursor (Mode 3) or 32 lines close together with a thin cursor (Mode 0). Mode 3 is the usual choice, being specially designed for text work.

Mode	Master (Mode 0–7)	Master (128–135)	Model B (with DFS)	Model B (2nd Proc)	B+ 128k (Mode 0–7)	B+ 128k (128–135)	Characters per line	Lines of text
0	8846	28926	5630	48366	4094	24574	80	32
1	8846	,,	5630	,,	4094	,,	40	32
2	8846	,,	5630	,,	4094	,,	20	32
3	12542	,,	9726	,,	8190	,,	80	25
4	18686	,,	15570	,,	14334	,,	40	32
5	18686	,,	15870	,,	14334	,,	20	32
6	20734	,,	17918	,,	16382	,,	40	25
7	27902	,,	25086	,,	23550	,,	40	25

Table 3.6 Memory available on different models of BBC Micro

Saving and Loading Your Text

As mentioned in Chapter 2, the **SAVE** and **LOAD** commands are used to save and load your work, and the format of these instructions is very simple:

SAVE TEXT <RETURN>

will save the current contents of memory in a file called **TEXT**, while:

LOAD TEXT <RETURN>

will load that file back into VIEW, wiping out anything in memory as it does so! To check that your work is saved properly, you can enter:

SCREEN TEXT <RETURN>

which will read the file called **TEXT** back in from your filing system - e.g. disc or tape - a bit at a time, displaying it on the screen. This process is primarily intended as a way of checking the layout of your text (especially in VIEW 2.1 and 3.0, where you can just type: SCREEN‹RETURN› to see the text in memory in its final format) but **SCREEN** can also act as a sort of 'verify' command.

Printing Out Your Text

If you have a printer, and have some text in the computer, you might like to try printing it out. Assuming that the printer is correctly set up and you are using version 2.1 of the software or later, you can make VIEW print the text straight from memory. In the case of the earlier 1.4 version you normally have to save the text first before it can be printed out. We will look at this in a moment, and deal first with VIEW 2.1, 3.0 and beyond.

If you are happy that there is paper in your printer, the first thing to decide is which of the two VIEW commands to use to print out your results. The commands in question are **PRINT** and **SHEETS**, and both are entered from the Command screen.

PRINT is usually used for continuous fanfold paper, as it causes VIEW to print the entire document without stopping. **SHEETS** is designed to work with printers which must be loaded with one sheet of paper at a time, and stops printing after each sheet, waiting for you to press a key on the keyboard before continuing. **SHEETS** can also be used for reprinting single pages of a long document, rather than having to print out the whole thing if you have only made one or two minor alterations. But for the time being, let's deal with the **PRINT** command.

Using PRINT

With all the versions of VIEW, if you enter **PRINT** from the Command screen, followed by a filename, the software will search the current filing system for the file and send it out to the printer a tiny piece at a time. This procedure does not affect any text you have stored in memory. The later versions of VIEW (2.1, 3.0, etc.) also allow you to print direct from the memory, without having to **SAVE** the file first, by leaving out the filename and simply entering:

    PRINT <RETURN>

whereupon your printer will leap into life. On the 1.4 version of VIEW, however, the usual way to print out the text is to save it first. This is easily done if you are using disc drives, but tends to be a very slow process if you are confined to a cassette system. The advantage of this method in VIEW 1.4 is that it imposes the discipline of having to make a copy of your final document, which is good news for anyone who is inclined to forget to save their work.

To get round the problem of tedious saving onto cassette all the time, Acorn produced an upgrade for 1.4 users which can be loaded into the micro in the form of a 'printer driver'. If you have the upgrade, this 'Memory Printer Driver' (as it is called) loads straight into the machine when you enter:

PRINTER MEMORY <RETURN>

from the command screen. Details of the Memory Printer Driver are available from Acorn Computers Limited.

VIEW's Page Layout

When VIEW prints out your text, it is automatically divided into pages of 66 lines each, out of which nine lines are left blank at the top and bottom of each page. This is the 'default' page layout, and it can be changed, but for the time being we will stick to the defaults!

Abandoning the Printing

If you discover that the printout is not quite right for some reason, you can stop the printing at any time by pressing the **ESCAPE** key. This will have an immediate effect on the screen - you will see the VIEW prompt appear again - but the printer will not necessarily stop straight away, because it has its own storage for text, known as a 'buffer', and will probably keep going until the buffer is empty. If you have a particularly slow printer, such as a daisywheel model, or a printer with a very large text buffer, it is sometimes tempting to switch the printer off at the mains, rather than wait for it to finish. Remember that if you do, you will lose any special print styles or margins that you have set up on the printer, and that these will have to be re-entered.

SHEETS

The second printout option available from VIEW is the **SHEETS** command. It is chiefly intended for use with printers requiring a manual paper feed. Its method of use is the same as that for **PRINT**, in that you must specify a filename to print from disc or cassette, and if you leave the filename out (except in the case of VIEW 1.4) the operation will be carried out on the text held in memory. When you enter the **SHEETS** command, you will see the prompt come up on the screen:

    Page 1..

This means that VIEW is ready to print the first page of your document, and is waiting for you to give the go-ahead. Check first that you have some paper loaded into the printer. If you then press the space bar, the micro will proceed to print out the first page. Pressing Q (for Quit) or **ESCAPE** at this stage will abandon the printout, while pressing M (for Miss) will cause page one to be missed out, and VIEW will offer up the next page for printing. In this way, you can select certain pages for reprinting after a few minor changes have been made, rather than going through a complete document. This facility offers a great saving in time, paper, and wear and tear on the printer!

Extra facilities such as bold and underline are available on some printers, and these can be controlled from VIEW using the VIEW Printer Drivers (see Chapter Five).

CHAPTER FOUR

Improving the Page Layout

There are two distinct levels at which page layout can be dealt with. The first is when you are actually entering the text; the second is controlled by VIEW when printing it out. In the first case, you can do things like altering the width of the ruler to suit your work, or defining your own **TAB** stops to lay tables out neatly. At the printout stage you can make VIEW centre text, govern the amount of space left at the top and bottom of each page, and add headers at the top of the page and footers at the bottom (including page numbering) if required. All the commands necessary to do these things are 'stored' in the text. Other possibilities include specific commands to suit the length and width of your paper, and to force a new page if required, rather than leave single lines or words straggling the next page. There is even the facility to print on both sides of a page, swapping the different sections of the headers and footers and the margins, so that you can bind your own books from your work. (We will look at this in Chapter Seven.)

Laying Out the Text

The main feature of the VIEW word processor that governs the way your text will look is the *ruler*. As the ruler affects text beneath it, you can put in a new ruler for a new layout at any time, and then redefine the subsequent page layout. To add a new ruler to your document, simply press the Default ruler function key (**SHIFT** *f5*), and a ruler will be inserted on the line where the cursor is positioned. If you want to enter your text in a 40 column mode that is easy to read, then change the layout to 74 characters per line in mode 3 or 0, this is simply done by changing screen mode, inserting a new ruler right at the top of your text, then re-formatting throughout the text to the new ruler width.

A default ruler is set by the software on start-up, depending on which screen mode you are in, but this can be overridden at any time, since a new ruler can be added and edited in just the same way as the text. Several characters are used to make up the ruler. Normally, full stops are used to indicate the ruler's length, and there are two full stops in the left-hand margin, indicating to VIEW that the line is to be used as a ruler. **TAB** stops are represented by stars, while the left and right limits for formatting the text are marked by < and> respectively. It is usual to use the full width of the screen, so you will see the< sign at the right-hand end of the default ruler. It is also possible to enter your own >sign, which will set a left-hand limit. Any text typed in on the line below a ruler with a >sign entered will begin at the left-hand mark, and wrap round as usual onto the next line when the right-hand limit is reached. This facility can be used to create indented blocks of text, as the marks equate to the left and right hand end-stops on a typewriter. Another typewriter-style facility is the use of the letter 'B' in the ruler, which will sound a beep whenever your text passes it.

A handy use of the < and > margin signs is to use only the right-hand half of the page for normal text, then go into the remaining margin on the left

```
F I.......*......*......*......*......*......*......*......*.....(
       (SHIFT f2), whereupon the cursor will shoot into the left-hand area
       automatically.  One thing you have to watch when using VIEW like this
       is that you don't type so much on the left-hand side that you enter
       the normal text area.  This will result in VIEW re-formatting the
       whole area, and messing up your layout.

       ......*......*......*......*......)......*......*......*.....(
       Working on Two Halves of the Page        One thing you have to watch
       ---------------------------------        when using VIEW like this is
                                                that you don't type so much on
                                                the left-hand side that you
                                                enter the normal text area.
       Comments and headings go on this         This could result in VIEW
       side of the screen.                      re-formatting the whole area,
                                                and messing up your layout.

       ......*......*......*......*......*......*......*......*.....(
       Figure 4.1                                                       ▪

       A good way to avoid problems using this technique is to remove the
       right-hand format sign from the ruler when you are satisfied with the
       text in that part of the screen, so that formatting is prevented in
       that area.  You will not be able to re-format this block at all,
```

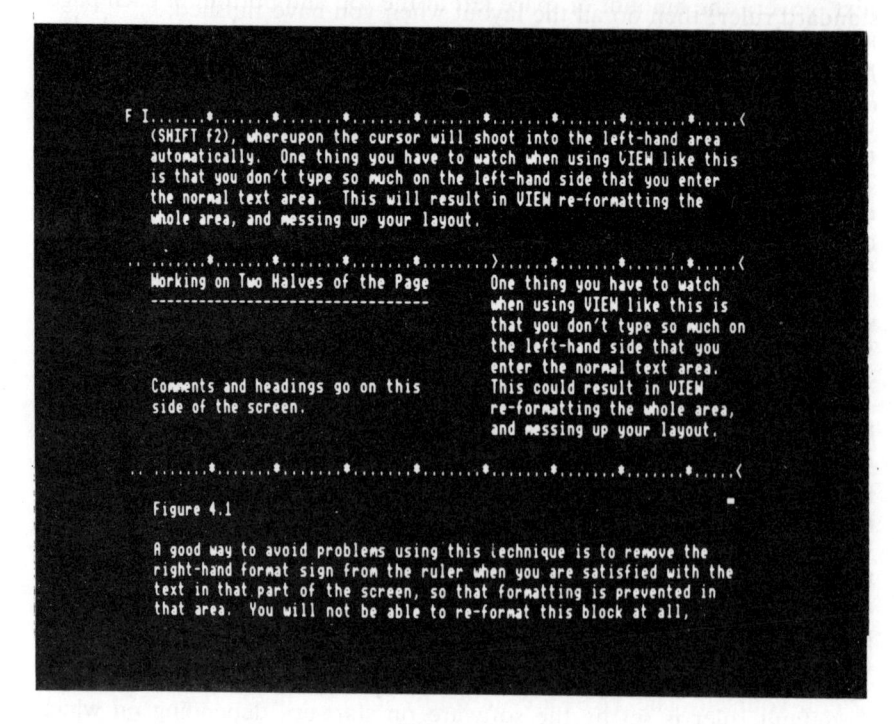

Figure 4.1

of the page to add headings and/or comments (see Figure 4.1). This can be useful when preparing presentations or scripts. VIEW 3.0 and beyond allow the cursor into the left-hand area at any time, but earlier versions require you to press the Release Margins function key (**SHIFT** *f2*), whereupon the cursor will shoot into the left-hand area automatically. One thing you have to watch when using VIEW like this is that you don't type so much on the left-hand side that you enter the normal text area. This will result in VIEW re-formatting the whole area, and messing up your layout.

A good way to avoid problems using this technique is to remove the right-hand format sign from the ruler when you are satisfied with the text in that part of the screen, so that formatting is prevented in that area. You will not be able to re-format this block at all, because VIEW will immediately incorporate all the left-hand comments in the main body of the text if you do!

VIEW's rulers are very versatile in that you can either plan ahead and set up a new ruler before you start writing, or change the text layout mid-stream by adding new rulers as you go. You can also enter all the text using a standard ruler, then do all the layout when you have finished.

Note: The top line of the VIEW text display always shows the ruler in operation. Pressing the **SHIFT** and **COPY** keys together will make a copy of the current ruler at the point in the text where the cursor is positioned.

Making Up Your Own Rulers

Any ruler that you incorporate in the text using the Default ruler function key (**CTRL** *f5*) can be edited exactly like text by placing the cursor on the ruler itself and either adding or deleting full stops, or the * **TAB** characters. This is also how you can add or remove the formatting limits (the > and< signs) and the B for a beep at the end of every line. One word of warning when making up your own rulers though: remember what the maximum number of characters is that your printer can print on one line. If you exceed this number with your ruler, the printer will print an extra line each time to get the rest of the line on, and this could wreck the layout of your text completely!

Using TABs

Like most normal typewriters, VIEW responds to **TAB**s, which can either be those present in the default ruler, or those set in a ruler you make up or edit yourself. The **TAB**s are shown by stars (*) in the ruler, and if you press the **TAB** key at the left-hand side of the keyboard, an invisible **TAB** character will be positioned on the screen at the cursor position, forcing the cursor, and any text entered after it, to the next **TAB** mark on the ruler. Text can then be entered as normal, or you can insert more **TAB** characters as required. Tables can readily be built up in this way, looking neat and tidy with all the columns lined up vertically. Besides being a quick way of entering tabular information, there are two major advantages of using **TAB**s for this sort of work. If you make any changes to the ruler, e.g. move the **TAB**s around by entering a new * on the ruler, and deleting an old one, the text columns under the ruler will automatically be re-formatted when you move the cursor under the ruler into the text area. Hence the gaps between the columns can be altered to get the best layout, even after all the data has been entered. Also, a tabbed block of text will not be ruined by re-formatting, whereas a table produced by leaving spaces between the entries will be completely reassembled (and usually ruined) if it should accidentally be formatted by VIEW. So it is actually much easier and safer to use **TAB**s properly.

The cursor behaves rather strangely when there is a **TAB** character present in the text, as it will cause the cursor to jump from one place on the screen (the location of the **TAB** character itself) to the place under the next * in the ruler. The way to remove a **TAB** character is to place the cursor under the first letter following it, and press the **DELETE** key. The preceding **TAB** will be deleted, and the text after the cursor will shoot back along the line to close up the gap.

Stored Commands

The second stage of controlling the exact layout of printouts from VIEW is achieved using so-called 'Stored Commands' embedded in the text. The effects of these commands cannot be seen at the writing stage - it is only during screening or printout that they are interpreted and used by VIEW to control the exact page layout. The Stored Commands fall roughly into three groups:

1. *Page layout.*

2. *Line layout.*

3. *Other extra commands.*

The last section contains commands which are useful for creating standard letters, and for generating files for integration and telecommunications use, and we will examine them in Chapter Seven.

The Stored Commands are entered by pressing the Edit Command key (**SHIFT** *f8*), which causes the cursor to jump into the extreme left-hand margin. Once you have entered the two letter command code, you can exit the margin by pressing RETURN. If you make a mistake, you will be able to keep typing in the narrow margin until the letters are correct (the cursor will oscillate between the two characters, allowing you to overtype) but you won't be able to use the **DELETE** key. To delete a command on any particular line, you should place the cursor on that line, then press the Delete Command function key (**SHIFT** *f9*). The command will then be erased from the margin.

The Stored Commands act from the point where they are entered, until another command is issued which changes or cancels their action. Where you wish a command to have effect all through a document, it is best to enter it right at the start of your work, before the text. That way the required page layout will take effect from the first printing line on the first page - any subsequent subsequent changes won't take effect until the following page.

The first section of useful Stored Commands - page layout - is the most immediately useful set of commands to learn, but before you start to use them, it is as well to consider the usual, or default, settings when VIEW prints a page (see Figure 4.2).

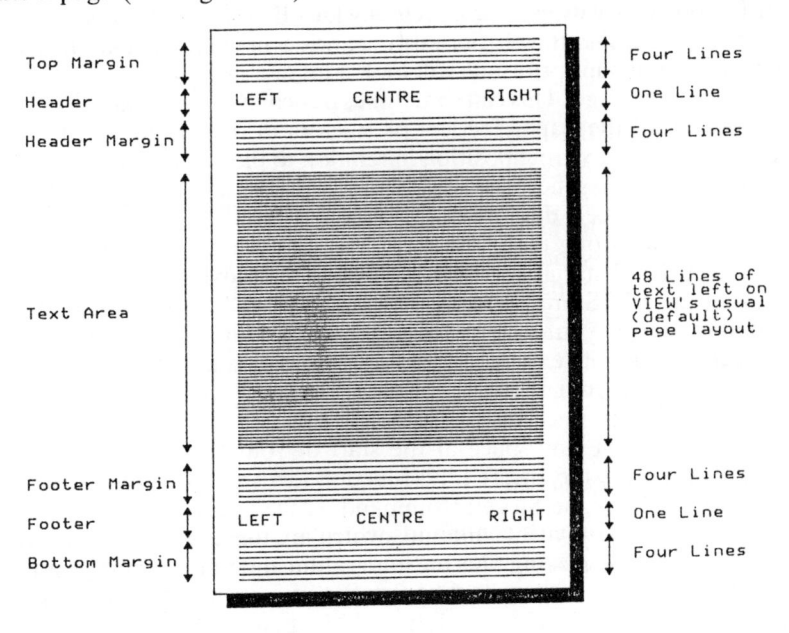

```
Top Margin          ↕                          ↕  Four Lines
Header              ↕   LEFT   CENTRE   RIGHT  ↕  One Line
Header Margin       ↕                          ↕  Four Lines

Text Area                                         48 Lines of
                                                  text left on
                                                  VIEW's usual
                                                  (default)
                                                  page layout

Footer Margin       ↕                          ↕  Four Lines
Footer              ↕   LEFT   CENTRE   RIGHT  ↕  One Line
Bottom Margin       ↕                          ↕  Four Lines
```

Figure 4.2 VIEW's default page settings.

Page Length (PL)

If you are using fanfold paper, you will find that it is most important to match the files you produce on VIEW to the exact length of the page. The default setting is to print 66 lines, but not all computer paper is exactly 11 inches long (true A4 paper can accommodate 70 lines) - and not all printers print six lines per inch - so you need some way of matching the printed output with the page length so that the printer always starts printing in exactly the same place at the top of each page. This is achieved using the **PL** Stored Command, which should be followed by a number giving how many lines long you wish each page to be. For example, to set the page length to A4 size you should press **SHIFT** *f8* and enter the **PL** Stored Command in the left-hand margin, then press RETURN and place the number 70 immediately following it on the same line, i.e.

PL 70

Left Margin (LM)

If you have already formatted your text to the default ruler length in mode 3 or 0, your text will be 74 characters wide. If your paper is A4 or 11¾ x 8¼ inches, the sheets will probably be wide enough to take at least 80 characters, and your printouts will look a lot neater if the text is positioned centrally on the page! This can sometimes be achieved physically, by altering the position of the paper feeders or tractors in the printer itself, so that the paper is in the correct position in relation to the print head for a centred printout. (The snag here can be that if you are also using a dot matrix printer to do screen dumps, or BASIC program listings, the paper may then be in the wrong place for them.) The alternative is to make VIEW insert a left-hand margin all the way through your text at the printout stage, by using the **LM** Stored Command. This command needs to be inserted right at the top of your text to act on the whole thing, but can also be used to indent blocks of text, as one or more **LM** commands can be entered anywhere within your text.

You may not have any space at the start of your text, so go right to the top line and press the Insert Line function key (*f6*), which will give you a blank line to enter the Stored Command. Once again, the command must be entered in the invisible margin on the extreme left-hand side of the screen display by placing the cursor on the new blank line, then press **SHIFT** (*f8*). The cursor will then jump sideways into the two character margin, and you can enter the letters **LM**, then press RETURN to leave the margin. Apart from the case of **CE**, **LJ** and **RJ**, VIEW will not print the line with a command on it, so it is no good typing any text on the blank line after the command. What VIEW does expect to see on that line, though, is a number to show how many blank spaces are to be inserted as a left-hand margin before the text itself on printing each line. By careful inspection of the results from your printer, you should be able to see roughly what space you need to leave to centre the text. It may be anything up to six or eight spaces, so enter your estimate on the line with the **LM** command in the margin, then try printing some text on a spare sheet of paper to see if the text is properly centred. If not, you can always press **ESCAPE**, and begin again by entering a new figure. Once you are happy with this, it is a simple matter to include the necessary **LM** command at the top of each document you intend to print.

Page Eject (PE)

While using **SCREEN** to check your text and page layouts, you may notice one or two untidy lines or words straggling at the beginning of a page, or a section heading at the bottom of one page, with its following paragraph on the next. Under these circumstances it is often useful to force VIEW to jump to a new page early, so that the resulting printout looks neater. This is achieved by putting in an extra blank line at the point where you wish the page eject to occur, or finding an existing blank line between paragraphs, and placing a Page Eject command (**PE**) on it in the margin. When you come to **SCREEN** the text again, you will see the effect of the new page break, and when your text is finished you can go through it adjusting the layout for the best results by adding **PE** commands wherever necessary.

The Page Eject command can be used in another way: if it is followed by a number on the same line in the text area, this is known as a 'conditional' Page Eject, where VIEW will only force a new page at the **SCREEN**, **PRINT** or **SHEETS** stage if there are less than the quoted number of lines left. Thus if you add the line:

PE 12

to your text just before a 12-line table or specially laid out section of text, VIEW will eject the whole thing if there are not enough lines to print it in one section. It is quite a good idea to put commands of this sort in at the writing stage as a precaution if you are not sure what the final layout and pagination of your work will be.

Line Spacing (LS)

Although all your work appears as single-spaced text when you are working on the computer with VIEW, it is possible to change the spacing at the printout or preview stages by using the Line Space (**LS**) command. As usual, this is placed in the left-hand margin using the Edit Command function key (*f8*), and once RETURN is pressed, adding a figure in the text area to tell VIEW how many extra blank lines to print between each text line. Hence the following:

LS 1

will give one blank line, or double-spaced text, which is very easy to work on at the proof-reading stage.

Top, Bottom, Header and Footer Margins

You may not want to print headers and footers on your document, so you may well need to reduce the number of lines left at the top and bottom of each page. This is often necessary, as VIEW's standard settings leave nine blank lines at the top of each page, and another nine at the bottom. Right at the top of each page there is a space controlled by the Top Margin (**TM**) command, then one line is left for the header itself, and directly beneath that, VIEW leaves another four blank lines for the Header Margin (**HM**). The layout at the bottom of each page is similar. The last four lines are the Bottom Margin (**BM**); above that one line is set aside for the footers, and immediately above that, lying between the footers and the last text line, is the Footer Margin (**FM**). **TM**, **HM**, **FM** and **BM** are all given default settings of four by VIEW, unless you specify otherwise.

A quick way to achieve a more efficient page layout if you do not intend to use the header or footer facilities, is to set both **HM** and **FM** to zero, by entering each as an Edit Command on a separate line at the start of your document, followed by a zero in the text area as follows:

HM 0
FM 0

A more useful page layout, which allows the proper use of headers or footers, might be:

TM 2
HM 3
FM 2
BM 3

Remember that VIEW leaves an extra line at the top and bottom for the headers and footers, and these lines are always present in your printout or **SCREEN**ing of the text, unless you are using VIEW version 3.0 or later, which includes an extra Stored Command to cancel them. (See Chapter Seven.)

Headers and Footers

Using headers and footers sensibly can give a very professional look to your work as they are each printed at precisely the same place on each page. They can be either text comments, or page or chapter numbers. VIEW splits the header and footer lines into three sections each: left, centre and right, and it expects to see three entries per line, although some of these can be left blank. (It is best to keep the three parts brief, so that VIEW can position them evenly across the page.) The forward slash character (/) can be used to separate the three parts (and is then known as a delimiter) on the lines defining the headers and footers. In the case of a header, you might want to give the chapter number, title and author of a work. To set up this example, first insert a blank line near the top of your text, then place the necessary Define Header (**DH**) Stored Command in the left-hand margin. This is done using **SHIFT** *f8*, entering the letters **DH**, then pressing RETURN as before. The first character you enter on the remainder of this line should be the forward slash, followed by the left-hand part of the header, then another forward slash, the centre section, a forward slash, the right-hand part, and finish the line with another forward slash. The line should look something like this:

DH /Chapter 4/VIEW/ Clive Williamson/

In fact, a number of different punctuation marks can be used as a delimiter, as long as you are consistent with their use on any single line. VIEW interprets the first character on the line as the delimiter, so you can get some very odd effects if you forget to put one in at the start of the line.

You can use the **SCREEN** function to check that your header will look correct at the printout stage. Note that the headers and footers are positioned relative to the current ruler, so if a short ruler is active you may get some strange results. If you do, insert a default ruler at a point in the text before the next page break. Another source of trouble related to this is the fact that the headers and footers will all be bunched together if they follow a ruler in which formatting has been disabled by removing the '<' character.

If you only require one or two parts of the header, you simply miss out the text part, but enter the delimiters as normal. Hence if you wanted to place the date in the top right of each sheet, you would use:

DH ///28.11.85/

and the software will see the left and centre sections of the header as being blank.

Footers are set up in exactly the same way as headers, again having three potential sections, only this time using the Define Footer Stored Command (**DF**). Using the footer facility is an ideal way of numbering the pages of your document. VIEW makes provision for you to do this by assigning a special register for page numbers during printout. A register is a place in the computer's memory set aside by the software to act as a counter, and each time VIEW prints a page, it adds one to the counter. In all, VIEW has 26 registers of this sort - one for each letter of the alphabet - and most of these are initially unspecified in their use. Two have been set aside to count line numbers (L) and page numbers (P), and it is the P register that we will use to generate our automatic page numbering. The split vertical line character (¦ in all modes except Mode 7, where it appears as ‖) is interpreted by VIEW as an instruction to print the contents of the register for the letter following it. Hence, the following line:

DF //¦P//

will cause the page number to be printed in the centre of the page on the footer line. We can make the page number look a little more prominent by printing a 'dash' either side, i.e:

DF //- ¦P -//

(The ¦ character is to be found on the shifted / key at the top right of the BBC Micro's keyboard, underneath the **BREAK** key.) The best plan where the same footer is needed all the way through a document is to place the **DF** command fairly near the top of your text, just under all the margin and the header definitions.

For the header and footer definitions to function fully, they must be placed before the first page break for which they are required. Thus a header definition needed on the first page of printout has to be stored before any text, while a footer can be defined at any point before the page break. Headers and footers can both be altered as many times as required during a long document, as long as the new footers are defined before the page break on the page where they are to appear, and the new headers defined at a point before the preceding page break.

Setting Registers (SR)

The page numbering does not have to start at page 1 - you can alter the number at which it begins for any number you like using the Set Register command (**SR**). Thus, if you wanted your page numbering to begin at 25, you would enter the Stored Command:

SR P 25

at the top of the document, or above the header or footer definition in which the P register is used.

Another good way of using a register is to set one up to print section or chapter numbers as well as the page number. In the case of a chapter, you could use the **SR** Stored Command to set the relevant chapter number, then print it out before each page number as follows:

```
SR C 1
DF //- ;C.;P -//
```

On printout, this will produce a sequence of footers:
— 1.1 — — 1.2 — — 1.3 —
and so on.

There are a couple of points to watch when using headers and footers. The first is that the ruler should be set to the same length throughout the text, or at least just before each page break, in order to obtain the left, centre and right components in the same position on each page. If you have shortened the ruler for any reason, it is best to add a new full-width ruler in the text at the point where the page break comes. Also, if you make an end section of a header or footer too long, you will again find the layout looking strange. VIEW can cope with a maximum of 64 characters in a header or footer definition, but expects them to be fairly evenly split, so that the middle section can be centred properly on the page. For this reason it is best to place the longest component in the centre of the line.

Creating a 'Start' File

By now you have probably used a relatively large number of Stored Commands to achieve the desired page layout. The final result may be similar to Figure 4.3.

```
LM 4
LS 1
TM 2
HM 3
DH /(left)/(centre)/(right)/
FM 2
BM 3
SR P 1
DF /(left)/- ;P -/(right)/
.. .......*........*........*........*........*........*........<
```
Figure 4.3

Obviously, this takes some time to enter each time you begin a new document, so the ideal thing is to create a 'start' file holding all the relevant details, then save that file (without any text) under the name **START**, so that it can readily be loaded back in and used as the starting point for future work. It is a good idea to include your usual text ruler in the start file, whether it be the default Mode 3 ruler, for example, or one you have designed yourself; you can then be sure that your results will be abolutely consistent.

Line Layout

Three Stored Commands that you may find useful at this stage are to do with the positioning of text on any particular line. They are:

Left justify text line *(LJ)*
Right justify text line *(RJ)*
Centre text *(CE)*

As before, these commands are only operative at the **SCREEN** or printout stage.

Left Justify (LJ)

If you place the **LJ** Stored Command in the left-hand margin, the contents of the line will always be printed to the left-hand side of the page. This is specially useful for printing number registers. It can also be used to protect something like an address in a letter from being formatted by mistake. If the parts of the address were on consecutive lines, and the block were formatted in error, the short address lines would be instantly strung together across the page as continuous text, ruining your layout. (An easier way of preventing this happening is to remove the right-hand formatting margin symbol on the ruler above the section to be protected, then insert a normal ruler underneath.)

Right Justify (RJ)

The Right Justify command (**RJ**) can be used whenever you want to align one or more lines of text with the right-hand margin at the printout stage. This can sometimes be useful if you are printing a date, address, an inset table, or some sort of list that has to be against the right-hand margin. As with other Stored Commands, a line with **RJ** on it cannot be formatted by mistake.

Centre Text (CE)

A very useful Stored Command is the one to centre any text on the same line as the command (**CE**). This is used to automatically centre any title, or section of text, at the screen or print stage. One thing to remember when using this command is that as with the headers and footers, VIEW centres the text by comparing it with the current ruler, so apparently odd effects can result if you have changed the ruler from normal for any reason.

Note: Other effects that you are likely to want to use at the printout stage involve special control of the printer to produce bold and underlined text, or different typefaces. These are governed by the VIEW Printer Drivers, and are dealt with in Chapter Five.

Creating a Help Page

By now we have looked at quite a few of the Stored Commands. They are all described in the VIEW manual, and if you have version 3 of VIEW you will also have a list of all the commands on a reference card. If you do not have the VIEW 3 reference card - and you are using disc drives - then you may find it useful to create one of your own, but one that can be displayed on the computer's screen whenever you need to see it. Figure 4.4 shows the sort of thing you can create on disc:

```
HM  0
TM  0
FM  0
BM  0
..  .........*.........................*...<
    VIEW Stored Commands and default values

    CE        Centre Text on line
    LJ        Left Justify line
    RJ        Right justify line
    CO        Comments (not printed)

    LM        Left Margin                   <0>
    LS        Line Spacing (-1)             <0>
    PL        Page Length                   <66>
    TM        Top Margin                    <4>
    HM        Header Margin                 <4>
    DH        Define Header /L/C/R/         <1>
    FM        Footer Margin                 <4>
    BM        Bottom Margin                 <4>
    DF        Define Footer /L/C/R/         <1>
    HE 0/1    Turn Headers off/on           <1>
    FO 0/1    Turn Footers off/on           <1>
    TS 1/0    Two-sided document on/off     <0>
    EP        Even Page eject
    OP        Odd Page eject

    DM ab     Define Macro (two letters)
    EM        End Macro definition
    SR        Set Register
    HT        Highlight Character
    PB        Page Breaks off/on            <on>
```

Figure 4.4

To make up the 'reference card' you need to begin a new file - call it **TEXT** if you like - and type in the details just as you see them here. (There are seven spaces separating each of the command letters from its description.) The figures in angled brackets are the default values of the command in each case. Once the text has been entered, **SAVE** the file under the name **HELP1**. To see the file simply go into the Command mode and enter:

SCREEN HELP1

whereupon the text will be read in from the disc and displayed on the screen, without actually affecting the running of VIEW. The page is designed to fit all the 40 and 80 character display modes on the BBC Micro. You could also make up similar help pages for the VIEW Command mode commands, or useful disc commands, to save you looking them up in manuals all the time (although some may prefer to print them out as home-made reference cards!).

CHAPTER FIVE

Printing from the VIEW Family

Beyond the standard printout described in Chapter Three, VIEW is capable of giving commands to many printers to control their more advanced functions (typically bold and underlined text), making your work look even more professional. These results are achieved by way of the VIEW Printer Drivers, which can be loaded into VIEW, ViewSheet or ViewStore at any time before the printing stage. The drivers send the correct control codes to the printer to make it switch bold or underlining effects on and off, and can offer additional, or 'extended' sets of features when used with some printers. Originally the Printer Drivers were available as a collection of drivers for specific printers, but now a Printer Driver Generator is also supplied, which can create customised drivers for printers not already supported by the software. The Printer Drivers and the Generator program normally come with VIEW 3.0, but must be bought as extras by Master owners, or by those with any other versions of the VIEW software.

Two of the function keys generate the bold and underline codes. **SHIFT** *f4* (called Highlight 1) gives underline (indicated by a dash on screen), while immediately next to it, **SHIFT** *f5* is used to control the bold effect (indicated by a star). Using the Highlight code once turns the effect on, while a second inclusion turns it off again. In View 3.0 the Highlight characters appear in reverse video, making them easier to spot. Highlight characters are ignored by the VIEW software when text is formatted, and so do not affect the finished line length at the **SCREEN** and **PRINT** stage.

Using a Pre-made Driver

A number of ready-made printer drivers are supplied with the Printer Driver Generator software. These are for the following printers:

```
F I.......*........*.......*........*.......*........*.......*........*.....<
  ⌂CHAPTER FIVE⌂

  ▌Printing from the VIEW Family▐

  Beyond the standard printout described in Chapter Three, VIEW is
  capable of giving commands to many printers to control their more
  advanced functions (typically ▌bold⌂ and ▌underlined▐ text), making your
  work look even more professional.  These results are achieved by way
  of the VIEW Printer Drivers, which can be loaded into VIEW, ViewSheet
  or ViewStore at any time before the printing stage.  The drivers send
  the correct control codes to the printer to make it switch bold or
  underlining effects on and off, and can offer additional, or
  'extended' sets of features when used with some printers.

  Two of the function keys generate the ▌bold⌂ and ▌underline▐ codes.  SHIFT
  f4 (called Highlight 1) gives ▌underline▐ (indicated by a dash on
  screen), while immediately next to it, SHIFT f5 is used to control the
  ▌bold⌂ effect (indicated by a star).  Using the Highlight code once
  turns the effect on, while a second inclusion turns it off again.  In
  View 3.0 the Highlight characters appear in ▌reverse video⌂, making them
  easier to spot.  Highlight characters are ignored by the VIEW software
  when text is formatted, and so do not affect the finished line length
  at the SCREEN and PRINT stage.
  ▪
```

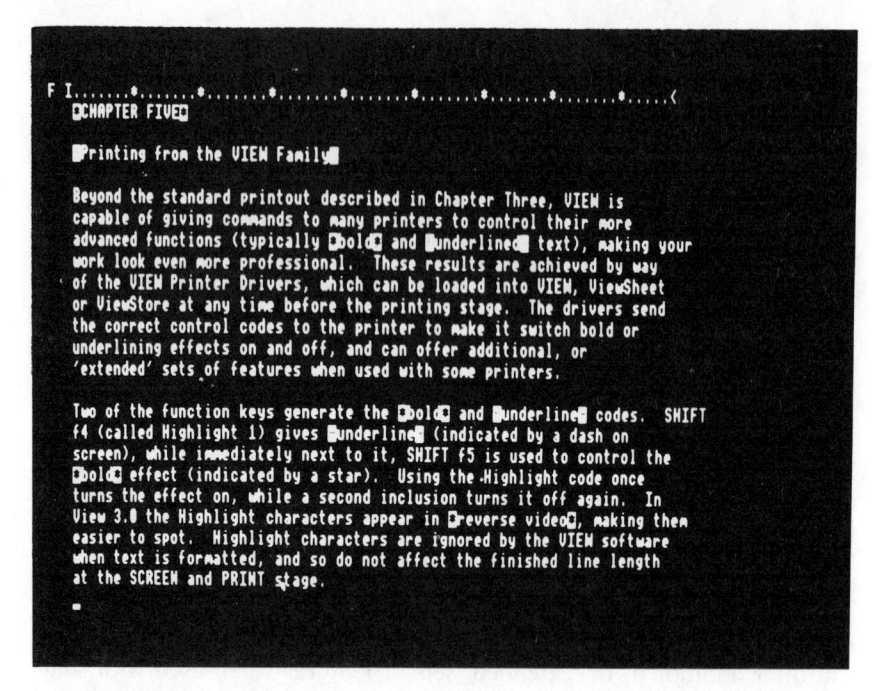

Figure 5.1 Typical screenful of text showing Highlight characters.

CHAPTER FIVE

Printing from the VIEW Family

Beyond the standard printout described in Chapter Three, VIEW is
capable of giving commands to many printers to control their more
advanced functions (typically bold and underlined text), making your
work look even more professional. These results are achieved by way
of the VIEW Printer Drivers, which can be loaded into VIEW, ViewSheet
or ViewStore at any time before the printing stage. The drivers send
the correct control codes to the printer to make it switch bold or
underlining effects on and off, and can offer additional, or
'extended' sets of features when used with some printers.

Two of the function keys generate the bold and underline codes. SHIFT
f4 (called Highlight 1) gives underline (indicated by a dash on
screen), while immediately next to it, SHIFT f5 is used to control the
bold effect (indicated by a star). Using the Highlight code once
turns the effect on, while a second inclusion turns it off again. In
View 3.0 the Highlight characters appear in reverse video, making them
easier to spot. Highlight characters are ignored by the VIEW software
when text is formatted, and so do not affect the finished line length
at the SCREEN and PRINT stage.

Figure 5.2 Printed results from the same text.

Facit 8105 (Daisywheel)
Ricoh Flowriter 1600 (Daisywheel)
Epson FX80 (Dot matrix)
Juki 6100 (Daisywheel)
JP 101 (Dot matrix)

These drivers are often suitable for a number of other models of printer. For example, many dot matrix printers now use the same control codes as the Epson range. If none of these drivers is suitable for your printer you can easily make one up using the Printer Driver Generator program.

The Drivers are loaded into the machine using the **PRINTER** command from the Command screen, e.g:

PRINTER FX4 <RETURN>

for the Epson Driver, or:

PRINTER JUKI4 <RETURN>

to load the Juki 6100 driver. Once a driver has been loaded, the Command screen will change to include the printer driver filename (e.g. Printer default will become Printer JUKI4), and you can proceed to print your text obtaining the extra functions supported by the driver concerned. Note: the Master Compact has the Epson Printer Driver as standard. This can be defeated by entering:

PRINTER <RETURN>

Extended Highlights

The extended features are available when using some some types of printer (such as the Epson range), where a variety of effects such as italic, superscript and subscript can be obtained with combinations of the two Highlight characters. At the outset the two Highlights are given codes 128 and 129 by VIEW, but to make Extended Highlights work you must first redefine Highlight 2 to a new code number (130) using the Stored **HT** command followed by the Highlight number and then the new code number you wish to give it; i.e:

HT 2 130

You can then obtain the following effects on your printer:

Highlight	Effect
-	Underline
***	Bold
*	Select extended character set, including accented letters
*_	Turn subscript on
**	Turn superscript on
**_	Cancel superscript or subscript
*--	Select alternate font
_	Italics
*---	Reset all functions to off
--	Used by ViewIndex (see Chapter Seven)

Microspacing

This sort of spacing is more often supported by daisywheel printers (such as the JUKI 6100). Here, the print head can be precisely controlled to produce even gaps between the words, making right-justified text far easier to read. This feature can be utilised by VIEW using the MICROSPACE command, which will operate if a suitable Printer Driver has been loaded. The default printing pitch is 10/120ths of an inch, giving 12 pitch letter spacing, but this can be altered by entering a different figure after the command. For example:

`MICROSPACE 12 <RETURN>`

will give 10 pitch printing.

Making Your Own Driver

If a Printer Driver does not exist for your type of printer, you will need to use the Printer Driver Generator software to create your own. It is run from BASIC by placing the Printer Driver disc in drive 0 and, while holding down the **SHIFT** key, briefly pressing **BREAK**. Once this is done, the Generator program is loaded and run automatically, and you should see the title page appear on the screen. The Generator consists of a series of questions to be answered about the printer you are using, relating to its general facilites, and the codes required to obtain the special effects. Before you try to answer the questions, it is useful to know one or two things about your model of printer. These include things like:

Does your printer have auto line feed?
Does your printer auto-bold?

Does your printer auto-underline?
(If not, can it be made to back space with a code 8?)
Does the your printer support microspacing?
What are the character codes needed to print the $ £ and signs?

To find out which character numbers are needed by the printer to give the $, £ and signs, you can usually consult your printer manual, which should contain a table of all the characters available, and the numbers or character codes required to print them out.

If you do not have a list like this, or you do but cannot actually understand it (and don't worry - you wouldn't be the first not to!) another way of finding out is to run a short BASIC program that prints all the character numbers from 32 to 126 and 160 to 254. Here is a listing to do so:

```
10 PRINT "     TURN PRINTER ON"
20 PRINT "(then press the SPACE BAR)"
30 input=GET
40 REPEAT UNTIL input=32
50 VDU 2
60 FOR N=32 TO 126
70 PROCprint
80 NEXT N
90 FOR N=160 TO 254
100 PROCprint
110 NEXT N
120 VDU 3
125 END
130 DEFPROCprint
140 PRINT N;" = "; CHR$(N);"    ";
150 ENDPROC
```

As with the Printer Driver Generator program, the BBC Micro should be running BASIC before you use this program. The results are printed continuously across the printer on consecutive lines. If you want to make them easier to read, delete the final semicolon in line 140. Each code number and the character it produces will then appear on a separate line.

Printing the Pound Sign

One of the chief problems encountered by people trying to print from the VIEW software without a Printer Driver is how to print the £ sign. If you have to include a £ in your text, you will more than likely find that it is printed as a single reversed inverted comma ('), which may prove rather frustrating if you are trying to print a financial report. The secret is often to replace the £ in your text with the hash sign (#), as this will generally produce the £ sign from a daisywheel printer with an English character set, and can also be set up to give a £ from most dot matrix models.

Printing the Pound Sign by Switching Fonts on the Epson Range

In the case of those dot matrix printers using Epson-style control codes, the hash (#) will often reproduce as a hash unless the character set inside the printer is switched from American (the normal, or default state) to English.

Before running the VIEW software, you can switch from the American character set to the English using the Printer Menu program from Chapter Two, or by entering:

```
VDU 2,1,27,1,82,1,3,3 <RETURN>
```

while still in the BASIC language. To switch back to the American set enter:

```
VDU 2,1,27,1,82,1,0,3 <RETURN>
```

Printing Several Files at Once

If you are saving your files on disc, you will find that **SCREEN**, **PRINT** and **SHEETS** will work when several different filenames are entered consecutively after the relevant command. Up to 33 are allowed - as long as each file name is only one character long - the names must all fit on one line of the screen display. The following example would print FILE1, FILE2 and FILE3 one after the other:

```
PRINT FILE1 FILE2 FILE3 <RETURN>
```

Any page numbering, headers, footers and other formatting details specified in the first of the files will be maintained throughout, unless you alter them in a subsequent file. The text will be printed without a break from one file to the next unless you deliberately include page ejects at the end of each file. The only precautions you must take are to ensure that the use of rulers is compatible through all the files to be printed, and to put a Page Eject command at the end of each file, if you wish the next to begin at the start of a new page. This technique can be very useful if you need to make a document up from standard sections, or if your files are broken up into small sections as a result of memory constraints (see 'Running Out of Memory' Chapter Six).

Printing Several Identical Copies

You may wish to print several copies of the same document, and although VIEW does not specifically ask how many copies you require at the printout stage, it is possible to make multiple copies nevertheless. Here you simply specify the same name over and over again when entering a list of files to be printed using **PRINT** or **SHEETS**, and VIEW will reprint the same file each time. Thus if you give the file a single character name you can print up to 33 copies in one go, this being the maximum number of separate characters that can follow the abbreviated printing commands on one line. Again, if you are not using footers in your document, you will probably have to include a Page Eject (**PE**) command at the end of the text, to ensure that each copy begins on a new page. A useful precaution if you are using automatic page numbering is to include a command to reset the numbering to one (or the required start number) at the start of each file. For example:

SR P 1

If you fail to do this, the page numbering becomes cumulative through each copy.

Printing Problems

Printing from Cassette with VIEW 1.4

If you use cassettes rather than disc drives, you should not experience any difficulties unless you happen to have the earliest version of VIEW (1.4). When printing from cassette, VIEW needs to turn the recorder on and off automatically, and reads in one small section (or 'block') of data at a time. Version 1.4 gives problems with some cassette recorders, as it only allows the minimum time to turn the recorder on and off. Some machines cannot stop and start fast enough, so the data is not read correctly from the tape. The way round this is either to upgrade to a later version of VIEW (preferably 3.0 or beyond) or to use the Printer Driver (called the Memory driver) specially created by Acornsoft to get round the problem. This is available direct from Acorn Computers, or as part of the Printer Driver Generator software (where the file is called **MPRINT**).

The Wrong Format on the First Page?

Sometimes when you are using headers and/or footers in your text, you can find that the first page looks all wrong. This is usually because you have left a blank line or some text at the top of your file, before the header and footer details. This can result in a first page without the expected formatting, or a complete blank page for no apparent reason. The way to cure this problem is to delete any blank lines, and place the header and footer definitions right at the top of the file. Move any spurious text below the Stored Commands.

Too Many Blank Lines at the Top and Bottom of Each Page

To prevent normal nine blank lines being printed at top and bottom of each page, you need to defeat the default settings for the header and footer margins. As explained in the previous chapter, VIEW usually leaves four blank lines each for top and bottom, header and footer margins, as well as one line each for the headers and footers themselves, it is often handy to turn all the margins off in order to make the best use of the available page length. This is especially useful if you are printing short documents or letters on single sheets of paper. To turn all the margins off, you should enter the following right at the top of your file:

TM 0
HM 0
BM 0
FM 0

using the Edit Command function key (**SHIFT** *f8*) each time to enter the letters, and pressing RETURN to make the cursor jump back into the text area to enter the zeros. You will find that VIEW 1.4 and 2.1 still leave one blank line at the top and bottom of each page: these are the header and footer lines, which cannot be turned off in this way. (VIEW 3 has a new Stored Command (**PB**) which is used to turn off all the Page Break effects. See Chapter Seven.)

CHAPTER SIX

Common VIEW Problems

Running Out of Memory

If you write long documents using Mode 3 or 0 on a Model B micro you will find that you soon run out of memory. The capacity is about 1500 words in Mode 3, and only 800 or so in Mode 0. The point at which memory runs out on a Model B+, B+128 or Master is much higher, at around 4000 words, and if you are using HI-VIEW or VIEW 3 in the the second processor, the capacity is roughly double that, or about 8500 words. Whatever system you are using, sooner or later you may find that you run out of space for your text. There is an indication of the amount of memory available in the machine on the top line of each of the VIEW software Command screens - 'Bytes Free' gives the number of characters the micro has space for in its memory - but if you are working continuously you may not notice that you are running out of space until you hear a warning 'bleep' from the micro. Early versions of VIEW then revert to the Command screen automatically, while the later versions (VIEW 3 and beyond) display an inverse (i.e. white on black) warning:

`Memory full - Press ESCAPE`

In either case, you will notice that most of the last line you typed has disappeared, as the software rejects the last 74 characters when this occurs. On a Model B, the answer may be to change to a 40 character screen mode, such as Mode 6 or 7, that will give you more space. This gives substantially more room for text, but you may have to write using a short ruler to make it easy to read by preventing the screen display from scrolling sideways. You can always re-format the work to the old wider ruler just before printout. In the case of the B+, B+128 and the Master micros, you will already have reached the maximum limit of memory. More drastic measures are called for, and you are faced with two alternatives - which also apply if you are using the Model B but desperately need to stay in an

80 column screen mode. Either you split your text by dividing it into a large first section to be saved as a separate file, then delete the saved portion and work on the remainder until the memory fills up to capacity again, or you can save the whole thing, and use an approach called Continuous Processing. The first of these options is often the more manageable solution, but you may find that the second method suits you best. Here is a description of the two alternatives.

Using Separate Files

Because VIEW lets you screen or print several files in succession, it is perfectly feasible to split a long document into manageable chunks. The **SCREEN, PRINT** and **SHEETS** routines will maintain the page layout and numbering set in the first file until they see something different, so strictly speaking there is no need to use a series of set-up instructions at the beginning of each file. However, it is often time-saving in the long run to place a standard page layout at the start of each separate file. If you have reached the limit of memory, the quickest way to establish a new file is to decide on a suitable place to split the text towards the end of the work so far. This could perhaps be at a point between paragraphs, but not right at the end of the text, in case you need to add any more later. First, **SAVE** the complete file (you could call this FILE1), and check that it is successfully saved by **SCREEN**ing it from the disc. To do so enter:

SCREEN FILE1 <RETURN>

As a precaution, you could lock this file using:

*ACCESS FILE1 L <RETURN>

If you are sure that it is properly saved, decide on a new filename for the second file (e.g. FILE2) and, in the case of VIEW version 3.0, change the working name of the file in memory using the **NAME** command. The section of text which you intend to keep as FILE1 can now be deleted. Place marker one on a spare line above the text at the start of the complete file in memory (i.e. just below the page set-up instructions) by pressing the Set Marker function key (**SHIFT** *f7*), and then pressing '1' when you see the 'MK' prompt appear at the top left of the screen. Then place the second marker at the point where you wish FILE2 to start (in this case press '2' when you see the prompt). Then delete the marked section using the Delete Block (**CTRL** *f0*) function key. (There is more about using markers in Chapter Seven.) If you have set the page register in the set-up, make sure you delete the instruction, as VIEW will automatically keep numbering the pages from the first file when you come to print the two files together.

You are now left with a much smaller file (FILE2) containing the format instructions, the page layout, and the chunk of text you typed in but which would not fit in FILE1. This file can now be added to in the normal way. When complete, FILE2 should be saved using:

SAVE FILE2 <RETURN>

Try SCREENing FILE2 from disc to make sure that you have saved the required section of text correctly, then lock it using:

*ACCESS FILE2 L <RETURN>

FILE2 now contains the second half of the text, so you can **LOAD** in FILE1 again to delete the portion of text that is now also held in FILE2. Again, this can quickly be done by marking the section and using the Delete Block function key. Once you have unlocked FILE1 (by entering *ACCESS FILE1 <RETURN>), you can re-save the final (shorter) version, and once both files are safely on disc you can check that the text still looks correct by screening the two files one after another using:

SCREEN FILE1 FILE2 <RETURN>

You will need to unlock FILE2 before you can resave anything in it. You can repeat this procedure as often as you like, then when you are happy with the way your files look at the **SCREEN** stage, you can print them out by listing all the file names consecutively, i.e:

PRINT FILE1 FILE2 FILE3. ..

and so on. Page numbers will continue correctly through the whole sequence (as long as you have not reset the page register in any of the overflow files).

Continuous Processing

When a file becomes too large to be held in memory in one go, the alternative to splitting it into short separate files is to save the whole thing in the longest form possible, then begin working on it in sections using a technique known as continuous processing. It is important to understand how this method works if you intend to use it, as it is only available to disc users, and can require careful planning of disc space. Once the text has been saved (we will call it OLDFILE), it can be reloaded for continuous processing with the **EDIT** command. This command requires that you specify first the name of the existing file, then a new filename for the edited and/or expanded text to be saved under. This second file will probably take up at least the same amount of disc storage space as the previous file, so you need to be sure that there is plenty of room on the disc you are using. You can do this by deleting any unwanted files on the disc, and using the *COMPACT command (but if you are using anything other than a Master Series machine, make sure there is nothing in the micro's memory first, as this procedure will destroy the contents of the memory!). If you have only one drive, the best thing is to save or transfer the file onto an empty disc, then use the **EDIT** command as follows:

EDIT OLDFILE NEWFILE <RETURN>

Better still (if you have more than one drive) begin the new file on a fresh disc in different drive. Using more than one drive it is possible to specify different drive faces at this stage, e.g.

EDIT :0.$.OLDFILE :1.$.NEWFILE <RETURN>

These measures are designed to prevent inadvertently filling the disc and getting a 'Can't Extend' error message, which may result in some of your work being lost.

In either case, VIEW will read in text from the OLDFILE until there is space for about 1200 characters left. You will then be able to use all the usual VIEW commands to edit the text in memory, and add to it until the memory is full again. Once you are happy with that section of text, you go to the Command page and type **MORE**, whereupon VIEW saves the current block of text in the NEWFILE, reads in the rest of the OLDFILE, and you can start making more additions and changes to the work. It will no longer be possible to use the **SCREEN** command, as the set-up instructions and any page numbering will probably be dependent on the previous section of text, which is no longer in memory, so this stage is only really suitable for adding or removing text, or general editing. Once you have finished the second section, you can either type **MORE** again, to save all the text into the NEWFILE, or if you need to go on, you can force VIEW to save only a part of the second section of text. This will give you space to make more additions, but leaves you with some of the previous work so that you can refer to it to get your bearings. The way to save only part of the text currently in memory is to set a marker (e.g. marker 1) at the point where you want the text to be split, then go to the Command screen and enter:

MORE 1

Using this method, you can go on adding to the file until the disc is full, in theory, but remember that while you do so you are not creating any backups of your work, which could be really dangerous if your disc developed a fault.

There are two ways to end a session of continuous processing. If you are certain that the OLDFILE is empty, (i.e. typing **MORE** gives the response 'Input file is empty'), or you just want to stop work where you are, then the usual way is to enter:

FINISH <RETURN>

which will transfer the remaining text in memory to the NEWFILE, and close both the new and old files. If you enter the **FINISH** command when there is still some text in the OLDFILE, this will automatically be added to the end of the NEWFILE before it is closed. The second, and more abrupt method of stopping work is to enter the somewhat more curt **QUIT** command. This will close both files without any of the safe transfer routines being carried out, so NEWFILE will not contain any text that was currently in the micro's memory, or the remaining text from the OLDFILE. Hence **QUIT** should only be used to abort a session, and never to end one where a lot of work has been done.

There are several important points to remember if you intend to use continuous processing:

1. It is only possible to preview or print the complete document once the new file has been completed, and if you must then make changes (e.g. to force new pages) you will have to go through the whole **EDIT** routine again, possibly many times.

2. Search, Change and Replace can only be used on the portion of text held in memory at any one time.

3. The 'Can't Extend' error message is pretty fatal, and could result in your losing a lot of valuable work. Hence the elaborate precautions to leave enough space for the new file on the disc.

4. It is not easy to make backups of your work until it is finished, and by then it may be too late.

For these reasons it seems better, on balance, to stick to saving manageable memory-sized chunks of text in separate files, but if you have a lot of very reliable disc storage space, you may prefer to use the latter continuous processing method. (Users of VIEW 3.0 will find that they can usually retrieve lost portions of text using the **READ** command in the event of an error message occurring during continuous processing.)

Can I Save a Section of Text?

Yes, you can place the required section of text between two markers (e.g. 1 and 2) then save it using the **WRITE** command:

WRITE TEXT 1 2

which will save a new file called **TEXT** having only the marked section in it. If you use the **SAVE** command in this way, or fail to set the markers properly, or define the markers incorrectly in the **WRITE** command, VIEW will save the entire contents of memory in the **TEXT** file. If you wish to incorporate one of these files in a new document, you should **READ** it back in (not **LOAD** it), i.e.

READ TEXT 1

VIEW will **READ** the file in at the end of the text, unless you set a marker first (e.g. marker 1), and specify it in the **READ** command as above.

Dealing with Error Messages

Three disc errors that can lead to difficulty are:

1. Disc Full. When there is not enough storage space left on a disc to save the marked text or file in memory.

2. Cat Full. The Acorn **DFS** can only cope with 31 filenames, so if you try to save any more you will be given this error message, and the file will not be saved.

3. Can't Extend. This message occurs when you are using the **WRITE** or **EDIT** commands with a file, and there is insufficient space on the disc immediately after the named file to accommodate an expanded version, and no room at the end of the disc for the **DFS** to save it elsewhere.

All the above errors can be remedied by inserting a new disc with sufficient space for the file in question. With a little knowledge of the Disc Filing System, you may be tempted to try to make space on the disc, either by using the *****COMPACT** command, or by copying the last file onto another disc (using *****COPY**), then deleting it to make space. THIS IS VERY DANGEROUS unless you know exactly what you are doing, as on many models of the BBC Micro the use of *****COMPACT**, *****COPY** and *****BACKUP** can destroy the contents of memory. Thus you could loose the very file you are attempting to save before you have made a copy of it on disc! It is only safe to use these disc commands when using the **ADFS**, or when using the **DFS** on any machine fitted with a second processor, as different areas of memory are then used for handling disc operations.

4. File Open. Sometimes if you inadvertently use the **ESCAPE** key during disc operations such as **READ** or **SAVE**, you may find that you cannot re-save a file under the same name because each time you get a `'File Open'` error message. This happens because the software has been interrupted before it can go through its usual routine of opening up the file for use, then closing it again. On later versions of the BBC Micro there is a *CLOSE command in the **DFS** to get round this problem, but if you have an earlier Model B and an early version of VIEW, you can achieve the same results by typing:

`QUIT <RETURN>`

as if you had been using continuous processing, and this will have no effect other than to properly close the offending file.

5. Locked. If you try to save or delete a file that has previously been protected by being locked using the *ACCESS DFS** command, you have to unlock it first by entering:

`*ACCESS filename <RETURN>`

To re-lock the file afterwards, you should enter:

`*ACCESS filename L <RETURN>`

6. No Text. This message will be seen if you try to **LOAD** a file into VIEW that is not in the correct VIEW format. The way round this is to use the **READ** command instead. The `' No Text '` error message also appears if you run VIEW 1.4 or 2.1 and fail to type **NEW** before pressing the **ESCAPE** key to go into Text mode. This trait was amended on later versions of VIEW, which automatically issue a **NEW** instruction as the language is run.

Problems with VIEW 1.4

The Cursor Sometimes Gets 'Stuck'

This is only a problem when using VIEW version 1.4. If you have **SCREEN**ed a file from disc to check how it will look on printout, the BBC Micro facility which holds the text at the bottom of each screenful is left operative. When you finish previewing the page layout and return to Text mode, you will find that the screen display will still 'lock up' at the end of each screenful of text if you try to move down through your work using the cursor keys. The micro is left in what is known as 'Page Mode'. This can be somewhat annoying, as you have to keep pressing the **SHIFT** key each time it happens (you will see the **SHIFT LOCK** and **CAPS LOCK** lights come on as an indication). To clear the problem, you must go into the Command screen, hold down the **CTRL** key, and briefly press the letter 'O' key. This turns Page Mode off, and you will find that the cursor will move smoothly up and down the text once more. Try to get into the habit of doing this each time you **SCREEN** a file, as it will save you much time and frustration later!

Words Join Up when I Re-format the Text

Sometimes when you have made corrections to a section of text, and you re-format it to tidy it up, you can find that words become unexpectedly joined together. This occurs if you happen to delete the wrong space between two words when the text you are working with is justified. There are two sorts of spaces in VIEW: a space which is typed in by hitting the space bar on the keyboard (this is known as a 'hard space'); and a space inserted by VIEW to pad out the text when justifying a line (known as a 'soft space'). The soft spaces are always inserted AFTER hard spaces, and if you delete a hard space by mistake, you may find that during subsequent formatting, VIEW will leave the hard spaces alone, but may delete soft spaces. This can give the undesirable result of running words together. Consequently if you want to delete spaces in formatted text, you should never delete the first space (you can delete subsequent ones, however).

Problems with VIEW 2.1

When running VIEW 2.1 on a BBC Model B+ or later, it is not possible to make full use of the extra memory available in modes 128 to 135. This version of VIEW was designed with the American BBC Micro in mind, and simply fails to recognise the 'shadow' memory, so the word processor will not run correctly. The listing given below will remedy the problem, and is known as a software 'patch'. When you type it in BASIC, then **RUN** it, a file will be saved on disc (or tape) called **XWORD**. (If the listing fails to work first time, you will see an error message on the screen, so you should be able to investigate the quoted line number and amend the incorrectly typed line. Repeat this process until the program runs successfully and saves the **XWORD** file onto your filing system.) Once you have done this, it is a good idea to save the BASIC listing - which will still be in the machine's memory - by entering:

    SAVE "PATCH" <RETURN>

This acts as a backup for all your hard work typing the listing in, and is best saved on a different disc. To use the file generated by the patch program, you should enter:

*XWORD <RETURN>

before running VIEW, whereupon the **XWORD** program will be loaded and run, correcting the problem. The program then runs VIEW automatically.

```
10 REM VIEW 2.1 PATCH
20 REM for BBC B+ and VIEW 2.1
30 REM (c) Acornsoft 1985
40 DIM MC%&100
50 xjmp=&4C
60 xshadow=&72
70 xreadhiorder=&82
80 xreadscreensize=&85
90 xreadresettype=&FD
100 osbyte=&FFF4:oscli=&FFF7
110 bytevec=&20A
120 codestart=&FFFF0C00
130 FOR I%=4 TO 6 STEP 2
140 O%=MC%
150 P%=codestart
160 [OPT I%
170 .setup
180 JSR setupvecs
190 LDA #xshadow
200 LDX #0
210 JSR osbyte
220 LDX #FNLO(word)
230 LDY #FNHI(word)
240 JMP oscli
250 .resetsetup
260 BCC notthistime
270 LDA #xreadresettype
280 LDX #0
290 LDY #&FF
300 JSR osbyte
310 TXA
320 BEQ setupvecs
330 LDA #247
340 LDX #0
```

```
350 JMP osbyte0
360 .setupvecs
370 PHP
380 SEI
390 LDX #1
400 .checkloop
410 LDA bytevec,X
420 CMP newbytevec,X
430 BNE notalreadysetup
440 DEX
450 BPL checkloop
460 BMI alreadyinstalled
470 .notalreadysetup
480 LDX #1
490 .setuploop
500 LDA bytevec,X
510 STA oldbytevec,X
520 LDA newbytevec,X
530 STA bytevec,X
540 DEX
550 BPL setuploop
560 .alreadyinstalled
570 LDA #248
580 LDX #FNLO(resetsetup)
590 JSR osbyte0
600 LDA #249
610 LDX #FNHI(resetsetup)
620 JSR osbyte0
630 LDA #247
640 LDX #xjmp
650 JSR osbyte0
660 PLP
670 .notthistime
680 RTS
690 .newbyte
700 CMP #xreadscreensize
710 BNE notscreensize
720 PHA
730 TXA
740 AND #7
750 TAX
760 LDY himemtable,X
770 LDX #0
780 PLA
790 RTS
```

```
 800 .notscreensize
 810 CMP #xreadhiorder
 820 BNE notourbyte
 830 LDX #0
 840 LDY #0
 850 RTS
 860 .notourbyte
 870 JMP (oldbytevec)
 880 .osbyte0
 890 LDY #0
 900 JMP osbyte
 910 .himemtable
 920 EQUB &30
 930 EQUB &30
 940 EQUB &30
 950 EQUB &40
 960 EQUB &58
 970 EQUB &58
 980 EQUB &60
 990 EQUB &7C
1000 .word
1010 EQUS "WORD"+CHR$13
1020 .newbytevec
1030 EQUW newbyte
1040 .codeend
1050 .oldbytevec
1060 EQUW 0
1070 ]:NEXT
1080 realend=codeend+MC%-(codestart AND
&FFFF)
1090 OSCLI"S.XWORD "+STR$~MC%+" "+STR$~
realend+STRING$(2," "+STR$~codestart)
1100 END
1110 :
1120 DEFFNLO(X)=X AND 255
1130 DEFFNHI(X)=(X AND &FF00)DIV256
1140 DEFPROCSAVE OSCLI"S.XWDSC "+STR$~P
AGE+" "+STR$~TOP:ENDPROC
```

The above listing was first published in *Acorn User,* July 1985.

CHAPTER SEVEN

Advanced Techniques

Speeding Up Your Work

A number of short cuts are made possible by the nature of the word processor software and the computer itself. For example, VIEW contains commands to help you look for specific words or phrases, or markers set within the text. It also allows abbreviations for some of the commands (e.g. **PRINT** becomes P; **LOAD** is L) and the latest versions of the software let you pre-define the name of the file you are working on, so there is no need to keep typing it in each time you save the text. It is particularly easy to save paragraphs or large sections of text that you need to use time and time again, and read them into a new file whenever they are required. The BBC Micro itself contains commands that can speed up the cursor movement as you gain confidence, and you can also make use of the red function keys to store often used commands or phrases.

Command Abbreviations

To improve your general efficiency when using VIEW, you may like to learn some or all of the abbreviations for the various commands used in the Command mode. They are shown in Table 7.1.

Unlike the disc commands, there is no need to follow the shortened version with a full stop, and if you should do so, VIEW may interpret the punctuation as the character used to separate the command from a filename (i.e. as a delimiter) and may produce error messages to the effect that it does not recognise the name of the file.

Speeding Up the Cursor

As you become more familiar with VIEW - and for that matter any of the other programs in the VIEW family - you will probably find the standard

Command	Abbreviation		
	VIEW 1.4	VIEW 2.1	VIEW 3.0
LOAD	–	L	L
SAVE	–	–	SA
SCREEN	–	–	SC
PRINT	P	P	P
SHEETS	–	–	SH
FORMAT	–	–	FOR
MODE	–	–	M
NEW	–	–	–
OLD	–	–	–
READ	–	–	RE
WRITE	–	–	W
EDIT	–	–	E
MORE	M	M	M
FINISH	F	F	F
QUIT	–	–	–
PRINTER	–	–	PRINTE
MICROSPACE	–	–	MI
COUNT	–	–	CO
CLEAR	–	–	CL
SEARCH	S	S	S
CHANGE	C	C	C
REPLACE	R	R	R
FOLD	N/A	–	FO
WILD	–	–	–
FIELD	–	–	FI
NAME	N/A	N/A	N
SETUP	N/A	N/A	SET

Table 7.1

speed at which the cursor moves around the screen a little on the slow side. This is easily rectified using two of the BBC Micro's ***FX** commands. ***FX** 11 governs the length of time before a key auto-repeats if it is held down, while ***FX** 12 controls the time between each auto-repeat. The default settings for these times are 32 and 8 hundredths of a second respectively, and it is unwise to reduce them too much or the slightest pressure on a key will enter lots of characters, or send the cursor whizzing all over the document, but they can comfortably be adjusted to 25 and 6 hundredths for a much more responsive 'feel'. The new parameters for the FX commands can be entered at any time from the Command screen:

*FX 11,25 <RETURN>
*FX 12,6 <RETURN>

Once you have speeded the cursor movement up, it is not wise to keep your finger pressed the on the keys when doing things like moving up through the text a screenful at a time or deleting lines, as the speed with which the micro remembers the key presses may cause you to overshoot, and accidentally destroy more text than you intended. If you wish to reset both the delay and auto-repeat times to normal, you should enter:

*FX 12,0 <RETURN>

Using Markers

VIEW has six markers in all - two of which are visible as inverse solid blocks - the others do not actually appear on the screen but can be located nevertheless. All markers can be used in a number of different ways. Some VIEW commands work either on the whole text or on a marked section, (**COUNT**, **READ**, **WRITE**, **FORMAT**, **COPY**, **SEARCH**, **CHANGE** and **REPLACE**), and you can also make use of the Go to Marker function key available from Text mode by pressing **SHIFT** *f6*. This can be very useful if you are referring to two or more different passages of text in a long file, since VIEW will give a tiny prompt for the marker number in the top left-hand of the screen when Go to Marker is pressed, allowing you to enter a number from 1 to 6. The cursor will then be positioned under the specified marker. This is a bit like the 'relocate' facility found on some electric typewriters, where the carriage moves to the point where you were last working after making a correction. If you happen to make a mistake when specifying a marker, such as asking for one that you have not yet set, the micro will 'beep' a warning, and the command will be cancelled. Markers 1 and 2 can be cleared from the text using the **CLEAR** command in Command mode. Markers 3 to 6 have to be physically deleted to remove them.

Writing with a Scratch Pad

It is often convenient to make notes somewhere as you work, rather as you might with pen and paper, and the word processor lends itself particularly to doing this! You can either write a set of notes as part of the text (to be deleted later), or you can set aside a special area for your notes in *comment lines*, which are ignored by VIEW at the printing stage. VIEW allows any two letter code to be inserted in the left-hand Stored Command margin, as long as it is not recognised as one of the usual commands, or previously defined as one of the VIEW macros (see the end of this chapter). In practice, it has become a convention to reserve the letters CO - standing for comment - to be used in this way. A set of spare lines can be inserted right at the top of the text, each with CO placed in the margin using the Edit Command function key (**SHIFT** *f8*). Your ideas can be written there, and then readily found by using the Top of Text keystroke. You can then flip instantly back to the end of the work by using Bottom of Text instead. If you are working elsewhere in the text, you may find it easier to set a marker at the point of text entry, then find it directly from the top of text by using the Go to Marker command (**SHIFT** *f6*), and entering the number of the necessary marker in response to the inverse MK prompt that appears at the top left of the screen.

Saving and Loading Portions of Text

By enclosing a section of text in markers it is possible to save only the marked section onto disc or cassette using the **WRITE** command. Suppose you have a set paragraph that you often use to begin or end a letter. Once it is written on the word processor, you can save it for use time and time again as a sort of building block. This is done by placing it within two markers (markers 1 and 2 are best, as they show up on the screen), and making a new file of the marked section only. Position the cursor at the start of the chosen paragraph, and press the Set Marker function key (**SHIFT** *f7*). You will be prompted for the number of the marker to be set. Press '1' and you will see the marker appear as an inverse character. Then move the cursor to the end of the paragraph - the blank line after it is a good place to choose - and set marker 2 in the same way. If you now go to the Command screen, you will see that an extra line has appeared at the bottom of the status display which says Marker(s) set 1,2. Now put a disc in the drive to take the marked section, and decide on a filename for it. We will call it PARA1 in which case the way to save it onto the disc is to enter:

WRITE PARA1 1 2

The numbers at the end specify the markers between which the area to be saved lies. If they are omitted, then VIEW will **WRITE** the whole of the file in memory to the PARA1 file, rather than just the marked section. So **WRITE** is roughly equivalent to the **SAVE** command, except that it can be used with markers, whereas **SAVE** cannot. (If you are using the **DFS** you may also notice that **WRITE** is considerably slower than **SAVE**!)

The corresponding equivalent of the **LOAD** command is **READ**, which enables you to retrieve files and add them to existing text in memory (unlike **LOAD**, which erases anything previously held in memory). **READ** used on its own e.g. **READ PARA1** will place the specified file at the end of the text already in memory. You may want to put it elsewhere, in which case you can set a marker at the point where you want the contents of the file to be inserted, and quote the marker number at the end of the **READ** command, e.g:

READ PARA1 1

In this way, you can assemble new work from often-used passages of text (changing them afterwards if required), or you can re-use complicated tables that you have already created, and generally save a lot of time. The **READ** command can also be used with files prepared from other programs, such as ViewSheet and ViewStore, in the preparation of reports. (See Chapter Fourteen.)

Finding Words in the Text

One of the difficult jobs made easy using a computer is that of finding specific words or phrases in a large text file in memory, and VIEW has no less than three different options available to do this, all with slightly different results. The simplest is **SEARCH**, which allows you to specify any text - a word, part of a word, or group of words - and locate every occurrence of it in the document. Next comes **CHANGE**, which will go through the text changing one string of characters for another automatically, and finally **REPLACE** shows you every occurrence of the string and gives the option of changing it or leaving it as it is.

SEARCH

To use the **SEARCH** facility, you go into the Command screen and enter the word you wish to find - let's say the word is 'aardvark' - as follows:

SEARCH aardvark <RETURN>

When you press RETURN, the software will begin to search for the the specified word - in this case aardvark - and if it comes up with a match within the text it will display the relevant section, with the cursor flashing under the sought-after word. You are then free to make any changes you wish, and then you can move on to the next occurrence of the word in the text by pressing the Next Match function key (**SHIFT** *f1*). If none is found, the software will return you to the Command screen. If the word is not present in the text at all, VIEW will stay in the command mode, and in the case of VIEW 3 will report no string found. In VIEW, the word or phrase you are looking for is always referred to as a 'string', and normally this string will be found by the software whether it is a word on its own, or part of another word. It can be found anywhere in the entire text (working from top to bottom) or you can set two markers and limit your search to the text between them, e.g:

SEARCH aardvark 1 2

will locate the string 'aardvark' anywhere between markers 1 and 2. A string does not have to be just one word - it can be a complete phrase, or any strange group of characters you like - but if you are looking for something with one or more 'space' characters in it, you have to adopt a slightly different approach. Because a space was used to separate the search command from the object of the search, VIEW assumes that a space character will also indicate the end of the search string. If you were now to search for a 'White Elephant' in your text, and entered:

SEARCH White Elephant <RETURN>

early versions of VIEW (i.e. 1.4 and 2.1) would actually be looking for the word 'white' rather than the whole phrase, because they would interpret the space between 'white' and 'elephant' as the end of the search string. VIEW 3 sees the word 'elephant' as a marker instruction, and would report that a 'Bad Marker' had been entered. So to look for a phrase that includes spaces, you must choose a different character to separate the **SEARCH** command from the thing you are looking for, e.g:

SEARCH/White Elephant/

This facility can solve the problem of a search for 'the' finding every 'then', 'these' and even 'theatre' in the text. If you are looking for a short word, you can use this facility to real advantage in the search, and include spaces like this:

SEARCH/ the /

in order to narrow the range of the search by being more specific with your specification. In effect, the character used as a separator (or delimiter, as it is known in the VIEW guide) can be almost any of the punctuation characters (! " # $ % & ' ( ) * + ,. or/) as long as it does not occur in the phrase you are searching for, and as long as you use it consistently throughout! The 'forward slash' (/) is a good one to choose as it is not often found in normal text, and it is available quickly from the keyboard without using the **SHIFT** key.

Change

By way of an advance on the **SEARCH** command, it is possible to make VIEW change every occurrence of a word or phrase into something else using the **CHANGE** command. Here you specify first the existing text you wish to change, then the thing you want it changed into, i.e.

    CHANGE aardvark wombat

would change every 'aardvark' into a 'wombat' throughout the whole text, or marked section. As with **SEARCH**, a phrase containing spaces must be enclosed between delimiters such as the forward slash:

    CHANGE/aardvark/white elephant/

If necessary markers can be set, and their numbers quoted after the instruction, but now the markers must be separated by the forward slash character also:

    CHANGE/aardvark/white elephant/1/2

There is a snag when using the **CHANGE** command, which is that unless you take care, it will work on words within words - often giving unexpected results. Say you want to change to disk:

    CHANGE disc disk

This may seem straightforward, but as well as altering the English spelling into American, you may well find that 'discuss' has become 'diskuss'; 'disclaim' has become 'disklaim' and so on! All rather embarrassing, unless you happen to spot the mistakes, or find them with the ViewSpell spelling checker. The answer may be to specify spaces in the **CHANGE** command:

    CHANGE / disc / disk /

or, if there is any doubt in your mind as to the end result, use the **REPLACE** command, which gives the option of changing one thing into another each time it locates the search item.

Replace

REPLACE works with exactly the same syntax as **CHANGE**, but instead of staying in the Command mode while the text is altered, it works more like **SEARCH** by showing you each occurrence of the search item with the cursor underneath it. You have the option of changing the text to the new string (by pressing 'Y' for Yes), or leaving it as it is (by pressing 'N' for No). Once you have pressed either key, VIEW moves on to present you with the next occurrence of the search string. Only when all the text has been checked does it go back to the Command screen.

Note: It is possible to cancel a **SEARCH**, **CHANGE** or **REPLACE** command at any time by pressing the **ESCAPE** key.

Wild Search

VIEW's search facilities can be extended to find other special characters. For example, all versions of the software let you look for the invisible **TAB** and **RETURN** characters in the text, and also let you specify single characters which can be used in a search to stand for anything at all. These are known as 'wild' characters, and on VIEW versions 1.4 and 2.1 they are used as follows:

? stands for any single character, so if you suspect that you have typed 'there' instead of 'their', you could enter:

`SEARCH / the?? /`

to allow you to check each spelling. This search would also turn up words like 'these' and 'theme'.

`SEARCH ~` (this is the 'tilde' sign, found near the **BREAK** key on the keyboard) will find all the **TAB** characters in the text.

`SEARCH ¦` finds all the RETURN characters in the text. (In Mode 7 this character appears as a double line (‖) on the screen.)

A snag that can occur using this facility is that you may actually wish to search for a ? ~ or ¦ sign, in which case there is a command that lets you change the wild characters. This is the **WILD** command, and it can be followed by up to three characters when entered from the Command screen. The first specifies the character to represent 'any character'; the second is the **TAB** character; and the third the RETURN character. Hence the 'normal' state for this command is:

`WILD ? ~ ¦`

but you can change any of these by entering the command with alternatives. If you want to change the ? into a # for example, you can enter either:

`WILD # ~`

or simply:

WILD £

because VIEW will assume you wish to leave the others unchanged if you leave them out. The software reads the number of characters you have entered after the command, and amends the default signs accordingly.

Version 3.0 of VIEW handles these wild characters differently. By interpreting the 'circumflex' character as a special search character, VIEW 3 gives a much wider range of search options, as follows:

^C	RETURN
^S	Hard space
^Z	Soft space
^T	TAB
^L	Left margin tab
^^	the ^ character
^-	Highlight 1
^*	Highlight 2
^?	Any single character

Distinguishing between Upper and Lower Case During a Search

So far, we have assumed that any searching or changing to be done is of unspecified case. In other words, searching for Aardvark will also find AARDVARK and aardvark, and any changes that are made retain the same case of the thing being replaced. Thus:

CHANGE aardvark elephant

will change also Aardvark into Elephant and AARDVARK into ELEPHANT. As soon as you need to do something case-dependent, such as replacing ViewSheet with ViewStore, you have a problem. At least you do with VIEW 1.4, because there is no way round it, but later versions of the software do allow you to specify the case of search strings. This is achieved using the **FOLD** command. When 'Folding' is on (i.e. in the default mode) case is ignored, and cannot be specified. If you turn the Folding off, however, by entering:

FOLD OFF <RETURN>

from the Command screen, the search becomes completely case-sensitive, and you can then obtain precise results. To restore folding to its default again, you type:

FOLD ON <RETURN>

and you can interrogate the software at any time by entering:

FOLD <RETURN>

from the Command screen, whereupon VIEW will report on the current state of the command (e.g. Folding off). (If you are using VIEW 3, you can enter 0 and 1 instead of **OFF** and **ON**.)

Copying Sections of Text

If there is a phrase, heading or complete paragraph of text you need to place at a number of different places in the text, one way of doing so is to place the relevant passage between markers, move the cursor to the new location where it is needed, then press the **COPY** key. VIEW will make a copy at the new cursor position, and you can move on and repeat this procedure as many times as you need to repeat the marked section. This facility can be extremely useful if you have a table format where the results are different, as you can copy the whole thing, then edit the new values into it.

Using the Function Keys

In addition to performing the range of operations shown on the function key strip in VIEW's Text mode, the BBC Micro's red function keys can be assigned extra duties which can significantly speed up your use of the VIEW software. Each key can be used in two ways: in Text mode they can be loaded with often used words and phrases, which can save a lot of time when you are typing; and from the Command screen the keys can generate complex or often-used sequences of commands. The BBC Micro can be given new 'definitions' for the contents of each function key using the *****KEY** operating system command. Running a language like BASIC, for example, once a key has been defined it can be used straight away to generate the necessary command or characters stored in it. In the case of the VIEW family, an extra command must be given to the micro first, in order to 'free' the contents of the keys. The defining of the keys is all done from the Command screen. You need to enter:

*FX 228,1

Then, to define a function key, you use the *KEY command, followed by the number of the key in question, and what you want it to do. Say you wanted the left-hand function key to hold a long word that you needed to use a lot throughout an article, such as 'staphylococcal'. To load the *f0* key with this, you should enter:

*KEY0 "staphylococcal" <RETURN>

The double quotes are not absolutely necessary, but they do make it clear to the micro that this is a phrase of text to be dealt with, and not a command. If you then go into Text mode, you can make the key print out its contents onto the screen by holding down both the **CTRL** and **SHIFT** keys at once, then pressing *f0*. You will then see the word or phrase appear on the screen as if it had been typed in! The second way of using the function keys is in the Command mode itself, where they can be used to hold command sequences. Say you want a single keypress to lock all the files on your disc. If you are using the **DFS**, this can be done using the command *ACCESS. To make key *f1* lock all the files in every directory, enter:

*KEY1 "*ACCESS *.* L ¦ M" <RETURN>

¦M is a way of making the key enter a 'RETURN' after issuing the instruction. (¦ is the symbol on the key at the top right of the keyboard. In Mode 7, this appears on screen as ⫿). To make use of this key in the Command mode, there is no need to hold down the **CTRL** and **SHIFT** keys. As long as you have already entered *FX228,1, simply pressing the function key on its own will generate the necessary characters, and the current disc drive will whirr into life, locking all the files on that drive. To unlock all the files, another key could be loaded with:

*KEY2 "*ACCESS *.* ¦ M" <RETURN>

which will unlock every file in every directory. Note: If you are using the **ADFS**, you cannot lock every file in every directory, but you can make KEY 1 lock all the files in the current directory using:

*KEY1 "*ACCESS * L ¦ M"

and similarly *KEY2 can unlock the files again if you enter:

*KEY2 "*ACCESS * ¦ M"

Out of interest, if you now try pressing *f0*, you will see your long word appear immediately, but notice that there is no carriage return - the cursor waits at the end of the word. You can remove the letters from the screen using the **DELETE** key, or simply press **ESCAPE** to return to the Text mode. Once in this mode, go to the end of your text, or somewhere where there is a gap, and try pressing **CTRL SHIFT** *f1* as before. You will see the *ACCESS command written on the screen, followed automatically by a carriage return to the next line. VIEW makes no sense of the instruction in this mode, and sees it simply as more text for the document.

Rather than type these function key instructions in each time you use the machine, it would be useful if they could be held in a file to be read in automatically when you begin work. You can edit a VIEW file like the one shown below, then make up a text only version (called **KEYS**, perhaps) which can be read in at any time by typing:

*EXEC KEYS <RETURN>

whereupon the micro will read in the set of definitions just as if they had been typed at the keyboard.

```
*KEY 0 "*DRIVE 0|M"
*KEY 1 "*DRIVE 1|M"
*KEY 2 "*DRIVE 2|M"
*KEY 3 "*DRIVE 3|M"
*KEY 4 "*ACCESS *.* L|M"
*KEY 5 "*ACCESS" *.* |M"
*KEY 6 "SCREEN HELP1:M"    (displays help file from page 59)
*KEY 7 "COUNT 1 2|M"
*KEY 8    ":S:A:G:@:@:@:M:S:@:D:@:@:@|M"(white
text, blue background)
*KEY 9    ":S:A:B:  :  :M:S:@:@:@:@:@| M"(green
text, black ground)
```

Once the text has been entered, you need to create a file which can be read into the Command screen from disc without any adverse effects. VIEW files are not 'pure' text - they contain special characters called control codes - which can upset the micro if you try to display them on the screen, rather than trying to **LOAD** the file into VIEW first. So you need to make a file of text characters only. This is known as as ASCII file (standing for American Standard Code for Information Interchange), and to generate a text-only file you need to **SCREEN** the file and make a copy on disc as you do so. First, press **ESCAPE** to get to the Command Screen, then place a suitable disc in the current drive (assuming you have more than one). Make sure that you have saved a copy of the above VIEW file first, in case anything should go wrong. (If you are using VIEW 1.4, you will have to **SAVE** the file first anyway.) Then enter:

*SPOOL KEYS <RETURN>

The disc will rotate, then stop. The micro has opened a file called **KEYS** on the disc, and will now feed anything that appears on the screen straight to it. Now **SCREEN** the file with the function key definitions, either from disc, or from memory. Once this is done, type:

*SPOOL <RETURN>

to close the **KEYS** file. Then type **NEW** and load the **KEYS** file into VIEW using the **READ** command as follows:

READ KEYS <RETURN>

READ is used instead of the normal **LOAD** command, because it is suitable for bringing text into VIEW that is not in the regular VIEW file format. If you now press **ESCAPE** to go into Text mode, you will see that the file has been read in, and you can go through it deleting any unwanted lines using the *f7* function key until you are left with the required block of text. Do not make any other alterations at this stage, but use the **SAVE** command to re-save **KEYS** in this final form. You will now be able to load all the key definitions into the micro by entering:

*EXEC KEYS <RETURN>

from the Command screen. Using a similar file, a complete 'auto-boot' sequence could be edited together for the BBC machine as follows:

```
*FX 228,1
*FX 202 48
*WORD
MODE 3
SETUP FI
NEW
PRINTER JUKI4
*KEY 0 "*DRIVE 0:M"
*KEY 1 "*DRIVE 1:M"
*KEY 2 "*DRIVE 2:M"
*KEY 3 "*DRIVE 3:M"
*KEY 4 "*ACCESS *.* L¦M"
*KEY 5 "*ACCESS *.*:M"
*KEY 6 "*SCREEN HELP1:M"
*KEY 7 "COUNT 1 2:M"
*KEY 8 ":S:A:G:  :  :M:S:  :D:  :  :@:M"
*KEY 9 ":S:A:B:  :  :M:S:  :  :  :@:M"
```

This can save a lot of time as it can be used at the start of each session to set the micro up to your usual way of working. *FX 202,48 turns off the CAPS LOCK, while SETUP FI sets VIEW's Formatting and Insert modes on, and Justification off (NOTE: for users of VIEW 3 only). You can include the instruction to load in a Printer Driver as well, as long as a copy of the driver is on the same disc.

The above file should be prepared as a text only file using the method described above, and finally saved under the name !BOOT. All that is needed then is to set an auto-start option on the disc by entering:

*OPT 4,3 <RETURN>

This will enable the BBC Micro to read in the contents of any file on drive 0 called !BOOT, as if they had been typed in at the keyboard. To 'boot the system' in this way, you simply press the SHIFT and BREAK keys simultaneously, releasing BREAK first.

Printing Books and Reports

If you wish to print on both sides of the paper to produce results that can be properly bound, VIEW contains three useful stored commands for doing so. The first is **TS**, standing for Two Sided document. This reverses the order of headers and footers on the even numbered pages, and can also print extra spaces in the left-hand margin of odd numbered pages to allow room for binding. The precise number of spaces to be left can be decided by trial and error at first, depending on the exact printer set-up and the method of binding you intend to use. The format of the **TS** command is as follows: to turn the effect on, you enter **TS** as a Stored Command in the left-hand margin as usual and follow it either with **ON** or 1:

TS 1

If you wish to leave a ten character left margin for binding, you would add the number 10 after the command, i.e.

TS ON 10

To turn the effect off you enter:

TS OFF

or **TS** 0, or delete the command altogether. The net result is shown in Figure 7.1.

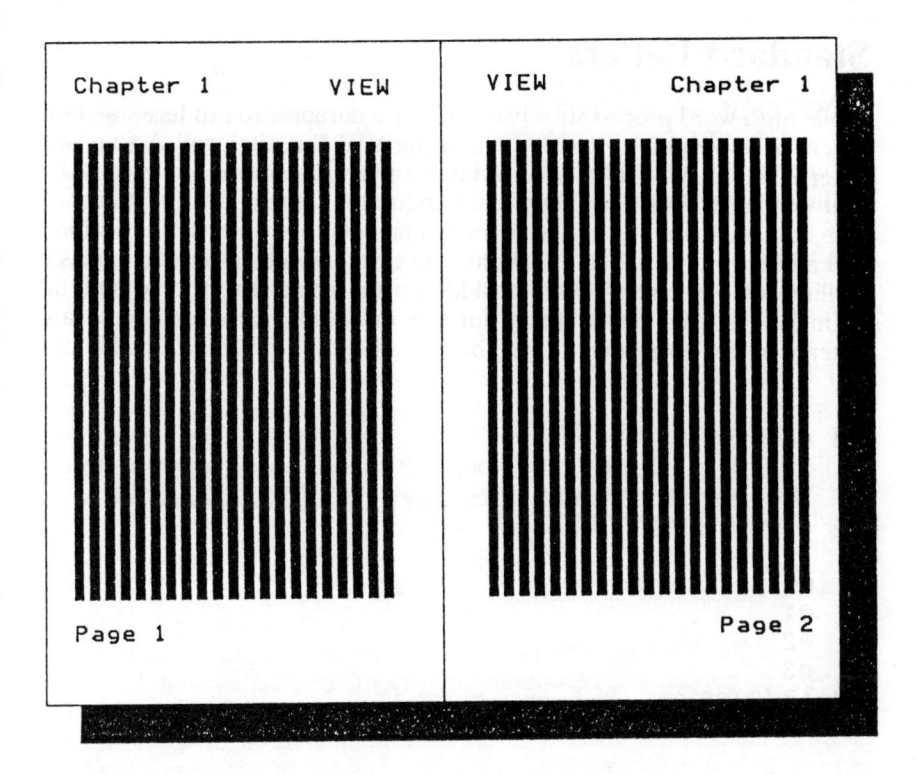

Figure 7.1 Effect of the TS Command

When using a single-sheet printer there is no problem preparing documents in this way, since it is only necessary to take each sheet out and turn it round before printing the next page. With continuous paper, however, you must print the odd pages first, using the **SHEETS** command to miss every other page. You then remove the paper, turn it round and feed it through again, this time printing the even numbered sheets on the reverse side. This way the finished work should be correctly page numbered, and printed on both sides of the paper.

The other commands which can be useful when preparing material for binding are Odd Page (**OP**) and Even Page (**EP**) page ejects. By inserting one of these Stored Commands it is possible to make VIEW give an extra Page Eject to either an odd or even numbered page. This means that something like a new chapter title or section heading can be made to appear on either a left or right-hand page without the need for an extra Page Eject after **SCREEN**ing the text, making the final printed work easier to scan through.

Standard Letters

While most word processors rely on links to a database to produce standard letters, it is possible to create them using VIEW on its own! A standard letter is any document such as a letter, invitation, or press release to be sent to a large number of people, which has the same body of text in each case but which requires different individual details (such as name, position and address) to be added every time the text is printed. VIEW contains a facility called a 'macro' which enables a main block of text to be built up to include special blank spaces for the individual parts, and these are entered in the form of a list at the end of the VIEW file. This list can

```
   DM AA
   .. ....*........*........*........*........*....<
   CE The Horticultural Society

      @0
      @1
      @2
      @3
   RJ 17/3/86



      Dear @4,

      Spring is with us once again, and I would
      like to remind you that along with the
      daffodils, your subscription to the
      society is due at the end of March.  I
      would be very grateful to receive your
      remittance of £@5 as soon as possible.

      Yours sincerely,




      Clive Williamson.
   PE
   EM
```

Figure 7.2 Typical VIEW Macro File to Produce a Standard Letter

either be built up from scratch and used time and time again, or in a more complex situation, could be generated by a database such as ViewStore. Once the complete file is screened or printed, VIEW will search automatically for the details necessary to complete each letter, and will fill them in to produce a series of customised and individual-looking results. This seems a little complicated at first, but in fact it is quite simple to master, so let's try a concrete example to see how the macros work. A fairly useful example for a standard letter is the sort of reminder that might be sent by a club secretary to tell members that their subscriptions are due at the end of the month (see Figure 7.2).

The idea is to set up a block of text to be the document itself, but with gaps left for the individual details to be inserted. In practice, VIEW can support 10 such gaps numbered from 0 to 9, and each number must be preceded by the '@' character for VIEW to recognise it as a place where the data is to be inserted into the text. The data itself comes from a different area of the file. So how do you set the macro up? First, the document is created in the form of a macro. This means placing a **DM** (Define Macro) Stored Command in the left-hand margin, then writing your text as usual, but inserting @0, @1, and so on (up to @9) in the places where you wish each version of the document to be different. At the end of the macro definition you should place an **EM** (End Macro) Stored Command in the left-hand margin. Notice that your macro must now be given a name, and this is done using any two letters (except those normally recognised by VIEW as Stored Commands) in the text area immediately following and on the same line as the **DM** command:

DM AA

Having defined the text part of the file, you simply add all the relevant details on separate lines after it, each line being started with a Stored Command matching that used to name the macro. In this case you would press **SHIFT** *f8*, enter **AA**, then press RETURN (i.e. the usual way of entering a Stored Command) then add each set of details on the same line as the command, e.g.

AA Dunroamin,14 Acacia Avenue,Hornsey,London N8,Miss Paxman,5.00

AA 36 Railway Gardens,Richmond,Surrey,,Mr and Mrs D.Allen,10.00

Notice that the six parts of the first example correspond to @0, @1, and so on up to @5, and that each part is separated by a comma. In the second set of details, the address is shorter, so an extra comma is inserted after 'Surrey' to indicate a 'blank' to be inserted for @3. If there are any commas in the items to be inserted, the relevant section should be enclosed in angled brackets to prevent VIEW misinterpreting the information. For example, you may want to insert a comma after the house number in the second details:

```
AA <36, Railway Gardens>,Richmond,Surrey,,Mr and Mrs D.Allen,10.00
```

If you try screening the example, you will see two the letters appear on separate pages, the first having the 'Miss Paxman' details, the second having those of Mr and Mrs Allen. (See Figure 7.3.) For the process to work successfully it is essential that all the additional details for each letter (including commas and angled brackets) fit on to one VIEW line - thus limiting the specific information to 132 characters per letter.

There is an important consideration when using the macro facility: text formatting is done before the insertion of the variable data, not afterwards. So if you use the justified format for your text you will find that the varying lengths of the inserts spoil the justification. Similarly, any long set of details inserted on an already full line will ruin the format of the text, whether justified of not, and could cause your printer to 'wrap the text round' onto an extra line. For this reason it is best if you try to place all the variable data on blank lines (as in the case of the address data @0, @1, @2 and @3 in the example), or on a line where you know there is enough space for whatever the insert is to be (e.g. @4, @5).

Another important point to consider if you need to prepare lots of names and addresses is that the macro, and the data used to produce the series of different documents, need not necessarily be in the same file. They can be stored separately, as long as the macro is read in from disc or tape first at the **SCREEN** or **PRINT** stage. Hence you can use different sets of data with the same macro file without the need to combine them into a single file, e.g.

SCREEN MACRO1 DATA1 DATA2 <RETURN>

Macros do not necessarily have to contain variables. They can be plain blocks of text - such as complicated headings or anything you intend to use more than once - and these can be defined as macros and called up when required at the printout stage.

Note that VIEW's macro facility can be made even more versatile by the addition of the ViewStore software, which has a special utility program to generate files in macro format from a database of information (See Chapter Twelve).

                The Horticultural Society

        Dunroamin
        14 Acacia Avenue
        Hornsey
        London N8
                                        17/3/86

        Dear Miss Paxman,

        Spring is with us once again, and I would
        like to remind you that along with the
        daffodils, your subscription to the
        society is due at the end of March. I
        would be very grateful to receive your
        remittance of £5.00 as soon as possible.

        Yours sincerely,

        Clive Williamson.

                The Horticultural Society

        36 Railway Gardens
        Richmond
        Surrey
                                        17/3/86

        Dear Mr and Mrs D.Allen,

        Spring is with us once again, and I would
        like to remind you that along with the
        daffodils, your subscription to the
        society is due at the end of March. I
        would be very grateful to receive your
        remittance of £10.00 as soon as possible.

        Yours sincerely,

        Clive Williamson.

Figure 7.3 Printed results from the VIEW macro.

For Master Users:

If you are using the version of VIEW supplied in a BBC Master Series 128 Micro, notice that the date (and even the time) can be added to the text automatically by 'date stamping' using the internal calendar and the 'D' and 'T' registers. To do this in the example, you would change the sixth line of the macro to read:

RJ ! D

Address Labels

The example of the standard letter in Figure 7.2 can be extended further to produce the printed labels to go with the set of letters. To do this, a new macro format is needed, but it can easily be based on the existing one. Sticky address labels for computer printers come attached to standard size pages, so as long as you are careful to work out how many lines are needed between the start of printing of each label, you can configure a LABELS macro file as shown in Figure 7.4.

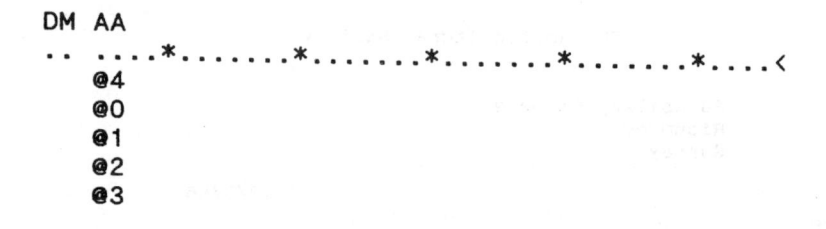

```
DM  AA
..  ....*.......*.......*.......*.......*....<
    @4
    @0
    @1
    @2
    @3




EM
```

Figure 7.4 VIEW Macro File to Print Labels.

Notice that three blank lines have been left between the last line of the address and the End Macro Stored Command. There could be more or less, depending on the exact size of the labels you buy. Just add or subtract blank lines until the first line of each address is printed in the same place on each label. This macro should be used with the same data set as the previous letter macro, so an exactly matching set of labels will be obtained. Thus it can be more efficient in the long run to keep all your data in a separate file, so that it can be used first with the file containing the letter macro, then with one containing the address macro.

```
Miss Paxman
Dunroamin
14 Acacia Avenue
Hornsey
London N8



Mr and Mrs D.Allen
36 Railway Gardens
Richmond
Surrey
```

Figure 7.5 Labels from Same Data as Used in Figure 7.3.

The only thing to watch out for when printing labels in this way is that you must set all the header and footer margins to zero at the start of the file, and use **SHEETS** to print out, remembering that you will have to reposition the address labels each time (because VIEW will still leave one unwanted line at the top and bottom of each page). Depending on the exact number of lines to each label, you may also find that some labels are cut in two by these unwanted blank lines. In fact, the whole thing sounds a bit hit and miss, but there is method in this madness, because on VIEW 3.0 it is possible to insert a new Stored Command to turn off all the headers, footers and unwanted lines completely. This is the Page Break command, and to work it must be inserted in the margin before the macro itself. The way of using this is to enter:

PB 0

whereupon the whole text, or in this case the set of labels, is reproduced without a break, so you should find no difficulty printing out the stream of labels either using **SHEETS** or **PRINT**. To restore page breaks to normal, you can either delete the Stored Command, or replace the 0 with a 1. (VIEW will also accept **ON** and **OFF** after the Stored Command, instead of 1 or 0.)

ViewSpell

A 70,000 word dictionary spelling checker called ViewSpell is now available for the VIEW word processor. This language is supplied separately in a plug-in ROM, or as part of the OverVIEW ROM cartridge expansion for the Master, and it allows the comprehensive checking of text files in conjunction with a large dictionary held on disc. Anything not found in the dictionary, or in extra dictionaries set up by the user of the software, is reported, and can be seen in context if required. ViewSpell also allows you to search the dictionary for words, using wild characters in the searches if required, and because it produces a list of all the words found in a document, it can be invaluable in the preparation of indexes.

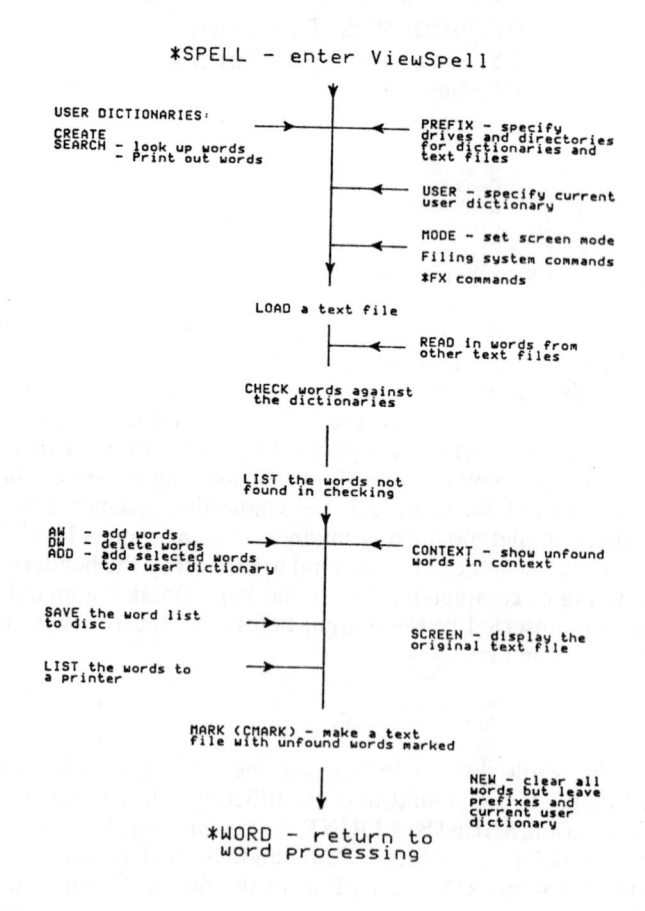

```
                    *SPELL - enter ViewSpell
                              |
    USER DICTIONARIES:         
    CREATE                    PREFIX - specify
    SEARCH - look up words    drives and directories
           - print out words  for dictionaries and
                              text files

                              USER - specify current
                              user dictionary

                              MODE - set screen mode
                              Filing system commands
                              *FX commands

                    LOAD a text file
                              
                              READ in words from
                              other text files

                    CHECK words against
                    the dictionaries
                              
                    LIST the words not
                    found in checking
                              
    AW - add words
    DW - delete words
    ADD - add selected words   CONTEXT - show unfound
          to a user dictionary words in context

    SAVE the word list
    to disc
                              SCREEN - display the
    LIST the words to         original text file
    a printer

                    MARK (CMARK) - make a text
                    file with unfound words marked
                              
                              NEW - clear all
                              words but leave
                              prefixes and
                              current user
                              dictionary
                    *WORD - return to
                    word processing
```

Figure 7.6 Summary of ViewSpell Commands.

102

ViewIndex

Another facility available for VIEW is a disc program that can be used to make indexes from text files. This is very useful if you are preparing your own magazines or complex reports. Key words or phrases can be marked in the text with double Highlight characters, then when the text is loaded into ViewIndex, to produced an index of page or section numbers. This can be edited and included in your document. It is even possible to merge several indexes if necessary.

```
Advantages of glass        12
Aseptic packaging          16
Bag-in-box                 19
Base cup                6,8,9
Beer                        8
Blank                      11
Bottle banks               18
Brand Names             22,23
Brik pack                  15
Cans                        5
Carbonation                 7
Cider                       8
Composition of glass       10
Computer Aided Design      11
Cullet                     13
Expanded polystyrene       20
Glass                      10
Gob                        11
Hermetic seal               7
Incineration               14
Insulation                 20
Lacquer                     6
Lamination                 15
Latex coating               8
Market research            22
Metal cans                  6
Packaging Liquids           1
Palette                    16
Paper Cartons              13
Parison                    11
PET bottles                 7
Polyester                   7
Polypropylene              28
Pressure vessel             9
Recycling                7,18
Ring pull cans             21
Semi-skimmed milk          21
Shelf-life              15,21
Surface treatment          12
Tetrahedron                14
Transport                   2
Unbreakable glass          12
```

SECTION TWO

THE SPREADSHEET

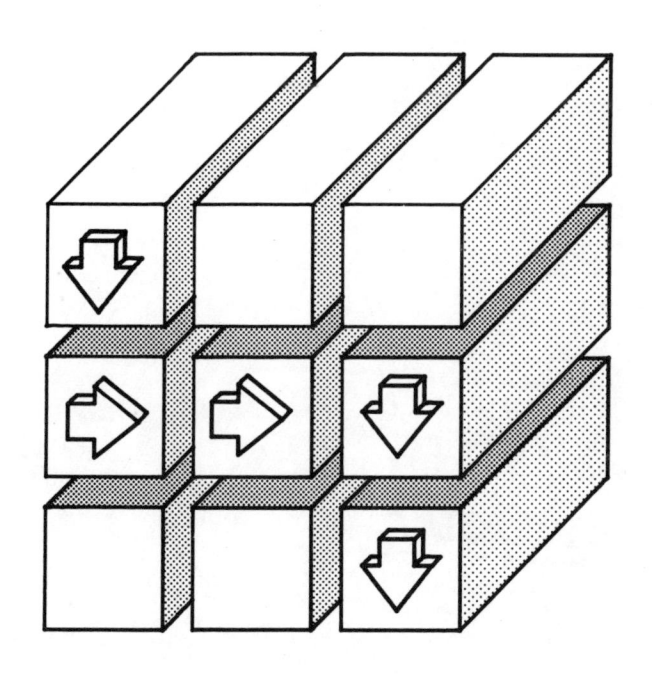

VIEWSHEET

CHAPTER EIGHT

ViewSheet

About Spreadsheet Software

The spreadsheet has rapidly established itself as the work-horse of modern day business computing. It is the perfect aid to anyone needing to perform masses of interrelated calculations, and has the major advantage that these calculations are performed almost instantly. The thing that takes time is the initial setting up of the spreadsheet calculation, or 'model', as it is also known. Spreadsheet software works by dividing up the computer's memory into lots of interrelated cells, or 'slots', which are laid out on the screen as a matrix or grid, every slot having its own grid reference. Each vertical column is identified by one or more letters of the alphabet, while each horizontal row is given a number. Thus A1 is the reference for the top slot, and C4 would be the location marked by a cross on Figure 8.1.

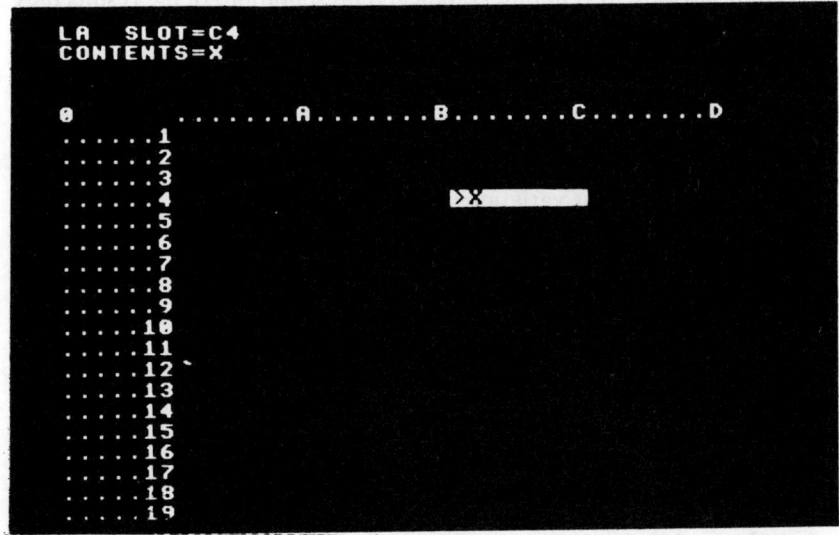

```
LA    SLOT=C4
CONTENTS=X


0         .......A......B.......C.......D
......1
......2
......3
......4            >X
......5
......6
......7
......8
......9
.....10
.....11
.....12
.....13
.....14
.....15
.....16
.....17
.....18
.....19
```

Figure 8.1 Spreadsheet Layout.

The slots may contain either text, a numerical value or a formula which enables calculations to be carried out using the contents of other slots. The formulae are not visible in the slots, but the results they produce are. There is always some way of moving the cursor from slot to slot, so that each location can be inspected or edited, and it is at this stage that the formulae become visible. An aid to defining a large spreadsheet is the 'replication' command, which allows the contents of one or more slots to be copied into selected areas of the grid. This copying can usually be done 'absolutely' (when each copy is identical to the original), or 'relatively' (when formulae are changed automatically to suit their new locations on the grid). Calculations performed by the spreadsheet are based on the contents of individual slots, and most normal mathematical functions can be used to create simple or complex formulae to act on the data entered on the sheet.

The complete grid is potentially much larger than the micro's screen can display in one go, so the screen area acts as a 'window' onto the sheet that can be moved around to view the contents of any group of slots. The maximum size of the spreadsheet is typically 100 slots wide by 255 down, but ultimately the factor limiting the total data that can be held by the spreadsheet is the amount of memory left over after the sheet has been defined by the software. For this reason, those sheets that are available for the BBC Micro as plug-in sideways ROMs are capable of supporting a larger grid, and can therefore perform much more complex operations than those programs which are run from the BASIC language. To further increase their usefulness, most spreadsheets now have some sort of associated software to generate graphical representations of the results they produce, either as graphs, pie charts or bar charts.

Because calculations can be carried out so quickly, and each sheet can either be saved or printed out many times over with different initial figures, the spreadsheet has become the perfect tool for experimenting with data. So-called 'what if?' analysis can be used to work out cash flow, budgeting and profitability against variations in the market or income by feeding in different sets of possible figures.

Dealing more with 'real' figures, the spreadsheet can be turned to scientific tables, or even simple accounting and home finance, and can also hold information such as insurance lists or catalogues where some maths needs to be performed. In fact a spreadsheet can act as a simple database, although most are not geared to actually sorting the data they contain (a decided nuisance for some applications!). A proper database like ViewStore would be needed for any task requiring more complex data handling.

The tabular nature of the spreadsheet makes it a useful aid when entering or calculating data for use in conjunction with a word processor like VIEW,

```
VA  SLOT=B13
CONTENTS=B5B11

0         A       B       C       D       E       F       G       H       I
......1 BUDGET 1986
......2
......3         JAN     FEB     MAR     APR     MAY     JUN     JLY     AUG
......4 ------  ------  ------  ------  ------  ------  ------  ------
......5 Gas     40                      60                      35
......6 Elect.          35                      40                              25
......7 Rates   45                      50      50      50      50      50
......8 Mort.   200     200     200     200     200     200     200     200
......9 Food    45      45      45      45      45      45      45      45
.....10 Milk    7.5     7.5     7.5     7.5     7.5     7.5     7.5     7.5
.....11 Papers  16      16      16      16      16      16      16      16
.....12 ------  ------  ------  ------  ------  ------  ------  ------
.....13         )353.5  303.5   268.5   378.5   358.5   318.5   353.5   343.5
.....14
.....15 Salary  380     380     400     400     400     400     400     400
.....16 B/F     0       26.5    103     234.5   256     297.5   379     425.5
.....17 ------  ------  ------  ------  ------  ------  ------  ------
.....18 Balance 26.5    103     234.5   256     297.5   379     425.5   482
.....19
```

Figure 8,2 Budget analysis using a spreadsheet.

so even if you don't feel that you need to use a spreadsheet directly in your business or home applications, you could well find a wealth of indirect uses for this sort of software.

What to Look For in a Spreadsheet

1. Large memory capacity to hold complex models, preferably with 80 column display.

2. The facility to have a number of different portions of a large sheet visible on screen at the same time (perhaps by setting up different 'windows' on the sheet).

3. Extensive commands for setting up a sheet quickly by copying similar formulae over a large area, with or without changes. (This is known as 'replication'.)

4. A wide selection of mathematical functions for calculations.

5. The facility to protect areas of the screen from accidental deletion, or alteration, by yourself or others using the sheet.

6. The possibility of using data from the sheet in a word processor to produce tables and reports.

7. Some way of deriving graphic output from figures calculated by the software (in the form of pie charts, bar graphs, etc.).

8. The ability to combine different small sheets into one large one, so that areas can be developed and tested separately.

ViewSheet

Getting started with ViewSheet is a relatively simple matter. First, place the ViewSheet function key strip (Figure 8.3) under the clear plastic holder over the keyboard, and once the chip is fitted inside the machine, you type:

*SHEET<RETURN>

to make it run; you will then see the ViewSheet Command Header on the screen. This consists of several status lines in the top left-hand side of the screen showing the amount of free memory, the name of the file you are editing ('No file' at first), and the current screen mode. The format of this Command screen display is similar to that of VIEW, ViewSpell and ViewStore. Pressing the **ESCAPE** key at this stage will make the display change to the spreadsheet itself: a blank screen with letters marked across the top, and numbers going down the left-hand side. These are the references that make up the coordinates for each slot, so that the first slot is A1, A2 is below it, B2 to the right of A2 and so on. At this stage, slot A1 shows as a white (or inverse) box, while all the other slots are black and 'invisible'. The white box is the ViewSheet slot cursor (i.e. the point at which data can be entered on the sheet) and if you now use the cursor keys to go right or down, you will see the white box begin to move around the sheet accordingly. Notice that as you move the cursor, the slot display on the top line of the screen changes to show the reference of the slot currently occupied by the cursor. If you reach the bottom or right-hand limit of the screen, the letters or numbers will alter, showing that you have moved away from what is effectively the top left corner of the sheet. ViewSheet has the potential of displaying a grid 255 slots wide by 255 slots down (A1 to IU255) so there is plenty of room in which to move the cursor about! Like VIEW, you can enter your data on the sheet in this Sheet mode (which is equivalent to VIEW's Text mode) then go back to the Command screen at any time by pressing **ESCAPE**.

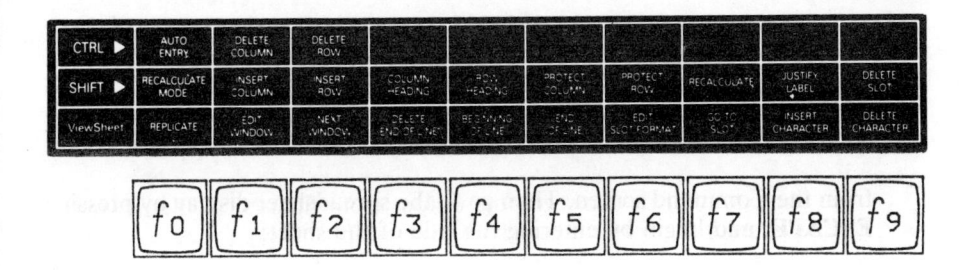

Figure 8.3 The ViewSheet function key strip.

So what about entering some data? The first thing to remember is that ViewSheet tries to interpret everything you enter as one of three things:

1. A label.
2. A number.
3. A formula.

Hence anything entered in a slot will be analysed by the program, and used accordingly. This method of operation is a quick and easy one when it comes to entering most data, but it can lead to some difficulty and unexpected results at times when the software interprets your entries incorrectly.

Starting a Simple Spreadsheet

As already indicated, there are masses of uses for a spreadsheet program, but it is probably best to think in terms of something simple as a first example to work through. Rather than opt for the usual 'home finance' budget analysis found in many books on spreadsheets, the example chosen here is a small sheet to check and estimate gas, electricity and telephone bills. This can be used to show several of the major features of ViewSheet, as well as serving a fairly useful purpose once it has been built up. A good habit to get into when setting up a new spreadsheet is to give it a name straight away using the **NAME** command. Here, for example, we could specify the filename 'BILLS' by entering:

`NAME BILLS <RETURN>`

from the Command screen. You will see the name appear in the 'Editing file' part of the status display. Now you are ready to begin. As the sheet is a simple one, it can be developed on most BBC machines in Mode 0 without fear of running out of memory. If your monitor will display 80 characters successfully, you will find that Mode 0 is the best display for spreadsheet work, as it shows the maximum number of characters on the screen at any one time. If you are not yet in Mode 0, enter:

MODE 0 <RETURN>

from the Command screen. Then go to the spreadsheet display by pressing **ESCAPE**, and begin by entering the title of the sheet:

BILL ESTIMATOR

in slot A1. There is no need to place this in quotes, as is the case with some spreadsheets, since ViewSheet automatically interprets the phrase as a label, and justifies it to the left of the slot. Immediately you will run into a problem, however, as the title you have used is too long to be displayed in its entirety. This is because each column of the default ViewSheet display is only seven characters wide, so that although the whole phrase has been successfully stored away, only part of it is visible!

The problem can easily be rectified by making use of the 'window' facility in ViewSheet to alter the displayed width of the columns. Windows provide a flexible method of 'viewing' different parts of a large sheet, or simply altering the basic format of the initial screen display. To make alterations to the current window, press function key *f1*, and you will be given the prompt Window? on the third line of the display, asking which number window you wish to edit. There are 10 screen windows in all (and a further 10 printer windows, which are explained later), but the default which is in operation when you begin is Window 0, so press the 0 key (then RETURN to enter it) and you will see the parameters for this window appear on lines three and four, just above the sheet itself.

Wi	TopL	BotR	Pos	Cw	Bw	Fmt	Opt
0	A1	I26		7	7	FRM	

Lots of different parameters make up the window format (eight in all), but the exact details of these do not matter for the time being - all we need to do is alter the width of the columns - and this is achieved by amending the figure 7 under the Cw heading (standing for Column Width). Normal cursor movement in ViewSheet using the cursor keys, on their own or with the **SHIFT** keys, moves the large 'slot cursor' around the sheet. To use the small flashing cursor that appears near the top of the display on line four where the window parameters are you must hold the **CTRL** key down and press either the left or right cursor keys. Use this method to place the flashing cursor under the figure 7 beneath Cw, and overtype the 7 with 15. When you press RETURN, the window details disappear, and the screen display is re-drawn showing only four complete columns, each 15 characters wide. (If you press **ESCAPE** instead of RETURN, the changes you have made are cancelled, and the window left unchanged.)

```
LA   SLOT=A1
CONTENTS=BILL ESTIMATOR


            ..............A...............B................C...............D
......1 BILL ESTIMATOR   Version 1.0
......2
......3
......4                  GAS            ELECTRIC         PHONE
......5
......6 Reading                547
......7 Previous               424
......8 Units used             123
......9 Calorific value       1016
.....10 Therms used         124.968
.....11 Unit cost              0.37
.....12 Actual cost        45.51000001
.....13 Standing charge     9.899999999
.....14 VAT                    0
.....15 TOTAL              55.41000001
.....16
.....17
.....18
.....19
```

Figure 8.4

Now you are ready to continue entering the categories down the left-hand side of the sheet as in Figure 8.4. Notice that once you have entered something in a slot, the cursor remains on that slot until you move it manually with the cursor keys. The quickest way to enter data is to make use of ViewSheet's auto-entry facility, whereby the slot cursor can be made to move right or down automatically whenever RETURN is pressed. Thus, as you enter the contents of A2, the cursor can be made to jump to A3, and so on. The selection of this mode of entry is made using function key **CTRL** *f0* (Auto Entry). If you press this key combination once, you will see the letter R (standing for move Right) appear in the top left of the screen display. Press the key a second time and the R is replaced by a D (standing for move Down) which is what you need in this case. The cursor keys still function in the usual way should you need to go back and amend or re-enter anything. When you wish to turn the Auto Entry off, simply press **CTRL** *f0* again, and the D will disappear, cancelling the effect altogether. You will see that all the text labels are justified to the left of their slots, whereas when you enter numerical data, it will be justified to the right.

Don't worry if you happen to miss one of the categories out - you can always insert an extra row by placing the slot cursor on the line below where you want it to be, then pressing **SHIFT** *f2* (Insert Row). The rest of the display will be moved down and renumbered to accommodate the extra row. When you have entered all the categories, take the cursor back to B4, turn off the Auto Entry, and put in the headings for each column (from B4 to D4).

Once the headings have been put on the sheet, you can begin to add the formulae that will perform the calculations, and the figures they need to work on. You could try entering the current and previous readings from your gas bill in B6 and B7 respectively. As long as these are purely numerical, they will be interpreted as values by the software, which will display them as such on the sheet. The difference comes when entering letters followed by numbers, which are interpreted as formulae. They are not displayed on the sheet directly, and only become visible when you move the cursor into the relevant slot, whereupon they are shown in the 'contents' section at the top of the screen. Thus, if you enter B6-B7 in B8, you will see the formula displayed on the screen itself. What you do see is the result of the calculation, as ViewSheet looks up the contents of B7 and takes them away from B6. Thus, with the figures given in the example, the figure 123 is shown in the slot. Normally, the whole sheet is recalculated automatically whenever a new entry is made, so there is no need to do anything special to make ViewSheet carry out the mathematics. (If necessary, you can turn the automatic calculation off,and force recalculation by hand, but this is explained later and is not needed for small sheets.) When the maths are simple, as in the example here, it might seem reasonable to work out the sums in your head, but in the long term, especially with large models, the spreadsheet decidely comes into its own.

The remaining formulae for the gas calculations are: B8*B11 goes in slot B12, a zero in slot B14 (because there is no VAT on gas at the time of writing) and the tricky one is B8*B9/1000 in slot B11. Notice that a star (*) is used as the multiply sign, rather than the usual 'times' (x) sign! The latter formula is used to work out the number of therms supplied to you, based on the calorific value of the gas at the time! Finally on our example sheet, entering B12B14 in slot B15 gives 'the sum of B12 to B14', a useful function that is often used in spreadsheets where columns of figures must be added. If you now add the final data - the unit cost of the gas (in pounds, not pence, or the bill will be astronomical) and the standing charge - you will see the final result in slot B15, and this will, we hope, tally with the actual amount of the bill.

Although the formulae are reasonably simple, and would not take long to repeat in the columns for electricity and the telephone, it is a useful exercise to copy them across into the other columns using a spreadsheet technique known as 'replication'. The idea is that the contents of one slot can be copied or replicated into others, either exactly as they are, or (in the case of formulae) with a change according to where they are on the sheet. Copying without change is known as 'absolute' replication, while copying with changes is called 'relative' replication. To copy the formulae in column B, the replication must be relative, so that the references to column B are changed to C in the electricity column, and to D in the telephone column. For example, to copy the contents of slot B8, you should press the Replicate function key (*f0*) then enter the slot you wish to act as the source for the copying (B8), then a dash, and then the references of the first and last slots to be copied into, i.e :

B8 - C8D8

When you press RETURN, the formula in the source slot will be shown on the editing line, with a flashing solid cursor over the first letter in the formula and prompt above: R)elative, N)o change?

As the replication needs to be relative here, press 'R' and you will see the cursor move on to the next letter in the formula with the same prompt. Press 'R' again, and ViewSheet will begin working out the correct formulae and placing them in the specified slots. The range in which this copying is done can be a row, a column, or an area, so the replication function is powerful and can save a lot of time when setting up a spreadsheet. For practice, try replicating the other formulae sideways across the sheet, then enter the other meter readings to check first the sheet itself, then when you are sure it is working properly, the accuracy of the bills themselves. The therms calculation is not needed for the telephone or electricity bills, but telephone bills attract VAT, so you will have to add the formula for the VAT calculations in slot D12. This is:

(D12+D13)*0.15

Make sure that you include brackets round the slot references so that the multiplication acts on the sum of D12 and D13, rather than on D13 alone, then adding C12. The former gives the required answer (14.415) while the latter gives 2.9175, because of the precedence given to mathematical operators as follows:

1. Brackets.
2. Multiply and divide.
3. Add and subtract.

Note: There is more about operator precedence in the next chapter.

Improving the Look of the Example Sheet

By now you should be getting more confident about using the cursor keys and the sheet itself, and you might like to try improving the layout of the model a little. This is easily done by adding lines and spaces where necessary, so that the overall result looks more pleasing to the eye and is easier to read. For example, a row of equals signs (=) could be used to double underline the title and a row of hyphens under the headings to separate them from the figures on the sheet. You could type in a row of 15 hyphens in A5, then replicate them across B5 to D5. To separate the totals, you could add an extra row above the totals line using the insert row function key, and put a dashed line across the sheet there too. Another point is that the titles would look better if they were right justified to line up with the columns of figures beneath, and this can be done using the Right-justify Label function key (**SHIFT** *f8*) once the cursor has been placed in the slot to be altered (i.e. B4, C4 and D4). The improved version is shown in Figure 8.5.

```
LA   SLOT=A1
CONTENTS=BILL ESTIMATOR


              ............A...............B...............C...............D
......1 BILL ESTIMATOR  Version 1.1
......2 ===============
......3
......4                         GAS             ELECTRIC            PHONE
......5 ---------------- ---------------- ---------------- ----------------
......6 Reading                 547             15141               6000
......7 Previous                424             14427               4467
......8 Units used              123               714               1533
......9
.....10 Calorific value        1016
.....11 Therms used         124.968
.....12 Unit cost              0.37           5.32E-2              5E-2
.....13
.....14 Actual cost       45.51000001         37.9848         76.65000001
.....15 Standing charge    9.899999999      7.810000001            19.45
.....16 VAT                         0                0            14.415
.....17 ---------------- ---------------- ---------------- ----------------
.....18 Total             55.41000001         45.7948           110.515
.....19
```

Figure 8.5

The Numerical Format

A final refinement can be added to the sheet by altering the way numbers are displayed. Normally they appear on the screen to ten significant figures, which is perfectly suitable for the readings and cost per unit but doesn't look right at all when displaying pounds and pence. The techniques available here are either to change the format of the whole sheet (which is not really suitable in this case, as the example model needs a mixture of formats) or better, but more tedious, to alter the formats of the individual slots. For example, you can place the cursor on B18 and press the Edit Slot Format function key (*f6*) whereupon you are shown a set of letters on the editing line. Initially, the slot formats are all represented by FRM. The letters meaning:

F)loating point. R)ight justification. M)inus signs for negative numbers.

In this case, to show pounds and pence, we need to delete the F and replace it by D2, meaning 'show a decimal display to two decimal places'. In theory you can specify anything up to 9 decimal places, but in practice you would rarely require this level of accuracy. Change all the money slots in column B to the new D2RM format. If you then copy the formulae across the other two columns once more, you will find that the new slots are replicated with the new format. This latest version, including some more refinements in the layout, is shown in Figure 8.6.

```
LA   SLOT=A1
CONTENTS=BILL ESTIMATOR


            .............A...............B...............C..............D
......1  BILL ESTIMATOR      Version 1.2
......2  ==============
......3
......4  28.2.86                 GAS            ELECTRIC           PHONE
......5  ---------------       --------        --------         --------
......6  Reading                 547             15141            6000
......7  Previous                424             14427            4467
......8  Units used              123               714            1533
......9
.....10  Calorific value        1016               -                -
.....11  Therms used         124.968                -                -
.....12  Unit cost              0.37            0.0532            0.05
.....13
.....14  Actual cost           45.51             37.98           76.65
.....15  Standing charge        9.90              7.81           19.45
.....16  VAT                    0.00              0.00           14.42
.....17  ---------------       --------        --------         --------
.....18  Total                 55.41             45.79          110.51
.....19  ---------------       --------        --------         --------
```

Figure 8.6

Protecting Your Work

It is a good idea to protect any slots on the sheet that contain formulae, so that you can't accidentally enter figures in the slots and ruin the calculations! Two of the function keys can be used to turn on protection of individual columns (**SHIFT** *f5*) and rows (**SHIFT** *f6*), thus preventing your overwriting of the contents either by direct entry or by accidental replication of something into one of the slots. On the finished model (see Figure 8.6) it is worth protecting column A and rows 8, 11, 14, 16 and 18. To achieve this, place the cursor somewhere on column A (say A8) and press **SHIFT** *f5* (Protect Column). You will see that the usual dotted line at the top of the sheet showing the width of column A has become a solid line, indicating that protection is now in operation. As row 8 is one of the rows to be protected, leave the cursor where it is and press **SHIFT** *f6* (Protect Row), and this will turn on protection for that row as well! Then move the cursor to rows 11, 14, 16 and 18, and repeat the operation each time. If you need to make any later alterations to a protected row or column, you will have to turn off the protection first. This is done by pressing the relevant function key a second time, as each key acts as a 'toggle' or switch between protection being on and off. If you try to replicate into a protected area, ViewSheet will behave as if the replication was successful - no error is reported - but the replication will not have occurred in the protected slots.

```
LA   SLOT=A1
CONTENTS=BILL ESTIMATOR


              _____A...............B...............C...............D
......1 BILL ESTIMATOR      Version 1.2
......2 ===============
......3
......4 28.2.86                        GAS          ELECTRIC         PHONE
......5 ----------------            --------        --------        --------
......6 Reading                        547            15141           6000
......7 Previous                       424            14427           4467
_____8 Units used                    123              714           1533
......9
.....10 Calorific value               1016              -               -
_____11 Therms used               124.968              -               -
.....12 Unit cost                     0.37           0.0532           0.05
.....13
_____14 Actual cost                 45.51           37.98           76.65
.....15 Standing charge               9.90             7.81           19.45
_____16 VAT                         0.00             0.00           14.42
.....17 ----------------            --------        --------        --------
_____18 Total                      55.41            45.79          110.51
.....19 ----------------            --------        --------        --------
```

Figure 8.7

Deleting Unwanted Rows and Columns

If you insert a row or column in the wrong place, you will find that you cannot then delete it using the expected keys (Delete Column - **CTRL** *f1*; Delete Row - **CTRL** *f2*) because a second level of protection applies to the whole sheet, preventing accidental deletions. This has to be disabled using a command from the ViewSheet Command screen. Press **ESCAPE** to get to Command mode and enter:

PROTECT <RETURN>

ViewSheet will respond with the current state of protection, i.e. the default setting:

Protection on

The same command can be used to turn protection off and on for the whole sheet, so to turn it off and hence allow deletions of whole rows or columns from your work, you should enter:

PROTECT OFF <RETURN>

Having done this you can delete things at will, but if anyone else is using the sheet it is wise to make sure you turn the protection back on with the reverse command:

PROTECT ON <RETURN>

just in case they press the wrong key and wipe some of your valuable work!

Printing Out the Sheet

Because of the instantly alterable nature of the spreadsheet, the above example can be used to feed in estimates or actual readings so that you can see the results straight away. Thus the basic framework can be used over and over again as a kind of advanced calculator. 'Hard copy' (in other words a printout on paper) can simply be obtained on an 80 column printer, as the entire sheet is contained on one Mode 0 screen. A larger sheet could require substantial alteration and setting up of the printer windows, and this procedure is explained later. If the column width were still the default seven characters you could print your results straight away, but having changed window 0 it's essential to change the printer window to match this screen window, so that the entire contents of each column are seen on paper. You first need to edit the printer window P0 to have the same column width as the screen window, i.e. 15 characters. While you are editing P0, you might like to try tidying the printout further by suppressing the reference numbers and letters that form the borders to the printout. This is done by entering T (for Top) and S (for Side) in the options section of the window definition.

```
Wi  TopL  BotR  Pos  Cw  Bw  Fmt  Opt
P0  A1    I26        15  7   FRM  TS
```

Having done this, you can go to the Command mode and try **SCREEN**ing the sheet. You should only see the contents of the sheet, not its borders, and the full 15 characters should be displayed in each column. There is a slight complication at this stage, however, in that the whole sheet appears to be very oddly spaced! As this was not the intention, it may well prove somewhat annoying. The reason is that the printer window is still set to display the default area (which in Mode 0 is A1 to I26) but now the columns have been made wider, the output is too wide for both the screen and an 80 column printer. Since we only have data on the sheet as far as D19 so far, it would make sense to edit the printer window to show only A1 to D19. Try returning to the sheet and doing so now.

```
Wi  TopL  BotR  Pos  Cw  Bw  Fmt  Opt
P0  A1    D19        15  7   FRM  TS
```

If you try the **SCREEN** command once more, you will now see a neat display with normal line spacing, and you are ready to print the results. The way to print the ViewSheet screen is to turn on the printer, make sure it is correctly loaded with paper, then enter the same command as you would in VIEW to print:

PRINT <RETURN>

ViewSheet will act on the specification for the Printer Window P0, producing something similar to Figure 8.8.

```
BILL ESTIMATOR                Version 1.2
===============

28.2.86                GAS         ELECTRIC        PHONE
---------------     --------      ---------      --------
Reading                547           15141          6000
Previous               424           14427          4467
Units used             123             714          1533

Calorific value       1016              -             -
Therms used        124.968              -             -
Unit cost             0.37          0.0532          0.05

Actual cost          45.51           37.98         76.65
Standing charge       9.90            7.81         19.45
VAT                   0.00            0.00         14.42
---------------     --------      ---------      --------
Total                55.41           45.79        110.51
---------------     --------      ---------      --------
```

Figure 8.8

CHAPTER NINE

Spreadsheet Applications

The Spreadsheet as a Calculator

As already mentioned, the Bill Estimator example given in Chapter 8 is rather like employing the spreadsheet as an advanced, customised calculator. ViewSheet can readily be adapted to many applications of this type in the home, in business, and also in schools. The calculator approach can be usefully employed to produce tables of results, such as the Exam Marks Analyser shown below. Here the results entered in a matrix of slots produce totals and averages from a classful of pupils' marks, as well as the highest mark obtained for each question (see Figure 9.1).

```
LA   SLOT=A1
CONTENTS=CLASS


         ........A........B........C........D........E........F.........G
......1  CLASS OF 86                        V1.0              Marks out
......2  ===== =====                                          of 10
......3
......4          Name     Question1     2         3         4      TOTAL
......5                   ---------  --------- --------- --------- ---------
......6       1  Nicki        8         9         8         8         33
......7       2  SaraJane     8         6         9         9         32
......8       3  Dave         4         8         7         8         27
......9       4  Barbara      7        10         8         7         32
.....10       5  Robin        6         8         9         6         29
.....11       6  Elizabeth    7         7         9         7         30
.....12       7  Fenella      5        10         7         8         30
.....13       8  Barry        7         6         9         8         30
.....14       9  Ian          6         8         6         7         27
.....15      10  Ellen        8         5         9         8         30
.....16      11  Merrill      5         7         8         8         28
.....17
.....18  HIGHEST MARK         8        10         9         9         33
.....19  AVERAGE MARK      6.45      7.64      8.09      7.64      29.82
.....20
.....21
.....22
.....23
.....24
.....25
.....26
```

Figure 9.1

As in the previous example, it is necessary to edit the default screen window to show more characters in each column than the initial seven. In this case a minimum of nine are needed to display the longest names and the contents of slot G1 (Marks out). The entry of the formulae is fast and straightforward, but note that this sheet uses two of the more interesting mathematical functions found in ViewSheet: **MAX** (or maximum value) and **AVERAGE**. These functions work by inspecting a specified range of slots on the sheet, so the required range must be placed in brackets after them. If you forget the brackets, ViewSheet will think that you are entering text, and will display the function in the slot as such. As the overall format for the sheet is floating point, and the averages would thus be shown to ten significant figures, it is best to set the format of slot C19 to D2RM before replicating it across the range D19 to G19. It may seem odd to use replication to place the students' numbers in the first column, but it is a little quicker than entering them all by hand, especially if the class is a large one!

The formulae contained on the sheet are as follows:

A7: A6+1 then**:**
replicate A7 from A8 to A16 (relatively).
G6: C6F6 then**:**
replicate G6 from G7 to G16 (relatively).
C18: MAX(C6C16) then**:**
replicate C18 from D18 to G18 (relatively).
C19: AVERAGE(C6C16) then**:**
set format of C19 to D2RM using function Key *f6*.
replicate C19 from D19 to G19 (relatively).

All the replication on this sheet is relative, as there are no fixed numbers to be incorporated into the calculations. It would be easy to expand the sheet to show percentages, if required, but first let's try printing the sheet out. As before, it is essential to change the printer window to match the screen window so that the entire contents of the sheet are seen on paper. You must first edit the printer window P0 to have the same column width as the screen window (i.e. nine characters), then adjust the window to the size of your sheet (A1 to G19). Finally turn the Top and Side borders off by inserting T and S in the Opt column.

```
Wi  TopL  BotR  Pos  Cw  Bw  Fmt  Opt
P0  A1    G19        9   7   FRM  TS
```

Having done this, you can go to the Command screen and try **SCREEN**ing the sheet. You should only see the contents of the sheet, and the full nine characters should be displayed in each column. As the TS options are active there will be no borders printed. The printout should appear as in Figure 9.2.

```
CLASS OF 86                              V1.0                    Marks out
===== =====                                                      of 10
         Name        Question1      2          3          4       TOTAL
         ----        ---------  ---------  ---------  ---------  -------
      1  Nicki           8          9          8          8        33
      2  SaraJane        8          6          9          9        32
      3  Dave            4          8          7          8        27
      4  Barbara         7         10          8          7        32
      5  Robin           6          8          9          6        29
      6  Elizabeth       7          7          9          7        30
      7  Fenella         5         10          7          8        30
      8  Barry           7          6          9          8        30
      9  Ian             6          8          6          7        27
     10  Ellen           8          5          9          8        30
     11  Merrill         5          7          8          8        28

HIGHEST MARK             8         10          9          9        33
AVERAGE MARK           6.45       7.64       8.09       7.64     29.82
```

Figure 9.2

The next stage with this sheet could be to add an extra column that calculates the marks as percentages, as well as the total marks out of 40.

H6 : G6*100/40 then: Edit the format of slot H6 to D2RM to match the others. Replicate H6 from H7 to H19 (relatively). Delete contents of H17 using **SHIFT** *f9* (formula not needed here).

To print out the larger sheet, you first need to edit the printer window to include the 'H' column (i.e. BotR should be H19). If you now try to screen the results, you will see that the odd spacing has returned, as in the example in Chapter Eight, because the output is eight columns of 10 characters (there is a space between each nine character column). This unfortunately forces the extra line on the screen again, so you may have to take steps to prevent it! If your printer will print more than 80 characters per line there is no problem. If it will not, then return window P0 to its original size (i.e. printing A1 to G19), then alter the next printer window (P1) to place the new column next to it on printout, but with a width of only seven characters. So window P0 should still look like this:

```
Wi  TopL  BotR  Pos  Cw  Bw  Fmt  Opt
P0  01    G19        9   7   FRM  TS
```

while P1 should look like this:

```
Wi  TopL  BotR  Pos  Cw  Bw  Fmt  Opt
P1  H1    H19   R0   7   0   FRM  TS
```

Since you only want to print out one column, TopL and BotR values should be H1 and H19 here, to match those in window P0. Notice that you have to make an entry in the 'Pos' column this time. Pos stands for 'position', and sets the position of one window relative to another. In this case P1 needs to go to the right of window P0 (hence the entry R0), but you can also place a window beneath a previous one if necessary. This is dealt with more fully in Chapter Ten. If you now try screening the sheet, you will see the two windows join invisibly to produce a printout of the desired width for an 80 column printer.

Tables and Price-Lists

Another example of the 'spreadsheet as calculator' is in producing tables of results, either for printing out on their own, or for inclusion in word processed files. Here is an example of a price-list which makes use of the computer's ability to perform a large number of calculations, taking the slog out of what would be a very lengthy process if done by hand, even with the aid of a calculator.

The example here is a price-list for picture framing. It is a rather specialised application but it does illustrate new points about replication and printing out only part of a whole sheet. Half the sheet is taken up with data used in calculating the final results, so the printout is adjusted to avoid all the 'background calculations', and concentrates purely on the price list to be shown to clients. The sheet is used to calculate the price of individual framing orders based on the cost of: the raw materials (glass, hardboard backing and mounting); the size of the frame; and the chosen style of frame (known as the 'moulding' in the trade). The formulae used here are a little more complex than those in the previous examples, and are explained fully below. The screen layout is shown in Figure 9.3.

The example is restricted to one screenful, but it could have been made to show a much wider range of frame styles and/or sizes. The sheet is split into four distinct parts. The top five lines hold the title of the sheet and the costs of basic materials: glass and hardboard backing for the frames, and the cost of adhesive tissue for mounting the picture before it is framed. A total for the material costs is calculated in slot C5, this being an area price per square foot of materials used. The second part of the sheet is from row 7 to row 13, and deals with calculating the cost of the materials actually used for a given size of frame, adding this to an amount for the labour involved in assembling the frame, and a small sum for the eyelets and string needed to hang the finished picture. The third part of the sheet is the area from A15 to A25 which holds the cost of the different styles or categories of frame moulding available, while the last part, from B15 to

```
........A.......B.......C.......D.......E.......F.......G.......H.......I
......1  FRAME PRICES
......2  ===== ======
......3
......4           COSTS:  GLASS=    1.00  MOUNT=   0.30 BOARD=   0.20
......5           TOTAL:  1.50 per sqr foot
......6
......7           SIZE:   1.25    1.50    1.75    2.00    2.25    2.50    2.75
......8           -------  ------  ------  ------  ------  ------  ------  ------
......9           EXTRAS: 0.20    0.25    0.30    0.35    0.40    0.45    0.50
.....10           G/M/B:  0.59    0.84    1.15    1.50    1.90    2.34    2.84
.....11           LABOUR: 4.00    4.50    5.00    5.50    6.00    6.50    7.00
.....12           -------  ------  ------  ------  ------  ------  ------  ------
.....13           TOTAL:  4.79    5.59    6.45    7.35    8.30    9.29   10.34
.....14
.....15  STYLE    SIZE     15"     18"     21"     24"     27"     30"     33"
.....16  COSTS    -------  ------  ------  ------  ------  ------  ------  ------
.....17   0.40    A        5.79    6.79    7.85    8.95   10.10   11.29   12.54
.....18   0.45    B        5.91    6.94    8.02    9.15   10.32   11.54   12.81
.....19   0.55    C        6.16    7.24    8.37    9.55   10.77   12.04   13.36
.....20   0.60    D        6.29    7.39    8.55    9.75   11.00   12.29   13.64
.....21   0.70    E        6.54    7.69    8.90   10.15   11.45   12.79   14.19
.....22   0.80    F        6.79    7.99    9.25   10.55   11.90   13.29   14.74
.....23   0.95    G        7.16    8.44    9.77   11.15   12.57   14.04   15.56
.....24   1.00    H        7.29    8.59    9.95   11.35   12.80   14.29   15.84
.....25   1.20    I        7.79    9.19   10.65   12.15   13.70   15.29   16.94
.....26           -------  ------  ------  ------  ------  ------  ------  ------
```

Figure 9.3

I26, uses all the figures on the sheet to calculate the entire cost of a frame for any size and style of moulding.

The important points on this sheet are that both relative and absolute replication are required to set it up, and that large sections of the sheet do not appear in the final printout. The latter idea is fundamental to producing large and complex spreadsheet models which are easy to read and work on, as well as giving concise final results.

The sheet is set up as follows:

Enter the labels in the area A1 to I13, using the Justify Label (**SHIFT** *f8*) function key to make the entries look neater, and copy the dotted line by replicating B8 from C8 to I8, and from B12 to I12.

Edit screen window 0 to have a format of D2RM as follows:

```
Wi  TopL  BotR  Pos  Cw  Bw  Fmt   Opt
P0   A1   I26        7   7   D2RM
```

Enter the costs of materials (per square foot) in slots D4, F4 and H4.

`C5: D4+F4+H4`
(the total cost of materials per square foot).
`C7: 1.25`
(the frame size in feet is shown in decimal, i.e. 15").
`D7: D6+0.25`
then: replicate D7 from E7 to I7 (relatively). (i.e. enter D7-E7I7 then press R once for D7 = R)elative replication).
`C9: 0.20`
(the cost of extras such as eyelets and string).
`D9: C9+0.05 then:`
replicate D9 from E9 to I9 (relatively).
`C10: (C7/2)^2*C5`
This formula for the actual cost of materials used is based on the maximum area for a rectangle being the case of a square:

$$\left\{ \frac{\text{sum of two sides}^2}{2} \right\} \times \text{the cost of materials per sq ft}$$

Replicate C10 from D10 to I10 : C7 = R)elative; C5 N)o change.

`C11: 4.00`
(the amount of labour on the smallest size of frame)

`D11: C11+0.50`
then: replicate D11 from E11 to I11 (relatively). (This sets up an ascending scale of labour charges.)

`C13: C9C11` then: replicate C13 from D13 to I13 (relatively). (The sum of the materials for each frame size.)

Enter the labels in the area A15 to I26 (right-justify B15 to I15 using **SHIFT** *f8*).

Replicate the dotted line in B8 from B16 to J16 and from B26 to J26.

Use auto-entry down (**CTRL** *f0*) to enter the frame moulding styles between B17 and B26, the the price per foot for these mouldings in A17 to A26.

`C17: (C7*2*A17)+ C13`
then: replicate C17 from D17 to I17 {R);N;R)}

Replicate each formula on row 17 downwards; i.e. replicate C17 from C18 to C25 {N);R);N)} then: repeat from column D to column I. This can best be done using ViewSheet's facility to replicate from a row range to a column range. Replicate from row range C17I17 to column range C18C25. ViewSheet will present each formula from slots I17 to C17, and you will have to press {N);R);N) for each one.

Finally you will need to set up a suitable printer window that shows only the final results table from B15 to I26, so edit window P0 as follows:

```
Wi  TopL  BotR  Pos  Cw  Bw  Fmt   Opt
P0  B15   I26        7   7   D2RM  TS
```

Having done so, the final SCREENed results from the sheet should look as shown in Figure 9.4.

```
SIZE     15"     18"     21"     24"     27"     30"     33"
-------  ------  ------  ------  ------  ------  ------  ------
  A      5.79    6.79    7.85    8.95   10.10   11.29   12.54
  B      5.91    6.94    8.02    9.15   10.32   11.54   12.81
  C      6.16    7.24    8.37    9.55   10.77   12.04   13.36
  D      6.29    7.39    8.55    9.75   11.00   12.29   13.64
  E      6.54    7.69    8.90   10.15   11.45   12.79   14.19
  F      6.79    7.99    9.25   10.55   11.90   13.29   14.74
  G      7.16    8.44    9.77   11.15   12.57   14.04   15.56
  H      7.29    8.59    9.95   11.35   12.80   14.29   15.84
  I      7.79    9.19   10.65   12.15   13.70   15.29   16.94
-------  ------  ------  ------  ------  ------  ------  ------
```

Figure 9.4

These results can either be printed out separately, or added to a word processed file written on VIEW so that the price-list includes a proper heading and instructions on how to use the table, or details of any special charges. (See Chapter Fourteen for instructions on how to do this.)

Tables of the kind shown in Figure 9.4 can be designed in all sorts of sizes, depending on the capacity of the paper and printer you intend to use. Replication makes light work of setting up the model, and any changes in the cost of basic materials are instantly reflected throughout the sheet. While the above model is unlikely to be specifically useful to many users of ViewSheet, it does serve to illustrate the possibilities, once the mathematics of a problem are known. If the above sheet was wholesale, and a retail version were required, the complete sheet could be replicated to include a percentage mark-up, and a printer window set up that would only print the retail area of the sheet. The formula for a certain percentage, A%, would be:

$$\frac{\text{Previous price} \times (A + 100)}{100}$$

so if a slot is set aside to hold the required percentage mark-up (e.g. A29) the formula to go in slot C31 is:

`C17*(A29+100)/100`

Notice that the brackets are needed here to prevent the multiplication taking place before the addition. C31 should be replicated from D31 to I31, with C17 copied R)elatively and A29 with N)o change; then copy each formula downwards to row 39 using the row range to column method (i.e. replicate from C31I31 to C31C39). Again, the replication is R);N) this time. It is a good idea to turn Protection on at this stage, since you can no longer see the whole sheet, and would not notice immediately if you made a mistake in the replication range, and erased or altered something elsewhere. The full table is shown in Figure 9.5.

```
.......A.......B.......C.......D.......E.......F.......G.......H.......I
.....15 STYLE    SIZE    15"     18"     21"     24"     27"    30"    33"
.....16 COSTS   ------- ------- ------- ------- ------- ------- ------- -------
.....17  0.40    A       5.79    6.79    7.85    8.95   10.10   11.29   12.54
.....18  0.45    B       5.91    6.94    8.02    9.15   10.32   11.54   12.81
.....19  0.55    C       6.16    7.24    8.37    9.55   10.77   12.04   13.36
.....20  0.60    D       6.29    7.39    8.55    9.75   11.00   12.29   13.64
.....21  0.70    E       6.54    7.69    8.90   10.15   11.45   12.79   14.19
.....22  0.80    F       6.79    7.99    9.25   10.55   11.90   13.29   14.74
.....23  0.95    G       7.16    8.44    9.77   11.15   12.57   14.04   15.56
.....24  1.00    H       7.29    8.59    9.95   11.35   12.80   14.29   15.84
.....25  1.20    I       7.79    9.19   10.65   12.15   13.70   15.29   16.94
.....26         ------- ------- ------- ------- ------- ------- ------- -------
.....27
.....28 Percent
.....29  40.00   SIZE    15"     18"     21"     24"     27"    30"    33"
.....30         ------- ------- ------- ------- ------- ------- ------- -------
.....31          A       8.10    9.51   10.99   12.53   14.14   15.81   17.55
.....32          B       8.28    9.72   11.23   12.81   14.45   16.16   17.94
.....33          C       8.63   10.14   11.72   13.37   15.08   16.86   18.71
.....34          D       8.80   10.35   11.97   13.65   15.40   17.21   19.09
.....35          E       9.15   10.77   12.46   14.21   16.03   17.91   19.86
.....36          F       9.50   11.19   12.95   14.77   16.66   18.61   20.63
.....37          G      10.03   11.82   13.68   15.61   17.60   19.66   21.79
.....38          H      10.20   12.03   13.93   15.89   17.92   20.01   22.17
.....39          I      10.90   12.87   14.91   17.01   19.18   21.41   23.71
.....40         ------- ------- ------- ------- ------- ------- ------- -------
```

Figure 9.5

Once the new headings have been entered, and the underlines copied (e.g. B26 from B30 to I30 and B40 to I40) you are ready to alter the printer window P0 to print the final, retail, version of the sheet:

```
Wi  TopL  BotR  Pos  Cw  Bw  Fmt   Opt
P0  B29   I40        7   7   D2RM  TS
```

giving results as shown in Figure 9.6.

SIZE	15"	18"	21"	24"	27"	30"	33"
A	8.10	9.51	10.99	12.53	14.14	15.81	17.55
B	8.28	9.72	11.23	12.81	14.45	16.16	17.94
C	8.63	10.14	11.72	13.37	15.08	16.86	18.71
D	8.80	10.35	11.97	13.65	15.40	17.21	19.09
E	9.15	10.77	12.46	14.21	16.03	17.91	19.86
F	9.50	11.19	12.95	14.77	16.66	18.61	20.63
G	10.03	11.82	13.68	15.61	17.60	19.66	21.79
H	10.20	12.03	13.93	15.89	17.92	20.01	22.17
I	10.90	12.87	14.91	17.01	19.18	21.41	23.71

Figure 9.6

The Spreadsheet as Database

Because of its mathematical abilities, ViewSheet lends itself to being used to store data, and to carry out calculations on that data. Thus it is possible to set up simple insurance lists and small-scale accounting systems without the need to look to a fully-fledged database to do the job. A little thought is needed at the planning stage, as it is vital that the data be stored and displayed in the most suitable way for later use. It should be pointed out that there are disadvantages to making the spreadsheet work like this. The sheet lacks the ability to sort and select data, and gives slightly less convenient data entry than would be possible with a proper database program. There is also a limit to the amount of data that can be conveniently stored, as the spreadsheet's capacity is largely memory-dependent, rather than being based on the amount of disc storage available (as would be the case with a database like ViewStore).

An Insurance List

This example is designed to fit the full screen width available on VIEW in Modes 0 and 3, showing the serial number, details, purchase date and value of home or office contents for insurance purposes. Each entry takes up one line, making it easy to insert or delete entries. Details can be added in date order, and could be divided up by room if required to make an inventory easier. As the list grows, it is likely to exceed the size of a single screen, so when printing out it will probably be necessary to edit the printer window to show the whole thing. To give the best display, you really need to set each column width differently, so the sheet as shown in Figure 9.7 uses four different windows at the printout stage.

```
LA   SLOT=A1
CONTENTS=01.04.86


..............A................B....................C...............D
..1 01.04.86            Version 1.0
..2
..3                     INSURANCE LIST
..4                     --------------
..5
..6 Date                Item (Office)          Serial No.            Value
..7 -----------------   ------------------     -----------------   ---------
..8 28.03.86            Computer                    663576            500
..9 28.03.86            Disc Drives                 123456            400
.10 28.03.86            TV Monitor                 7756438            300
.11 28.03.86            Discs                                          65
.12 01.04.86            Printer                    1000267            215
.13
.14                                                                 --------
.15                                            SUBTOTAL=               1480
.16 Date                Item (Kitchen)         Serial No.            Value
.17 -----------------   ------------------     -----------------   ---------
.18 29.03.86            Coffee Maker                                   30
.19 29.03.86            Kettle                                         15
.20 29.03.86            Microwave Oven              5760              200
.21 01.04.86            Mugs x 30                                      45
.22
.23
.24                                                                 --------
.25                                            SUBTOTAL=                290
.26                                            ==================
                                               TOTAL=                  1770
```

Figure 9.7

The first thing to do when creating this sheet is to change window 0 as follows:

```
Wi  TopL  BotR  Pos  Cw  Bw  Fmt  Opt
0   A1    I26        18  3   FRM
```

so that there are four columns of 18 characters on the screen. This should be enough to see what is going on in the Item column, where longer details than usual will typically be needed. Place the headings on the sheet. For speed you can replicate the dashes at A7 from B7 to D7, and from A17 to D17, although to look neat at the printout stage you should really add more dashes to B7 and **B17**. You can replicate the range of headings from A6D6 to A15 and across (i.e. A6D6-A15), then add the subtotal and total headings. There are only three formulae on this sheet:

D5 : D8D12   D15 : D18D22   D26 : D14+D24

The first two give the sum of the contents of each room, while the third is the simple addition of the two subtotals. You could have many more room subsections than this if you were itemising the contents of a house, for example. Using the Insert Row function key you can make new additions anywhere on the sheet to update the contents of a particular room, and as you do so the subtotals and total will re-adjust automatically, as the cell references in the formulae change accordingly.

When it comes to printing out this sheet, the neatest results will be obtained by defining four different printer widows, one for each of the columns of data held on the sheet. Each column can then be set to its optimum width: Date, Serial No., and Value need not be so wide, but the Item column could probably do with being wider, to allow a full description. In addition, the fourth column 'D' can be set to show pounds and pence by altering its format. Assuming the list finishes at row 26, the set of windows is as follows:

Wi	TopL	BotR	Pos	Cw	Bw	Fmt	Opt
P0	A3	A26		8	0	FRM	TS
P1	B1	B26	R0	30	0	FRM	TS
P2	C1	C26	R1	10	0	FRM	TS
P3	D1	D26	R2	10	0	D2RM	TS

Use the **SCREEN** command to check that the above values give a printout that appears as in Figure 9.8.

```
          INSURANCE LIST
          --------------

Date      Item (Office)                    Serial No.      Value
--------  -----------------------------    ----------    ----------
28.03.86  Computer                             663576        500.00
28.03.86  Disc Drives                          123456        400.00
28.03.86  TV Monitor                          7756438        300.00
28.03.86  Discs                                              65.00
01.04.86  Printer                             1000267        215.00
                                                          ----------
                                              SUBTOTAL=    1480.00

Date      Item (Kitchen)                   Serial No.      Value
--------  -----------------------------    ----------    ----------
29.03.86  Coffee Maker                                       30.00
29.03.86  Kettle                                             15.00
29.03.86  Microwave Oven                         5760       200.00
01.04.86  Mugs x 30                                          45.00
                                                          ----------
                                              SUBTOTAL=     290.00
                                                          ==========
                                                 TOTAL=    1770.00
```

Figure 9.8

You can either print the list as it stands, or *SPOOL it as a file onto disc for inclusion in a VIEW report (see Chapter Fourteen). Remember as you add to the list that you must adjust all the printer windows to show the maximum extent of the data on the sheet so that if, for example, you had added so many records that the Totals line was on row 50, you would need to change the '26' in every printer window into a 50.

It might seem an attractive idea at first to amend the screen display to match the printout, but if you set up a series of screen windows to do the same thing, you find that you can no longer move readily around the sheet, as you have to keep pressing the Next Window function key ($f2$) to move sideways across the sheet. In Chapter Ten we will expand this database to act as an accounts package, where a number of screen windows can usefully be set up.

ViewSheet's Mathematical Operators and Functions

By now you have met and used a number of mathematical symbols like addition (+), subtraction (-), division (/) and so on. These are known as 'òperators', because they 'operate on' or have an effect on, one or more items in the computer. Table 9.9 shows the mathematical operators on the BBC Micro.

Operator	Sign	Example	Result
Raise to a Power	^	2^3	8
Multiplication	*	5*4	20
Division	/	100/10	10
Addition	+	7+2	9
Subtraction	–	5–2	3

Table 9.9

Note that the '-' sign can also be used to give negative values to particular numbers, as well as its use in addition and subtraction, e.g :

-5 -2= -7

To avoid any ambiguities when using these operators, brackets can be used, as the normal mathematical rules of precedence apply; i.e. anything in brackets is worked out first, then 'powers', then multiplication and division and finally addition and subtraction. By way of an example, the following equation could give the wrong result when entered into ViewSheet unless brackets are used:

$$\frac{-5+4}{2} = 4.5$$

It may be tempting to enter the equation as:

5+4/2

but because the computer performs the division first, it will give the answer as 7, so for the addition to be carried out first, the sum must be placed in brackets:

(5 + 4)/2

which will yield the desired result of 4.5

ViewSheet uses types of operators other than purely mathematical ones, and it will follow a strict order of precedence when using them. The operators are divided into five groups, and those within each group have equal priority. If several operators from the same group are used on a single program line then the computer deals with them in order; i.e. from left to right.

Group One

Brackets	()
Functions	Such as **SIN**, **COS**, **AVERAGE**, **MAX**, etc.
Unary minus	Acts on one number, making it positive or negative.

Group Two

^ (or ↑)   Raise to the power.

Group Three

*   Multiplication.

/   Division.

Group Four

+   Addition.

−   Subtraction.

Group Five (conditional operators)

=   Equal to.

<>   Not equal to.

<   Less than.

>   Greater than.

<=   Less than or equal to.

>=   Greater than or equal to.

ViewSheet's Mathematical Functions

A full list of the functions available in ViewSheet is given in the ViewSheet User Guide, together with details of their use. The functions are listed here for reference:

ABS	Absolute value.
ACS	Arccosine.
ASN	Arcsine.
ATN	Arctan.
AVERAGE	Calculate average value.
CHOOSE	Choose a particular value in a list.
COL	Column number of slot. **COS** Cosine.
DEG	Convert from radians to degrees.
EXP	Exponent.
IF	Used with conditional operators above.
INT	Integer.
LN	Natural logarithm.
LOG	Logarithm to base 10.
LOOKUP	Finds value in one range depending on result in another.
MAX	Maximum value in a range.
MIN	Minimum value in a range.

PI	Value of pi.
RAD	Converts from degrees to radians.
READ	Reads from disc file.
ROW	Row number of slot.
SGN	Gives sign of a number.
SIN	Sine.
SQR	Square root.
TAN	Tangent.
WRITE	Write to disc file.

CHAPTER 10
Advanced Use of Viewsheet

ViewSheet's Windows

Windows are very useful – indeed vitally important – in the manipulation of data on the sheet so that it can be viewed or printed in the most suitable way. A spreadsheet may be much larger than the visible screen area and ViewSheet's screen windows can be defined to show important parts of the calculations taken from several places in the sheet. At the printout stage windows can also control the precise size and layout of the final printed results.

Notice that the examples in Chapter Nine use the W directory. It is often helpful as a reminder to give a window's file the same name as the ViewSheet file itself, but in the W directory (signifying a Window file) instead of the normal one. (In the case of the ADFS, the W directory would have to be created as a new directory in that containing your ViewSheet files.) When you are editing a window definition, the action of pressing RETURN enters or confirms the new window, and causes ViewSheet to check that it can make sense of the parameters you have entered. If something vital has been left out, the software may interpret your entry so that it can make sense of it, and this can sometimes produce some odd results. If, for example, you have already edited window 1 to a format of D2FM, but fail to specify the Bw (Border width) of the new window, ViewSheet will reject the entry with a 'beep', and the flashing block cursor will appear over the D of D2FM!

```
Wi TopL BotR Pos Cw Bw Fmt   Opt
P1 B1  B10  R0  8     D2RM TS
```

It is not immediately apparent that the Bw figure is missing, because ViewSheet is looking 'down the line' for the mistake. It takes the 2 in Fmt as the Border width it needs, then and queries the **D2FM** as an error. The 2 is effectively missing from this section, having been used already. To rectify the problem you need to add a value for Bw as follows:

```
Wi TopL BotR Pos Cw Bw Fmt   Opt
P1 B1  B10  R0  8  0  D2RM TS
```

Although you have probably used ViewSheet's windows quite a lot by now, it is worth running carefully through their exact details at this stage so that you can become well versed in their capabilities. There are eight parameters in total, some of which are optional:

The Window Parameters

The windows are edited by pressing the Edit Window function key (*f1*), which brings up the prompt:

    Window?

in the third line of the screen display. Once you enter the relevant number, the window is displayed as a set of parameters, and the headings associated with each one:

    Wi TopL BotR Pos Cw Bw Fmt Opt
    0 A1   I26   7 7 FRM

Wi : Window number

Up to 10 screen windows are available (numbered 0 to 9) and these should be used in sequence. A further 10 printer windows (P0 to P9) can also be defined to control the exact layout at the **SCREEN**, **PRINT** or **SHEETS** stage.

TopL and BotR : Top left and Bottom right slots of window

When you start up in ViewSheet, the default values for window 0 are always those that can be accommodated in the current mode, so Mode 0 gives a top left value of A1 and a bottom right of I26, while Mode 3 shows A1 to I19, Mode 7 A1 to D19, and so on.

Pos : Position of the window

Windows 1 to 9 must be given a position relative to a previous window specified. They can either be right (R) or below (B) an earlier window, as long as there is space to put them there. You need to specify the number of the window you wish the new window to be positioned next to, e.g. R0.

The 'Pos' parameter for window 1 could be R0 (right of window 0), while window 2 can either be B0 (below window 0) or B1 (below window 1) since ViewSheet applies a little logic to where the window will fit, and would put it in the same place anyway. If you try to display more windows than will fit on the screen, the software will make adjustments accordingly, either by leaving them out or by reducing their size. Note that using the H or V options it is possible to link windows so that their contents scroll together horizontally or vertically. To move the slot cursor from one window to another it is necessary to press the Next Window (f2) function key.

If you decide to put a new window on the screen, you must first make sure you have enough room for it. If necessary you may have to edit earlier windows to fit it in. This is especially relevant when you begin using new windows, because before you can add window 1, 2, and so on, you must edit the default window 0 to leave space for subsequent additions.

Cw : Column width

Can be set from 3 characters up to the full screen width less two characters. This will be 18, 38 or 78, dependent on the screen mode. A single space is left between each column.

Bw : Border width

This parameter governs the width of the row headings down the left-hand side of the display. The minimum is 2 characters, the maximum 15.

Fmt : Format for numerical values

The way in which numbers are displayed in a particular window can be altered in the same way as that of individual slots, or the entire sheet, i.e.

F (Floating point) or D (Decimal places).
R (Right justification) or L (Left justification).
M (negative values have minus sign) or B (negative values shown in brackets).

The default setting for the format is FRM. A typical example of using this facility is to change the display to two decimal places, rather than floating point, i.e. D2RM (as seen in some earlier examples).

Opt : Options available for the window

H Horizontal scrolling, linked with other windows having the H option set.
V Vertical scrolling, linked with other windows having the V option set.
S Turns off the side border (i.e. the row headings).
T Turns off the top border (i.e. the column headings).
C Chart facility. This displays asterisks instead of the value in the slot;

one asterisk for each unit of the value. (Negative values appear as exclamation marks(!)).

Printer Windows

These behave in exactly the same way as screen windows, except that the total size of the group of windows is not limited to the micro's screen display. The maximum working area is 255×255 characters (subject to the capacity of the printer you are using). You can check the results of your printer window definitions by **SCREEN**ing the sheet in memory, but note that if the width of the sheet exceeds 80 characters, the lines will wrap round producing rather a strange result on the screen. This can only act as an indication, and the best course then is to actually print the sheet in order to see how it looks.

There are other minor differences between screen windows and printer windows:

1. The maximum width for a column becomes 253 characters.

2. Two new codes can be placed in the Opt section of the window parameters. '1' stands for Highlight 1, and '2' for Highlight 2. Including either of these causes the whole window to be printed in the relevant highlight, as long as the current printer driver supports it. You can load Printer Drivers into ViewSheet in the same way as you can with VIEW, and so obtain the full range of bold, underline and any other options supported by the Printer Driver, such as control of printing the £ sign (see Chapter Five).

3. Printouts wider than 80 characters can often be obtained on dot matrix printers by buying a wide printer or, in the case of an 80 column printer, setting the print style to Elite or 15 pitch. (The codes for these can be included in the printer set-up program given in Chapter Two, or in a Printer Driver.) On a daisywheel, you may be able to load paper sideways for a wider printout, or set the printing to 15 pitch, changing to a 15 pitch wheel if one is available for the machine.

Saving the Window Definitions

ViewSheet provides two commands for loading and saving the complete set of window definitions. **SW W.ACCOUNT** saves the current set of window definitions in a file called 'W.Account'. **LW W.ACCOUNT** loads a file called 'W.Account' containing the window definitions previously saved under that name. Although ViewSheet saves the current windows if you use the **SAVE** command, you may find it useful to save an alternate set that gives a different screen or printer layout of the same sheet.

One potential problem with ViewSheet is that once you have set up a large number of windows, there is no command to de-activate them all other than editing each one in turn, or changing to another screen mode and back again. Hence you may find the 'alternate set' of windows useful, and one possibility is to save a blank set when you first switch the spreadsheet on. If you call this something obvious, like W.OFF, you can always load this into the sheet to reset all the windows, but remember to save the complex definitions as a separate file first, or you could lose all your hard work.

Designing Spreadsheets

There are a number of points to bear in mind when designing a spreadsheet:

1. Try to set aside an area for entering variable data on the sheet (preferably in the top left corner). Design this area like a form, so that it is easy to read and understand.

2. Work out a rough design for the sheet on paper first, and in the case of a large sheet, make notes as you go along. It is often difficult to remember and visualise the entire sheet, and this approach can save a lot of time in the long run.

3. Place headings and instructions on the sheet whenever you can, to make the model easier to follow when used by others (or by yourself if you come back to it some time later).

4. Keep calculation areas away from data entry areas. Use the **PROTECT** command; Protect Row and Protect Column function keys; to preserve valuable work and guard against incorrect replication.

5. Keep related data on the same row or column so that, if necessary, it can easily be deleted without affecting anything else.

6. Every time you make an entry, ViewSheet normally recalculates the entire spreadsheet. It is important to realise that it does this from left to right, row by row, so if you refer at the top of the sheet to a slot further down you will probably find that you obtain misleading results. ViewSheet may not have carried out all the necessary calculations for the later slot. Hence the data and formulae should be arranged so that any references are to slots back up the sheet, or to the left on the same line.

7. As the sheet grows larger, you may find the time taken to perform the recalculation annoying, as you cannot enter any data while this is happening. If you find you are being delayed in your work, you can turn off

the automatic recalculation (using **SHIFT** *f0*, labelled the Recalculate Mode). You can always force a recalculation when necessary by pressing **SHIFT** *f7* (Recalculate). When you have finished designing your sheet and entering data, automatic recalculation can be switched back on by pressing **SHIFT** *f0* again.

8. If you are using complex mathematical formulae, try one or two test calculations by hand to check that you are getting the correct results from the sheet. A mistake in a formula, or in replication, could produce totally misleading results.

9. Include a title, version number and the date somewhere on the sheet, so that you can recognise the work easily.

Problems Using ViewSheet
A % Sign Appears in Some of the Slots

This is an indication that the number to be displayed in the slot is too long to fit into the current display format, so rather than show the number in part, ViewSheet prints the % sign as an indication of the problem. The solution is to alter the width of the column using a screen window, or to alter the display format, either for this single slot, or for the entire sheet. If you move the slot cursor into the offending slot, you will see its contents correctly displayed in the **CONTENTS=** section at the top of the screen.

Small Errors in the Mathematics

Sometimes allied to the problem above, it is not uncommon to find very small errors creeping into the calculations, so that what should be a whole number or straightforward decimal suddenly acquires a string of zeros and a one after the decimal point. There is an example of this in the second Bill Estimation illustration in Figure 8.5, where the Actual Cost of the Telephone has acquired a very long number! These seemingly odd displays can be cured by reducing the precision of the display on the entire sheet using the **FORMAT** command from the Command screen. For example, you could enter D5RM instead of FRM, so that all the figures on the sheet are rounded up to five decimal places instead of nine!

Complex Examples on ViewSheet
Accounting

An extension of the insurance list given in the Chapter Nine is a simple accounts spreadsheet, entering first the income, then the expenses, and calculating a current balance. This is a useful illustration of changing one model into another, hence saving time. The same layout and printer windows used in the insurance list can be used as a starting point for this application. The only real changes required are new headings for income, expenditure and balance, and the change in the formula necessary to work out the final balance at the end of the sheet. The beauty of doing your accounts using windows in this way is that you can see precisely what effect each entry has on the final balance. The initial layout is shown in Figure 10.1, although the data in some slots is too long to be shown in full in this format.

```
A   SLOT=A101
CONTENTS=*BLANK*


0        ...............A................B...............C...............D
..1  28.03.86           Accounts Sheet     Version 1.0
..2
..3                     VANDENBERG ANTIQUE *1985-86*
..4                     ================== =========
..5  INCOME
..6  ======
..7  Date               Item               Invoice No.        Value
..8  ------------------ ------------------ ------------------ ------------------
..9  28.03.86           Repairs to Frame   10001                    50
.10  28.03.86           Supply Coins (I Ch 10002                    75
.11  28.03.86           Sale of Towel      10003                    10
.12  28.03.86           Sale of Tea Chests 10004                    65
.13  01.04.86           Photograph of Stat 10005                   300
.14  01.04.86           Boxed Butterfly Se 10006                    45
.15
.16
.17

.37
.38
.39                                                           ------------------
.40                                TOTAL INCOME=                   545
.41  EXPENSES
.42  ========
.43  Date               Item                                  Value
.44  ------------------ ------------------                    ------------------
.45  28.03.86           Computer                                   500
.46  28.03.86           Disc Drives                                400
.47  28.03.86           TV Monitor                                 300
.48  28.03.86           Discs                                       65
.49  29.03.86           Flash Gun                                  200
.50  29.03.86           Journalism Course                          200
.51  30.03.86           Stationary                                  30
.52  29.03.86           Coffee Maker                                30
.53  29.03.86           Repairs to Trolley                          15
.54  29.03.86           Microwave Oven                             200
.55  01.04.86           Mugs x 30                                   45
.56
.57
.58

.98
.99
.10
.10                                                           ------------------
.10                                TOTAL EXPENSES=                1985
.10                                                           ==================
.10                     (INCOME)-(EXPENSES PROFIT=                -1440
.10
```

Figure 10.1

(You will notice an odd effect – the row numbers in the 100s are incomplete – this results from reducing the side border width to three, but it is necessary if you are to use the maximum column of 18 characters shown in the example.) A large number of extra rows has been inserted to allow enough space for entries under Income and Expenses throughout the financial year. The sheet data ends (somewhat arbitrarily) at row 104 – you could allocate as much space as you liked for your data. ViewSheet has a maximum of 255 rows, and if you are going to divide memory up beforehand you need to think about the proportions initially allocated to each heading. Depending on the exact nature of the business, it is probably reasonable to allow about 50 rows for income, 190 for expenses and the rest for totals, headings and the balance calculation. You could leave a few spare rows to cover any you need to insert when setting the sheet up and using it. If the entire sheet is already allocated and you try to add any extra rows, the computer will 'beep' to indicate an error. Then you have to delete rows from one area before you can add them to another!

There is no problem scrolling up and down through the sheet, but you may find it helpful to use the screen windows to show all the relevant sections on the screen at once. These divide into five groups: the sheet heading; income data section; income total and expenses heading; expenses data; profit area; and the following windows set the whole thing up on the screen as shown in Figure 10.2.

The sheet heading:

```
Wi  TopL  BotR  Pos  Cw  Bw  Fmt  Opt
0   A3    D8         18  3   FRM  H
```

Income data:

```
Wi  TopL  BotR  Pos  Cw  Bw  Fmt  Opt
1   A9    D11   B0   18  3   FRM  HT
```

Income total and expenses heading:

```
Wi  TopL  BotR  Pos  Cw  Bw  Fmt  Opt
2   A39   D44   B1   18  3   FRM  HT
```

Expenses data:

```
Wi  TopL  BotR  Pos  Cw  Bw  Fmt  Opt
3   A45   D47   B2   18  3   FRM  HT
```

Profit area:

```
Wi  TopL  BotR  Pos  Cw  Bw  Fmt  Opt
4   A101  D104  B3   18  3   FRM  HT
```

The whole sheet can be scrolled in any of the windows, but it is far quicker to move around by pressing the Next Window function key ($f2$) to do so. Notice that an H is present in each of the screen window definitions. This is so that the whole sheet will scroll sideways if you wish to add any extra data to the right (i.e. in column E and beyond), or if you accidentally take the slot cursor off to the right.

```
A    SLOT=A101
CONTENTS=*BLANK*

0   ...................A....................B....................C....................D
..3                     VANDENBERG ANTIQUE *1985-86*
..4                     ===================  =========
..5 INCOME
..6 ======
..7 Date                Item                 Invoice No.          Value
..8 ------------------- -------------------  -------------------  -------------------
..9 28.03.86            Repairs to Frame     10001                                  50
.10 28.03.86            Supply Coins (I Ch   10002                                  75
.11 28.03.86            Sale of Towel        10003                                  10
                                                                  -------------------
.39
.40                                   TOTAL INCOME=                                545
.41 EXPENSES
.42 ========
.43 Date                Item                                      Value
.44 ------------------- -------------------                       -------------------
.45 28.03.86            Computer                                                  500
.46 28.03.86            Disc Drives                                               400
.47 28.03.86            TV Monitor                                                300
                                                                  -------------------
.10>
.10                                   TOTAL EXPENSES=                            1985
.10                                                               ===================
.10                      (INCOME)-(EXPENSES PROFIT=                              -1440
```

Figure 10.2

An important thing to remember if you are setting up windows like this is that as soon as you add or delete any rows or columns, the window definitions (unlike the formulae on the sheet) DO NOT CHANGE to take account of this, and so they must all be changed by hand. Hence the need to set this accounts sheet up in such a way that it will need the minimum of alteration. When it comes to printing out the accounts, similar printer windows are used to those in the insurance list in the previous chapter:

```
Wi  TopL  BotR  Pos  Cw  Bw  Fmt  Opt
P0  A3    A105       8   0   FRM  TS
```

```
Wi   TopL   BotR   Pos   Cw   Bw   Fmt   Opt
P1   B3     B105   R0    30   0    FRM   TS

Wi   TopL   BotR   Pos   Cw   Bw   Fmt   Opt
P2   C3     C105   R1    10   0    FRM   TS

Wi   TopL   BotR   Pos   Cw   Bw   Fmt   Opt
P3   D3     D105   R2    10   0    FRM   TS
```

The full contents of the sheet can be **SCREEN**ed or printed out at any time, but the printout will contain large gaps unless you ***SPOOL** the results into an ASCII file and **READ** them into VIEW to remove the blank lines. (This is described in Chapter Fourteen.) Alternatively you could delete the gaps on the sheet and adjust the window sizes for the final printout. (Note that windows of this sort could be used for the screen display, but they would substantially slow down data entry, as you would have to keep moving to the 'Next Window' using function key *f2*.) Figure 10.3 shows a sample printout from the sheet.

```
              VANDENBERG ANTIQUES INC.        *1985-86*
              ========================        =========
INCOME
======
Date          Item                            Invoice No    Value
--------      ------------------------------  ----------    ----------
28.03.86      Repairs to Frame                    10001         50.00
28.03.86      Supply Coins (I Ching)              10002         75.00
28.03.86      Sale of Towel                       10003         10.00
28.03.86      Sale of Tea Chests                  10004         65.00
01.04.86      Photograph of Stately Home          10005        300.00
01.04.86      Boxed Butterfly Set                 10006         45.00
                                                            ----------
                                   TOTAL  INCOME=              545.00
EXPENSES
========
Date          Item                                            Value
--------      ------------------------------  ----------    ----------
28.03.86      Computer                                         500.00
28.03.86      Disc Drives                                      400.00
28.03.86      TV Monitor                                       300.00
28.03.86      Discs                                             65.00
29.03.86      Flash Gun                                        200.00
29.03.86      Journalism Course Fees                           200.00
30.03.86      Stationary                                        30.00
29.03.86      Coffee Maker                                      30.00
29.03.86      Repairs to Trolley                                15.00
29.03.86      Microwave Oven                                   200.00
01.04.86      Mugs x 30                                         45.00
                                                            ----------
                                   TOTAL  EXPENSES=           1985.00
                                                            ==========
                         (INCOME)-(EXPENSES)=  PROFIT=       -1440.00
```

Figure 10.3

Expanding the Sheet Further

You may find that you run out of memory using the sheet to store data in this way – it is only really suitable in this form for small-scale accounting – but there is a way round the problem. Using a special feature of ViewSheet, you could set up separate sheets to contain income and expenditure, with the income totals carried forward in something called a 'linking file' to the expenses sheet, where the overall balance is calculated. For really complex accounts, the number of sheets could be expanded still further, with separate sheets for quarterly or monthly figures, and extra columns could be added to deal with VAT. If you are working with several files, linked or otherwise, it is useful to create the spreadsheet model without any data entered on it, then save the blank model so that it can be used as a starting point for each sheet of figures. Blank sheets saved in this way are sometimes known as 'masks', and you may find that masks you have created are of use to other people running ViewSheet, as well as yourself.

Tying Sheets Together

As mentioned above, sheets can be tied or linked together, so that results from one sheet appear in another. It is possible to create a completely linked system for the purposes of accounting or stock control, so that an entire year's figures can be kept on manageable monthly sheets. You can 'cascade' results from one sheet to the next, so that there is no need to carry lots of data forward by hand each time. This is achieved using a ViewSheet facility called 'linking files', but can only be set up if you are using disc drives.

```
STOCK   CONTROL
======  =======

Item   Stock  Reorder  Order   Cost     Cost of  Delivery Number   Stock     Number  Sales   Link
       B/F    Level    Number  Per Item Order             In Stock Value     Sold    Value   Totals
------ -----  -------  ------  -------- -------- -------- -------- --------- ------- ------- ------

BASIC    20     10       0       70        0        5        2       140       23     1610     2
BCPL      8      4       0      100        0        4        4       400        8      800     4
C         6      3       0      200        0        3        1       200        8     1600     1
FORTH    12      6       0       75        0        6        2       150       16     1200     2
LISP     16      8       0      100        0        8        6       600       18     1800     6
LOGO     20     10       0      100        0        5        4       400       21     2100     4
PASCAL   16      8       0       80        0        8        4       320       20     1600     4
PROLOG   14      7       0      100        0        5        1       100       18     1800     1
------ -----  -------  ------  -------- -------- -------- -------- --------- ------- ------- ------

                       ORDER TOTAL=    0     STOCK TOTAL=    2310
                                                  TOTAL SALES=    12510
```

Figure 10.4 Printout from 'Working month' example spreadsheet

Stock control provides a good example of this technique, which seems a little daunting at first, but in fact is quite simple – and powerful – once you get the hang of it. The sheet shown in Figure 10.4 is a working month of figures for a mythical computer software company. Formulae are mostly straightforward, being entered on row 10 and replicated (relatively) downwards in each case.

Do not start to enter this sheet yet, because the quickest method in the long run is to build up a spreadsheet mask which will act as the starting point for each month's new sheet. The design for the mask is as shown in Figure 10.5.

```
        ........A........B........C........D........E........F........G........H........I........J........K........L
......1 LINKING FILES          V. 1.0              MASK : 1986
......2
......3 STOCK   CONTROL
......4 ::::::: :::::::
......5
......6 Item    Stock    Reorder  Order    Cost     Cost of  Delivery Number   Stock    Number   Sales    Link
......7         B/F      Level    Number   Per Item Order                     In Stock Value    Sold     Value    Totals
......8 -------- -------- -------- -------- -------- -------- -------- -------- -------- -------- -------- --------
......9
.....10 BASIC            10       0        70       0                          0                 0        0        0
.....11 BCPL             4        0        100      0                          0                 0        0        0
.....12 C                3        0        200      0                          0                 0        0        0
.....13 FORTH            6        0        75       0                          0                 0        0        0
.....14 LISP             6        0        100      0                          0                 0        0        0
.....15 LOGO             10       0        100      0                          0                 0        0        0
.....16 PASCAL           8        0        80       0                          0                 0        0        0
.....17 PROLOG           7        0        100      0                          0                 0        0        0
.....18
.....19 -------- -------- -------- -------- -------- -------- -------- -------- -------- -------- --------
.....20
.....21                           ORDER TOTAL=     0         STOCK TOTAL=    0
.....22
.....23                                                                           TOTAL SALES=   0
```
Figure 10.5 The mask design

Most of the text fits into eight character columns, so edit the screen window 0 to read:

```
Wi   TopL  BotR  Pos  Cw  Bw  Fmt  Opt
0    A1    H26        8   4   FRM
```

You are then ready to put in the headings and dashed lines. Reorder Level, Delivery (i.e. the number delivered), Cost per Item and Number in Stock are all to be entered by hand. As the reorder level will probably be the same on every sheet, these figures should be put on the mask to save typing them on every time. The Stock B/F (i.e. Stock Brought Forward) column has the starting levels entered on this sheet by hand: these figures will be replaced by those from the previous month in later sheets. The other columns have formulae which are all entered in row 10, then in all cases are replicated relatively downwards from row 11 to row 17.

D10 : IF(C10>B10,C10-B10,0)

This formula checks whether the current stock level is below the reorder level (is C10 greater than B10?), and if so places the quantity to be reordered in D10 (the quantity is the second value in the statement, given by C10-B10). If the stock level is higher than the reorder number and no extra stock is required, then D10 takes the third value in the statement, i.e. zero.

F10 : D10*E10 (The cost of the order is the number of units required multiplied by the cost per item.)

I10 : H10*E10 (The value of the stock is the number in stock multiplied by the cost per item.)

J10 : B10+G10-H10 (The number sold equals the stock brought forward plus the number delivered minus the number now in stock.)

K10 : E10*J10 (The total value of sales for each different item.)

F21 : F10F17 (Sums the value of the order to be placed.)

I21 : I10I17 (Sums the value of current stock.)

K23 : K10K17 (Sums the value of the month's sales.)

Now comes the tricky part: all the formulae and data necessary for the mask have been added, all that it is left is to set up the formula that links from this sheet to the next. It is a good idea to save a copy of this spreadsheet under the name MASK, so that you always have a copy to use for future months. Do this now. Next, you must begin a file on the disc to hold the data to be carried forward – the linking file – and this is done using the **CREATE** command. **CREATE** will make a file up in the V. directory, so if you are using the ADFS filing system you will have to start a new directory using the ***CDIR** command:

*CDIR V <RETURN>

will set it up. This is not necessary under the old DFS. The way **CREATE** works is to allow you to create, or define, a file into which the contents of some of your spreadsheet's slots will be copied. Then the next sheet you set up will be able to read that data in, and make use of it as if you had typed it in yourself. In this example, you need to pass eight figures from one sheet to the next: the contents of the Number in Stock column. To **CREATE** the necessary file you must first give the number of the linking file you wish to make (this can be anything between 1 and 255 – so let this be number 1). Then you have to state the horizontal and vertical size of the data to be saved. Here you need to save an area one slot wide by eight slots down.

```
CREATE (file number) (horizontal size)
(vertical size)
```

so the command you need to enter is:

```
CREATE 1 1 8 <RETURN>
```

The disc drive should spin when you enter this as ViewSheet sets up the necessary file to hold the data, to which it gives the name:

```
V.VS1
```

The sheet so far can now be given a new name (using the **NAME** command) for the first month's figures, e.g. APRIL (see Figure 10.6). (Note that you should still have a copy under the name MASK somewhere on the disc.) Now you are ready to enter the formulae which will write the data from your first sheet into the file. ViewSheet uses a **WRITE** command to save data in linking files, which should not be confused with the VIEW command of the same name. In this case, **WRITE** is actually placed on the sheet itself, followed by four parameters:

```
WRITE (the number of the linking file)
(horizontal coordinate in file) (vertical
coordinate) (value to be placed in the file)
```

The horizontal and vertical coordinates available in the file correspond to the sizes specified using the **CREATE** command, so in this case there are 1x8 possible coordinates. Column L is a convenient place to set up the write instructions, so the first goes in L10. The formula to be entered is:

```
WRITE (1,1,1,H10)
```

being linking file 1, column 1, row 1, and the contents of cell H10, which is the value we wish to place in the file. The next slot down, L11, would then be:

```
WRITE (1,1,2,H10)
```

and so on. In fact there is an easier way to write the formula so that it can be replicated, and that is to use the ROW function to work out the vertical coordinate. In L10, ROW-9 would give the result 1, so ROW-9 in L11 gives 2, and so on. The formula in L10 then becomes:

    WRITE (1,1,ROW-9,H10)

and then L10 can be replicated relatively from L11 to L17. You will notice that as you enter the formula, or replicate it, the disc drive operates. This is because ViewSheet is now writing results into the linking file as it works them out, and this will continue as you update the contents of the sheet. Updating always takes place when you press **ESCAPE**, so be sure you do this when you finish working on the sheet, so that the final values are correctly stored in the disc file. Be sure you have saved a version of the APRIL file before moving on to the next month.

Having established the first working month (APRIL), you should then go on to set up the MAY file (see Figure 10.7), once again based on the MASK file that has been saved. In this sheet, and all subsequent ones, two linking files are used. The previous month's figures are read into the 'Stock Brought Forward' column, while a new file should be established to carry the 'Number in Stock' figures to the next sheet. If you now **LOAD** the MASK file, you can begin by placing the instructions to read the contents of V.VS1 into the sheet. ViewSheet's **READ** command is used to do this, and it works in much the same way as **WRITE**, except that there is no fourth parameter:

    READ (number of the linking file) (horizontal
    coordinate in file) (vertical coordinate in
    file)

so if you use the **ROW** function again, the formula needed in B10 of the MASK file is:

    READ (1,1,ROW-9)

Once again this is replicated from B11 to B17, although the replication will take place straight away this time, as there are no slot references in the formula. The disc drive will leap into action again, as the contents of V.VS1 are read in, and you will see them appear on screen. The entire sheet then recalculates on the basis of the new data. Remember to change the **NAME** of this new sheet to MAY, or whatever you choose, so that you do not destroy the MASK file by saving anything over it!

All that is needed to complete the chain is to set up another linking file from MAY into JUNE. The process is much as before, except that this file should be numbered '2', using:

    CREATE 2 1 8

which will set up V.VS2. Enter the following formula in L10:

WRITE (2,1,ROW-9,H10)

and again replicate L10 relatively from L11 to L17. Working in this way, monthly sheets can be kept for the entire year, and printed out individually whenever they are required. A suitable printout (as in Figure 10.4) could be obtained using the following printer window:

```
Wi   TopL   BotR   Pos   Cw   Bw   Fmt   Opt
P0   A3     L23          8    0    FRM   TS
```

One thing to note when using this method is that if you go back to a previous month's sheet and make any changes, these will not be reflected in the next sheet in the chain unless you load that sheet and 'force it' to read in the new data. This can easily be done by pressing the Recalculate function key (**SHIFT** *f7*), because the sheet checks the relevant linking file and reads in the stored data each time it recalculates.

```
        .........A........B........C........D........E........F........G........H........I........J........K.........L
......1 LINKING FILES          V. 1.1           APRIL : 1986
......2
......3 STOCK   CONTROL
......4 =======  =======
......5
......6 Item    Stock   Reorder  Order   Cost    Cost of  Delivery Number   Stock    Number   Sales    Link
......7         B/F     Level    Number  Per Item Order            In Stock Value    Sold     Value    Totals
......8 -------- -------- -------- -------- -------- -------- -------- -------- -------- -------- --------
......9
.....10 BASIC   20      10       0       70      0               20       1400     0        0        20
.....11 BCPL    8       4        0       100     0               8        800      0        0        8
.....12 C       6       3        0       200     0               6        1200     0        0        6
.....13 FORTH   12      6        0       75      0               12       900      0        0        12
.....14 LISP    16      8        0       100     0               16       1600     0        0        16
.....15 LOGO    20      10       0       100     0               20       2000     0        0        20
.....16 PASCAL  16      8        0       80      0               16       1280     0        0        16
.....17 PROLOG  14      7        0       100     0               14       1400     0        0        14
.....18
.....19 -------- -------- -------- -------- -------- -------- -------- -------- -------- -------- --------
.....20
.....21                                  ORDER TOTAL=     0       STOCK TOTAL=     10580
.....22
.....23                                                                           TOTAL SALES=     0
```

Figure 10.6 First month, with figures added to Stock Brought Forward column by hand

```
........A........B........C........D........E........F........G........H........I........J........K........L
......1 LINKING FILES            V. 1.2              MAY : 1986
......2
......3 STOCK    CONTROL
......4 =======  =======
......5
......6 Item     Stock    Reorder  Order    Cost      Cost of  Delivery Number   Stock    Number   Sales    Link
......7          B/F      Level    Number   Per Item  Order             In Stock Value    Sold     Value    Totals
......8 -------- -------- -------- -------- --------  -------- -------- -------- -------- -------- -------- --------
......9
.....10 BASIC      20       10       0        70        0        5        2       140       23      1610      2
.....11 BCPL        8        4       0       100        0        4        4       400        8       800      4
.....12 C           6        3       0       200        0        3        1       200        8      1600      1
.....13 FORTH      12        6       0        75        0        6        2       150       16      1200      2
.....14 LISP       16        8       0       100        0        8        6       600       18      1800      6
.....15 LOGO       20       10       0       100        0        5        4       400       21      2100      4
.....16 PASCAL     16        8       0        80        0        8        4       320       20      1600      4
.....17 PROLOG     14        7       0       100        0        5        1       100       18      1800      1
.....18
.....19 -------- -------- -------- -------- --------  -------- -------- -------- -------- -------- -------  -------
.....20
.....21                            ORDER TOTAL=      0      STOCK TOTAL=         2310
.....22
.....23                                                                        TOTAL  SALES=    12510
```

Figure 10.7 Working month example spreadsheet

SECTION THREE

THE DATABASE

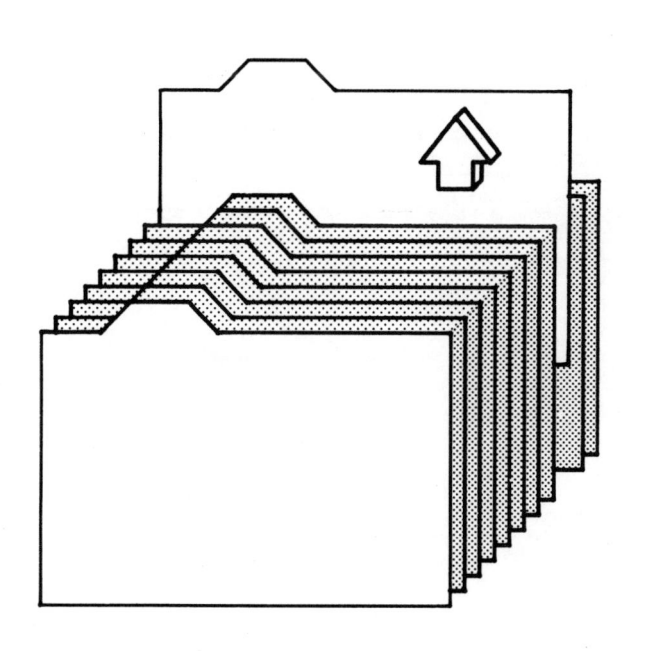

VIEWSTORE

CHAPTER ELEVEN

Introduction to ViewStore

What is a Database?

A database is a means of storing large amounts of information in such a way that it can be retrieved again quickly having been edited, sorted, or searched for specific data. Because of its flexibility, the database structure is now at the heart of most business software, including invoicing, order processing, stock control, accounting, sales and purchase ledgers and payroll packages.

The power of the computer database can readily be called upon when searching stored information for records which satisfy one or more criteria, so that, for example, a file of London employees could be searched for anyone who was between the ages of 20 and 40, earning more than £6000 and living in Croydon. As new records are added to a database, a sort facility can be used to re-assemble all the entries in alphabetical or numerical order. Databases are invaluable when they can be used with word processing software to produce standard letters, and some can generate a set of mailing labels to go with the letters automatically.

Some databases can also perform calculations, making them suitable for things like stock control, invoicing, and advanced accounting. These individual activities can sometimes be linked, so that several files become interactive and a change made to one file will automatically affect, or 'up-date' the others.

The terms used to describe an electronic database are similar to those in manual filing. A 'Record' is one set of details, equivalent to a single card in a card index. A number of separate sections, or 'fields' make up each record. The complete set of records concerning any one subject is called a 'file'.

A word of warning here: it is not always the best thing to computerise a box file or card index of data, or things like telephone directories, as the time taken to access really simple data from a computer store can sometimes make a complete mockery of the system! The best, and indeed most impressive results, come when large amounts of information have to be processed in some way, or a variety of different ways, and then the computer really comes into its own.

A versatile database program can be set up to handle information in the way the user requires, and gives access to that information in the form of printed reports or on-screen results. The reporting software can often be made to perform mathematical functions on the contents of the database automatically. Some databases can be linked to word processors to produce standard letters, and even more versatile reporting. Once a particular style of report has been prepared, the same routine the can be rerun after the addition of new data, or reconfigured to produce a new set of results with the minimum of effort.

Despite the obvious advantages of using a database, there are two important considerations when putting a body of data into a computer.

Firstly, the database needs some thought in its application if it is not to become a cumbersome version of a card index on the screen. No-one who travels would dream of giving up a tiny address book for a desk-bound computer version of the same thing! And if you only know 20 people, it's a bit of a bore switching the computer on every time you need to know one address or telephone number. Since a lot of time has to be spent keying in data, it is vital that a computer's power can be made to work for you once that data is stored inside. Maintaining a large database usually takes up a lot of time, so this form of information storage is only really useful in business terms if the data can be made available to a number of people, or if using the computer's power to carry out the searching and sorting for specific references which make the system cost-effective. These factors can make a database unsuitable for some applications in the home environment, as it can be quicker to write the information on file cards and refer to it by hand.

The second problem when in using a database is that the initial setting-up stage often has to be carefully planned, so that best use can be made of the data in store. Usually, the biggest headache with database software is knowing what you want it to do first! This can be very difficult if you are a first-time user. The correct 'specification' of a database: i.e. its configuration to accomplish a specific task; is vital if the stored information is to be used to maximum advantage. A useful feature to be found on some databases is a utility enabling already-entered data to be incorporated, or re-built, into a new database with different parameters. This means that any initial mistakes made in the specification of the database can be rectified later, without having to type all the information in again.

ViewStore

The ViewStore database is a ROM-based language for the BBC micro, and it is supplied with a range of Utility programs on disc, so to use the software you must have at least one disc drive and a suitable disc filing system fitted to your computer. ViewStore can display its data in two different ways, either as individual record 'cards', or in a spreadsheet-style tabular form (see Figure 11.1).

```
L Space 102    Indexed by Author
                                STAFF LIBRARY
Title

Author   Robinson  Lytle W.
Title    Edgar Cayce's Story of the Origin and Destiny of Man
Publisher  Neville Spearman
Classification    000.00
On Loan?  Y
----------------   ----------------   ----------------   ----------------
On Loan to?   Clive Williamson
Department    Computers
Room No.      402                        Date Purchased  2.2.85
Date Due Back: 6.7.86                    Price   £    4.25
```

```
L Space 26   Indexed by DATE
                            ACCOUNTS - 1985/86
Description of item:

DATE......ITEM.................................TAXCODE.OUTGOING.TYPE.INCOMING.7
28.03.86  Repairs to Frame                                    I     50.00
28.03.86  Supply Coins (I Ching)                              I     75.00
28.03.86  Sale of Towel                                       I     10.00
28.03.86  Sale of Tea Chests                                  I     65.00
28.03.86  Computer                              500.00 C
28.03.86  Disc Drives                           400.00 C
28.03.86  TV Monitor                            300.00 C
28.03.86  Discs                                  65.00 E
29.03.86  Flash Gun                             200.00 C
29.03.86  Journalism Course Fees                200.00 E
29.03.86  Coffee Maker                           30.00 E
29.03.86  Repairs to Trolley                     15.00 E
29.03.86  Microwave Oven                        200.00 C
30.03.86  Stationary                             30.00 E
01.04.86  Photograph of Stately Home                          I    300.00
01.04.86  Boxed Butterfly Set                                 I     45.00
01.04.86  Mugs x 30                              45.00 E
```

Figure 11.1 ViewStore card and spreadsheet layouts

ViewStore files can be read directly into the VIEW word processor, where they appear in the tabular format, with a TAB character between each field of data. This is an excellent way of manipulating the data in reports, as it allows very precise control over the layout of the text and tables, but to use this feature successfully it is important that careful attention is paid to the initial setting up of the database in a form suitable for VIEW.

Bearing in mind the complexity of ViewStore, its User Guide is quite adequate for learning to use the example Cars database supplied on the Utility disc that comes in the package, so the approach taken here is to take the reader through setting up a specific example of a database, learning about the software in the process. Figure 11.2 shows the ViewStore function keys strip for reference.

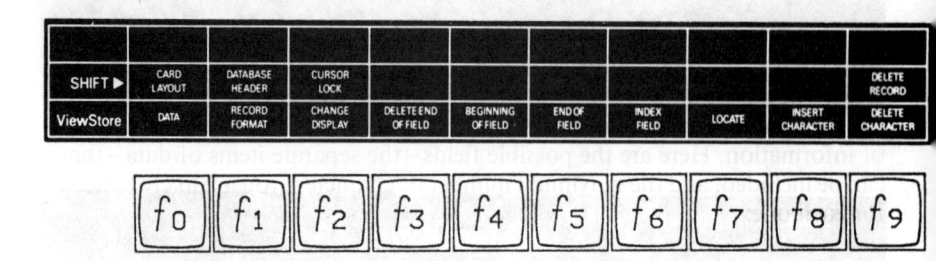

SHIFT ▶	CARD LAYOUT	DATABASE HEADER	CURSOR LOCK						DELETE RECORD
ViewStore	DATA	RECORD FORMAT	CHANGE DISPLAY	DELETE END OF FIELD	BEGINNING OF FIELD	END OF FIELD	INDEX FIELD	LOCATE	INSERT CHARACTER	DELETE CHARACTER

| f0 | f1 | f2 | f3 | f4 | f5 | f6 | f7 | f8 | f9 |

Figure 11.2 The ViewStore function key strip

Starting a Simple Database

Unlike VIEW and ViewSheet, it is not possible to use the ViewStore software without studying its documentation. In common with most other versatile database programs a good knowledge of its general operation is vital before you can undertake the design and use of your own databases. The example here is an expanded name and address file using the card index style of data presentation possible with ViewStore. This database can readily be expanded or adapted at the set-up stage (or later on) to form the kernal of a number of useful applications, such as personnel, salaries, or medical records. The general style of presentation and report generation is also applicable to other textual uses, e.g. in a library catalogue of books or discs, or as a store of specialist knowledge.

The basic name and address database finds a host of applications in small businesses and mail-order houses. The example here is expanded slightly beyond purely name and addresses to show some of the possibilities of ViewStore. Thus, a birthday section is included, so that you can search the information for anyone who has a birthday in the current or coming month, and a further extension is the option of selecting whether or not a Christmas card is sent. In either case, a selection of records can be made, either on screen or to be saved as a special 'select file', and the latter can then be used in conjunction with a ViewStore utility called 'Label' to print a set of sticky labels for the recipients of the Christmas or birthday cards. If this sounds a little impersonal, rest assured that the Label utility can produce results just as if they had been perfectly typed by hand! You can go beyond these facilities to produce a printed address or telephone list from the entries with the help of a Report utility, or you could produce standard letters in conjunction with the VIEW word processor using a VIEW Macro Generation utility.

Designing the Database

Because there are so many possibilities in using a database of this type, the structure of the final report should be carefully considered at the planning stage. The basic name/address/phone contents can to some extent be geared to the special requirements mentioned above by the inclusion of a few extra pieces of information. Here are the possible fields – the separate items of data – that can be included, and the maximum number of characters you are likely to need for each one:

```
SURNAME          (18)
FORENAME         (20)
TITLE            (15)   (this can be used to hold Mr, Mrs, etc.)
(COMPANY NAME)   (20)   (if you wish to include this now)
ADDRESS1         (25)
ADDRESS2         (25)
ADDRESS3         (25)
TOWN             (17)
COUNTY           (15)
POSTCODE         ( 8)
BIRTHDAY         ( 7)
CHRISTMAS CARD   ( 1)
PHONE            (17)
OTHER INFO?      (30)
```

If you are preparing this for business use straight away, you might like to change Birthday to Date of Birth, and add sections for National Insurance Number, Salary, Tax Code, and so on. The object of planning the database in this way

161

is to see roughly how many characters each record will require. The maximum number in the basic list is about 225, so an average number might be 180. When you set up the database, ViewStore will ask how much space to reserve on disc for the file, and this is easily worked out by multiplying the number of separate records (let's say about 100 names and addresses will do) by the maximum number of characters in each, plus a bit! The actual formula given in the ViewStore User Guide is:

Average characters per record × Expected no. of records × 1.1

For our example, this gives:

180 × 100 × 1.1 = 19800

and we could conveniently round this figure up to 20000. The other thing you need to know before you start designing the database (and this is often the tricky bit) is which of the fields you would like the software to act on when organising or ordering the data. (If you do get this wrong, don't worry, ViewStore lets you change it later.) Logically, you would probably like the information to be in alphabetical order, so SURNAME is one field that you should specify. BIRTHDAY might be another, and whether or not a CHRISTMAS CARD should be sent could be a third. When you set the database up, you will be asked to specify fields like this as Index fields, and to give each one a name. This is because separate files are created on disc to hold the details of the order in which the records should be shown for each field. You can choose a maximum of four such fields if you are using the DFS, and up to nine in the case of the ADFS. In this example, suitable filenames might be SURNAME, BIRTH and XMAS. Choose something you will recognise later. Having thought about all that, you are actually ready to set up the database!

Running ViewStore

You should select ViewStore by entering:

    *STORE <RETURN>

whereupon you will see the ViewStore Command screen (it is similar to those of VIEW, ViewSheet and ViewSpell). You should by now have made a backup copy of the ViewStore Utilities Disc supplied with the software. It is best to make a further working copy which contains only the U. directory files (Utility files) and F.REPORT, otherwise the files associated with the CARS database may take up so much room that you will be unable to begin anything of your own. If you only have one disc drive and you are using the DFS, you can copy all the Utilities by entering:

    COPY 0 0 U. <RETURN>

Then copy F.REPORT by entering:

    *COPY 0 0 F.REPORT

You could save your new files on this disc, or you could run the Utility, then swap it for a blank disc to hold your new database files. If you have more that one drive, however, you can leave the Utilities in drive 1 all the time, and put a blank disc in drive 0 to take the data. Using a new disc is advantageous because it leaves more space for the data you need to save. To configure ViewStore to work with two or more drives you can use the **PREFIX** command. This allows the specification of certain drives for certain types of file. Entering:

    PREFIX <RETURN>

will generate the response:

    PREFIX
    D)ata
    F)ormat
    I)ndex
    S)ort
    U)tility

As there are no prefixes to start with, these different files will all be loaded from, or saved to the current drive (assumed to be drive 0). You need to enter a different prefix to make ViewStore recognise the Utilities on Drive 1, so type in:

    PREFIX U:1. <RETURN>

The software will respond by showing the list again with the new prefix in place. To turn the prefix off again you should enter:

    PREFIX U <RETURN>

To create the database, you need to run a Utility called **SETUP**, so enter:

    UTILITY SETUP <RETURN> or U SETUP <RETURN>

(If you only have one disc drive, you should now replace the Utilities disc with the disc for your database.) The **SETUP** Utility presents a series of questions about the database you wish to start and, hopefully, by now you will be equipped to answer these. The first question asks whether you are setting up a database or a report (answer D); then you are prompted for a filename for the database (this should be not more than seven letters long if you are using the DFS). You could suitably call the file ADDRESS, and this will be saved automatically in Directory D. (Note that if you are using the ADFS, Directory D should already have been created using *CDIR, along with the other Directories used by ViewStore, i.e. F, I, R, S, and U.) You are then asked for the name of the Format File to go with this database. This is the file that holds all the information about how the data is displayed, and it is usual to give it the same name as the database itself. To do so, you can just press RETURN in reply. ViewStore gives it the name ADDRESS, but will save this file in Directory F. The next prompt if you are using the DFS is:

How many bytes to reserve?

One byte is needed to store each character, so you should enter the value already worked out, i.e. 20000. The next question asks for the number of records in order to reserve files of the correct length for the indexes; it is better here if you err on the generous side — say 120 here, just in case. The **SETUP** Utility then asks for the name of the first Index. This will be SURNAME in our example. The next question: Keysize, refers to the number of characters to be checked when sorting through the contents of all the SURNAME fields when making up the Index. The more you enter, the larger the size of the Index file and the slower the sort; too few will fail to distinguish between the entries when putting them in order. A reasonable number would be seven, which should be enough for most purposes. The Index questions are repeated again, and you can enter 'BIRTH' and '3' to allow birthdays to be selected by month. At the next Index prompt you can enter 'XMAS' and '1' to set up an Index of those selected to receive Christmas Cards. The Indexes will all be stored in Directory I. (If you were setting up this database for office use, you might prefer to call the BIRTH Index DATE instead, for Date Joined. The same keysize of '3' is needed for proper dates.) Once you have entered the final Index you require, you can press RETURN at the next prompt to terminate this section, whereupon ViewStore sets up all the files on disc and returns the '=>' prompt to the screen when it has done so. Your work is far from over, however, as you must now set up the database to the required format.

Defining the Database Format

All the new files created on the disc by the **SETUP** Utility are empty to begin with, so to start working on them enter:

LOAD ADDRESS <RETURN> or L ADDRESS <RETURN>

and ViewStore will load the database file and the format file, giving notice that
it has done so on the Command Screen header information. If you press
ESCAPE at this stage you will see the default spreadsheet style layout of the
database, which looks pretty unfriendly. The best thing to do now is to define
the precise form of the different fields, and this is done by pressing the Record
Format function key (*f1*). You are then presented with various headings. You
enter the details of your required format on this display. A full description of
the fields (one per column, talking in spreadsheet terms) is given in the
ViewStore User Guide under Creating a Database. You could refer to it, or
simply enter the details as shown in Figure 11.3.

```
L Space 21003
Field name                       Record format

Field name......Wid.T.S.D.Low limit..High limit.I.Key.Index name..........Prom
SURNAME          18  t y n                       y   7 SURNAME
FORENAME         20  t y n                       n     !
TITLE            15  t n n                       n
ADDRESS1         25  a y n                       n
ADDRESS2         25  a y n                       n
ADDRESS3         25  a y n                       n
TOWN             17  a y n                       n
COUNTY           15  a y n                       n
POSTCODE          8  a n n                       n
BIRTHDAY          7  a n n                       y   3 BIRTH            (Mon
CHRISTMAS CARD?   1  t n n                       y   1 XMAS             (Y,N
PHONE            17  a n n                       n
OTHER INFO?      30  a y n                       n
*                 0
-------------     0
-------------     0
```

Figure 11.3 The database format

Start on the top line in the Field Name column, with SURNAME. If you press
RETURN, you will be moved right to the next field in the display. After the
Index name column, the display can scroll sideways to the left to reveal two more
headings. The first is the Prompt section, where details can be added that will
be shown whenever the database field cursor enters a particular field. In this
case prompts are included for two fields: Birthday (Month,Date) and
Christmas Card (Y/N?). Moving the cursor right once more you will see the
Value List column, which holds any checks you wish the database to make for
legal entries. The lists are:

    For BIRTHDAY:
    JAN*,FEB*,MAR*,JUN*,JUL*,AUG*,SEP*,OCT*,
    NOV*,DEC*
    and for CHRISTMAS CARD:
    Y,N

Each star in the BIRTHDAY section stands for 'any group of characters' (this being one of ViewStore's 'wild' characters) and any entry that does not comply with one of the stated values will be rejected by the software with a beep and the warning `'Value not in list'`. The user will be shown this value list, and will have to delete the incorrect entry and begin again.

It is possible to delete any incorrect rows in the Record Format display using **SHIFT** *f9* (Delete Record): each row corresponds to the record for a single field. You can also go back and edit the data in this display, either by complete re-entry, or by editing in the style of ViewSheet, using **CTRL** with the left and right arrow keys to move the small flashing cursor within the separate fields. The Insert Character (*f8*); Delete Character (*f9*); Delete End of Field (*f3*); Beginning of Field (*f4*) and End of Field (*f5*) function keys all help with the editing at this stage. The thing you cannot do with this system is insert extra fields if you find you have forgotten one – except at the end of the list!

Moving the Cursor

The ViewStore cursor works in much the same way as that in ViewSheet. Here the usual left, right, up and down arrow keys move the block or field cursor around the display one 'slot' at a time, while editing within a particular slot is done with **CTRL** left and **CTRL** right, and the function keys mentioned above. **CTRL** up and down take the field cursor to the very top and bottom of the file, while **SHIFT** left and right move the cursor to the previous or next record, and **SHIFT** up and down move it up or down by one screenful at a time. All these movements operate in the same way on both the Record Format and the database itself.

It is worth noting at this point that the maximum size of a single record in ViewStore about 60,000 characters, although in practice this is limited to what can be held in the computer's memory at any one time. For example, a Model B could accommodate around 9000 characters (9k) in Mode 3 and 25k in Mode 7, while the Master Series 128 would manage 28k in any mode. When you have finished entering the specifications in the Format file, you might like to see how the database is looking. To do this you press the Data function key (*f0*). The display should now look as shown in Figure 11.4.

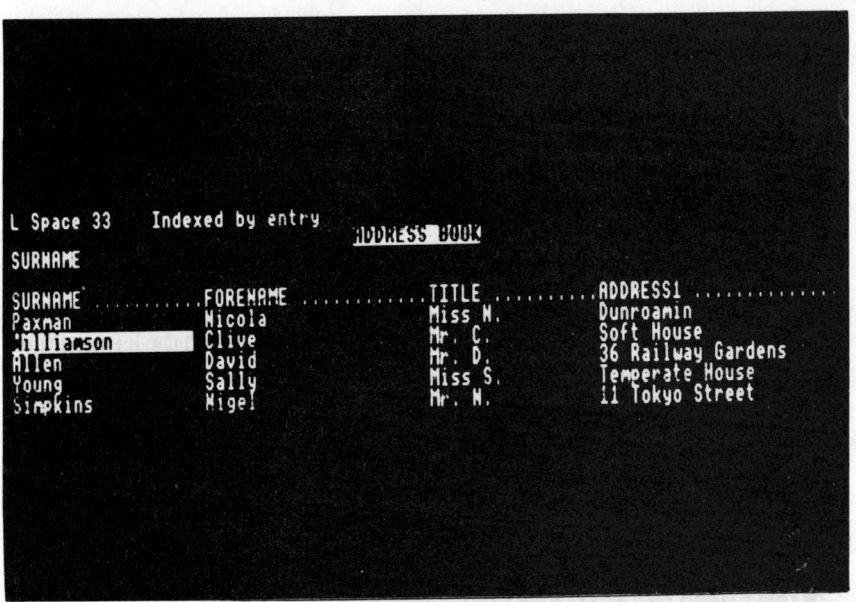

```
L Space 33    Indexed by entry    ADDRESS BOOK
SURNAME

SURNAME........FORENAME........TITLE........ADDRESS1........
Paxman          Nicola           Miss N.      Dunroamin
Williamson      Clive            Mr. C.       Soft House
Allen           David            Mr. D.       36 Railway Gardens
Young           Sally            Miss S.      Temperate House
Simpkins        Nigel            Mr. N.       11 Tokyo Street
```

Figure 11.4 The Spreadsheet version of the Address database

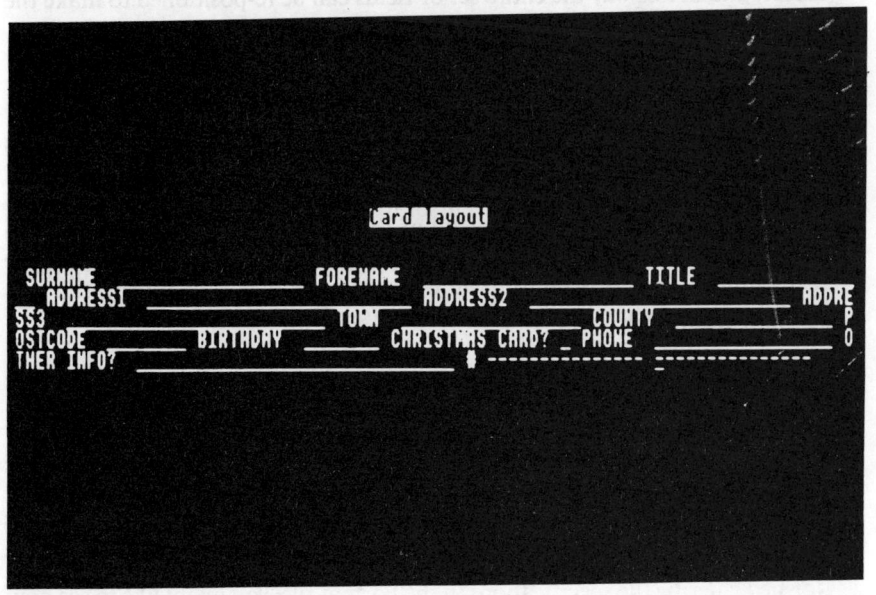

```
                          Card layout

SURNAME _____ FORENAME _____ TITLE _____
  ADDRESS1 _____ ADDRESS2 _____ ADDRE
SS3 _____ TOWN _____ COUNTY _____ P
OSTCODE _____ BIRTHDAY _____ CHRISTMAS CARD? _ PHONE _____ O
THER INFO? _____ # -------------- _____
```

Figure 11.5 The unedited card display

Do not enter anything as yet: as you can see, the layout is not really suited to displaying this sort of data. It would all be strung out sideways, involving lots of scrolling on the screen to see it in its entirety. The answer is to press the Change Display function key (*f2*) to alter the database to the card index display. When you do so, you will see a number of sets of field names appear all bunched together in a fairly illegible fashion (see Figure 11.5).

Fortunately ViewStore does allow you to edit this. The way to do so is to press the Card Layout function key (**SHIFT** *f0*), whereupon you are given the layout for a single record in an editable form. The extent of each field is shown by a solid line, and you can effectively 'pick the fields up' and put them where you like on the screen. To do this, place the cursor on any part of a field and press the **COPY** key.

You will see a star character appear at the head of the field you have marked. Now you can move the cursor to the place on the screen where you want the start of this field to be, then press **COPY** again. The field will be re-positioned at the cursor, and in this way the entire set of fields can be re-positioned to make the record card easier to read.

If you now press the Data key (*f0*) again you may see that the card display shows two records on screen at the same time. You may prefer only one to shown, in which case you should re-edit the Record Format, adding a new field name of a single hash (**#**) character at the end of the file, and setting its field width to zero. Go back to the Card Layout and use the cursor and COPY keys to move this 'dummy' field to a point more than half way down the screen; this will inhibit a second record from being shown (see Figure 11.6).

One final thing before you actually begin entering some data. You should now edit the Header Format to fix the screen mode of the display and details of the data storage. This is done by selecting the Database Header with **SHIFT** *f1*. Important features you can specify here are: the required screen mode (e.g. Mode 3 or 0 on a Model B; Mode 131 or 128 on a B+ or a Master Series); the type of display (C)ard or S)preadsheet); any title you wish to appear on the database; the number of extra bytes to be left spare after data has been entered in a record and so on. Full details of editing the Header Format are to be found in the ViewStore User Guide.

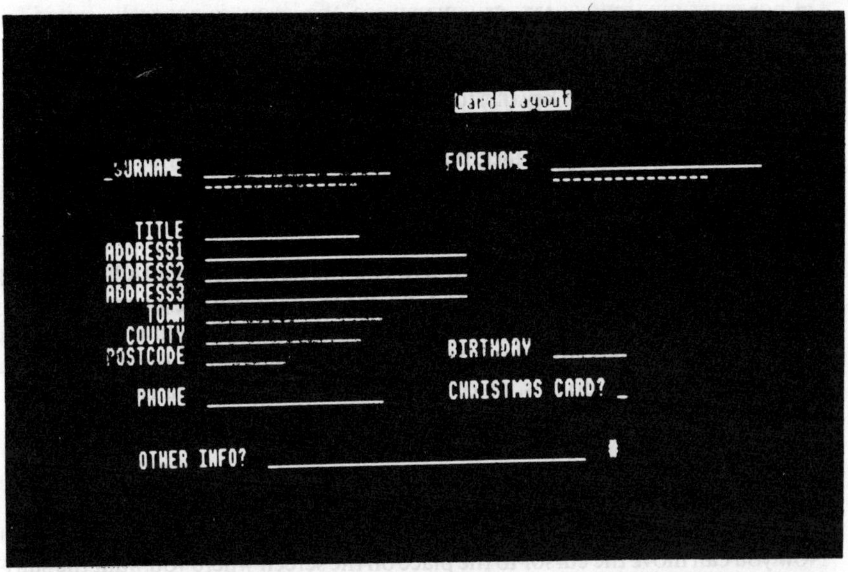

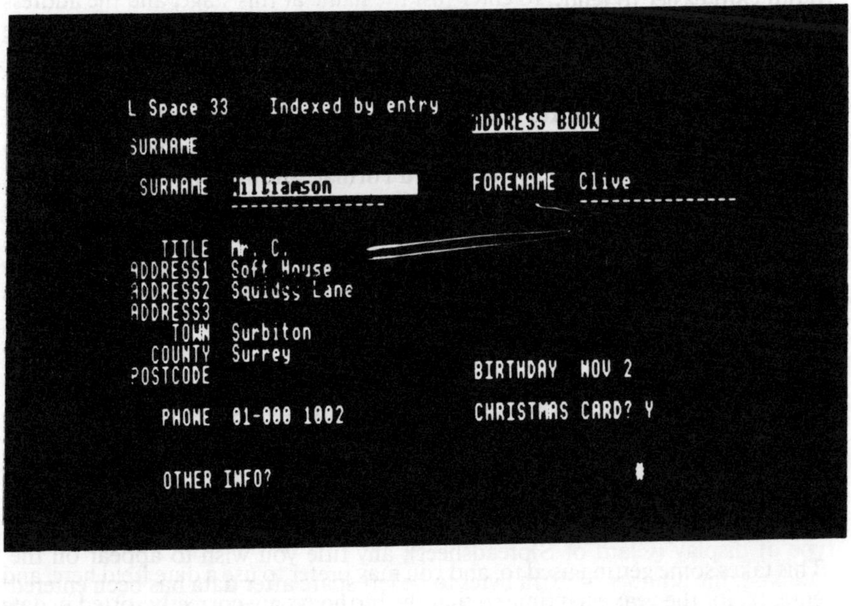

Figure 11.6 The finished card layout

Saving the Details So Far

While you have been doing all this work on the database, ViewStore has been operating the disc drive at intervals. This is because the software updates the disc files every time you press **ESCAPE**, and makes continuous access to the files as you move about the format files and the database itself. Thus the files are kept more or less up to date without the need to ever actually **SAVE** anything. This does mean one thing though, and that is you must *NEVER SWITCH THE MACHINE OFF WHILE YOU ARE WORKING ON A DATABASE.* Always return ViewStore to the Command screen by pressing the **ESCAPE** key (twice if necessary). (Pressing **BREAK** has the same effect.) This ensures that the data is definitely updated in full, and the files are all left in a safe condition.

Entering Data

After the long set-up procedure you are finally ready to start building up your database of names and addresses. Try to enter as much data as you can in one go for each new record, because once a record is entered (i.e. when you move on to the next one) there are only 30 characters spare as 'overflow'. Hence there may not be room, for example, to enter just the name at this stage, and the address some time later! When you have built up a few records at random, you may like to try indexing them in alphabetical order. Initially the records are only displayed in the order they were entered, but by activating one of the Indexes, you can change this so that the database is shown in the order of either the SURNAME, BIRTH or XMAS Index files. You will be given the option to choose which one if you press the Index Field (*f6*) function key. Having selected, say, SURNAME from this list, the disc operates and a `Reading` message appears on the screen. Almost immediately the Index is sorted and read in. Once the process is complete, you will will see the first sorted entry appear on the Card format, and you can then inspect the list in alphabetical order. This routine can be repeated for the other Indexes, although you should note that since these sorts are alphabetical, N for No will come before Y for Yes in the Christmas Card Index, and the months in Birthday will also be sorted into alphabetical order, i.e.:

```
APR, AUG, DEC, FEB, JAN, JUL, JUN, MAR, MAY, NOV,
OCT, SEPT.
```

This takes some getting used to, and you may prefer to use a date field here, and enter 00 for the year each time so that the birthdays are correctly sorted in date order. If you do this you will need to use a different prompt (e.g. `Date? DD.MM.00`) and value list (*.*.00)in the record format.

When you go on to add more records, you will find that they appear at the end of the file, and are not inserted in the correct place. In this case you can force a new sort by pressing the Index Field function key and re-entering the current Index field name.

Searching the Data

The quickest way of searching for a specific record is to press Locate (function key *f7*), whereupon ViewStore lets you enter a value to be searched for in the currently indexed field. Thus if you are indexed by Surname and need to know Santa Claus's telephone number you can enter Santa in reply to the prompt Value?, and the software will position the cursor on the 'Santa' record (assuming Santa Claus is in a SURNAME field in your database, of course). You can check the number, then use the cursor up and down keys to view the records either side of Santa Claus in the database if required. Thus you might find Rudolph by using the up cursor – although it is unlikely he would have a telephone!

If you need to find all the birthdays in June, you would change to the BIRTH Index, then use the Locate key and enter JUN. The cursor will be placed on the first record having a June birthday, and you can use the down arrow cursor to see if there are any more. Apparently strange things can happen here, because if there are no more June birthdays, you will find your cursor on the next nearest record alphabetically, which could be one with a JUL or a MAR entry. Unfortunately there is no '**No match found**' error message in ViewStore.

More Advanced Searches

The Locate routine is all right if you are happy to search under the Surname, Birthday and Christmas Card fields, but what about the rest? Suppose you need to find all your friends who live in Richmond town, or anyone in the county of Surrey, what then? You must resort to using the **SELECT** Utility, which can examine the whole database looking for values in any of the fields, and can also be given special criteria by which to search. Running this Utility allows you to generate a Select File of all the records it finds, and this can be used extensively by other ViewStore Utilities, such as the mailing **LABEL** routine.

A simple example of using **SELECT** would be to search for those of your friends who live in your home town. Suppose you are giving a party, and need to print mailing labels to send them all invitations. First, make sure the necessary database is actually in memory. Then, before you run the Utility, get ViewStore to give a list of all the fields in the database, just in case you need to refer to them. To obtain this, simply enter:

    LIST <RETURN>

and you will see the following information appear:
1	SURNAME	2	FORENAME	3	TITLE	4	ADDRESS1
5	ADDRESS2	6	ADDRESS3	7	TOWN	8	COUNTY
9	POSTCODE	10	BIRTHDAY	11	CHRISTMAS CARD?	12	PHONE
13	OTHER INFO?	14	#				

Now you are ready to enter:

    UTILITY SELECT <RETURN> or U SELECT <RETURN>

If you are using one drive and keeping the Utilities on a separate disc, you should first change discs, or else you will get an error message:

    U.SELECT not found
    Insert utility disc & hit a key

(Note that if you mistype the name of a Utility, you will also be given this error message, so press **ESCAPE** and re-enter the Utility name correctly.) Once **SELECT** is running, however, you are asked to specify whether you want the results to be saved in a Select F)ile on disc, or simply L)isted. If you choose L), then the options are whether the list should appear on the screen, or be sent to a printer. The best thing at this stage is probably to check that the results are correct by viewing them on screen.

Next you are asked for the criteria to be used in the selection. You can select according to the same set of conditional operators found in ViewSheet, i.e.

    =   equal to
    <>   not equal to
    >   greater than
    <   less than
    >=   greater than or equal to
    <=   less than or equal to

When using these operators you have to specify three things: the name of the field; the operator to be used; and the valued required in the search. You are not restricted to specifying things in full: you can use special wild characters to match either a single character (the question mark ?) or any group of characters (the star *). Hence if you want to look for people living in Richmond, you would enter:

    TOWN=RICHMOND

at the Select Criteria prompt. When you press RETURN, you will see
'Select Criteria' come up again, giving you the chance to enter more
criteria. Pressing **RETURN** again at this stage indicates that there are no more,
and ViewStore will begin selecting, and printing all the selected records on the
screen as it finds them. The results are in the form as shown in Figure 11.7.

```
ViewStore
Bytes free 26976
Editing D.ADDRESS
Format F.address
Screen mode 0

=)list
1    SURNAME        2   FORENAME        3   TITLE              4   ADDRESS1
5    ADDRESS2       6   ADDRESS3        7   TOWN               8   COUNTY
9    POSTCODE      10   BIRTHDAY       11   CHRISTMAS CARD?   12   PHONE
13   OTHER INFO?   14    *             15   ---------------   16   ---------------

=)U SELECT
SELECT
List or create select file (L,F)? L
Screen or Printer (S,P)? S
Select criteria? TOWN=RICHMOND
Select criteria?

Allen           David                  D.
Murrish         Olivia and Kevin       Mr. & Mrs. K.
Rooke           Steve                  Mr. S.J.
Williamson      Ralph                  Ralph

4 records selected out of 57
=)_
```

Figure 11.7 The results of a selection

If there are a large number of records, they will begin scrolling off the top of the
screen display unless you depress the **CTRL** and **SHIFT** keys simultaneously.
This provides a pause for you to read the screen. Notice that the Select Utility
only displays the first few fields of each record – as many as will fit across
the chosen screen mode. If you need to see any more than this you must use
ViewStore's Report Utility. Finally a message is produced on the screen to say
how many records were found that matched the criteria.

On a BBC Model B you may well get a '`Memory Full`' error message while
running the **SELECT** Utility if you are in Mode 0 or 3, in which case you should
change to Mode 6 or 7 to give the micro more memory space, then repeat the
process as before.

In addition to being displayed on the screen or printer, the results of these selections can be made into files suitable for use in the VIEW word processor, and details of how to do this are included in Chapter Fourteen.

Making Complex Selections

The **SELECT** Utility can be made much more advanced in its action by using more than one Select Criterion using the words AND and OR. Say you were compiling your own version of the telephone directory, and needed to find all those people living in Surrey or Middlesex whose surnames begin with E to K. At the Select Criteria stage you would enter:

```
Select Criteria?   COUNTY=SURREY
Select Criteria?   OR
Select Criteria?   COUNTY=MIDD*
```

(This 'wild selection' caters for both Middlesex and Middx!) Then:

```
Select Criteria?   SURNAME<=K
Select Criteria?   AND
Select Criteria?   SURNAME>=E
Select Criteria?   <RETURN>
```

After the last criteria enter RETURN only and the Utility will move to select the necessary records as before.

Making a Select File

If you answer F for F)ile to the initial **SELECT** Utility question, the routine is slightly different. Rather than showing any results on the screen, ViewStore will create a disc file holding all the selected records, and these can be sorted into alphabetical or numerical order if required. The resulting selection of your records can then be used when you are preparing reports using the **REPORT** Utility, or using any of the other ViewStore Utilities that act on the stored data. In this case, the **SELECT** Utility goes beyond the selection routine to ask which field or fields you wish the records to be sorted by, and whether the sort should be carried out in ascending or descending order.

After answering the Select Criteria questions, you may wish to sort the records first into those who should receive Christmas Cards, then those who shouldn't, and place each of these sections into alphabetical order. To do this you would enter:

```
Sort field?        CHRISTMAS CARD?
Sort field?        SURNAME
Sort field?        <RETURN>
```

ViewStore then asks whether the sorting should be in ascending or descending order. If you answer A, then the utility sorts all the nos before the yesses in the CHRISTMAS CARD? field, then sorts each section into alphabetical order by SURNAME. Rather than showing the results on screen, ViewStore simply stops work when the sort is done, and gives you back the cursor. The selected and sorted file is present on the disc (with the same name as the database, but in the S directory), and it can be used by the other utilities at any time if you answer Y)es to the prompt 'Use select file (N,Y)? Note that if you make any changes to the database they will not be included in the Select file unless you run the **SELECT** Utility again.

Obtaining Reports

Whether or not you have prepared a Select File when running the **SELECT** Utility, you can produce a simple report on screen of the first 80 characters of each record, or if you choose the printer option, you can specify the width of the paper, page length, and whether or not single sheets are required. The simple report will give the all the records or a selection, depending on whether a Select File is used. If you follow the **REPORT** Utility routine through without using a Report Format File (answer N)o to the prompt 'Use report format file (N,Y)?') you will see that this 'simple' report is not particularly suited to the chosen layout of your data in the name and address file. The key factor here is that the records are shown in the spreadsheet format, and are thus limited to the width of the screen (usually a maximum of 80 characters), or the specified paper width if you choose the printer option, so once again you are not going to see all the data from the database. There are some sorts of database for which this type of report is perfect (such as accounting applications) where you might use a spreadsheet style display for the database and limit the width to 80 characters anyway, in which case this form of reporting is perfectly satisfactory. If not, read on...

Complex Reporting

If you wish to see the entire contents of each record when selecting and reporting from the ADDRESS file, you must first establish a Report Format file so that you can make use of it at the 'Use report format file' stage of running the **REPORT** Utility. In this way you can display as much of the information in each record as you want, with any required layout for the screened or printed results. This approach gives a far more useful output than the simple report when there are a large number of significant fields in the database, but some effort is required to set the necessary Format file up in the first place.

To create a Report Format file for the address database, you should first enter:

UTILITY SETUP <RETURN> or **U SETUP <RETURN>**

and answer R in response to the prompt '**Set up database or report (D,R)?**' You are then asked for a file name for the report, and if you now enter:

ADDRESS <RETURN>

ViewStore will automatically create this new file in the R Directory. You must then load the file into memory by typing:

LOAD R.ADDRESS F.REPORT <RETURN>

The REPORT part is the special Format file included on the ViewStore disc, and needed for the editing of these Report files. Press **ESCAPE** to see this Report file displayed, and you will see a new header, similar in style to that when setting up the original database.

The idea of the Report files is to create a custom screen display or printer output that will show as much of each record as is required. The display will eventually be divided up into pages, and each page can be given a Header, and can show as many complete records as can be fitted on the page. There is also the facility to perform some maths on numerical fields, such as adding up subtotals and totals where necessary, and this can be see in the Accounts example in Chapter Twelve. For the time being, to get a full output from the ADDRESS file you need to set up a series of entries as shown in Figure 11.8.

The first column in the Report Format shows whether the line is to be: printed once per page as part of a header (H); printed every time a record is printed (R); a subtotal (S); or a total (T) line. The T is included in the example to force a spare line at the bottom of each page. In addition, you can specify the bottom margin (M) and page length (P) as required, on lines that won't actually be printed. Unlike the case of editing a new database format, you cannot delete lines here, but you can amend them and add new lines at the end of the format list, so take care how you add data, and try to plan the format carefully before you start.

The @ characters in the definition mark the places where data from the database records is to be inserted, and their numbers match the maximum number of characters specified in the original format for the ADDRESS

```
: Space 251  Indexed by entry
                          Report format definition
Type (C=comment,H=header,M=margin,P=page length,R=record,S=subtotal,T=total)

T.  ..............................................................
H                    REPORT : ADDRESS DATABASE
H                    ------------------------
H
R   SURNAME: @@@@@@@@@@@@@@@@@@      FORENAME: @@@@@@@@@@@@@@@@@@
R            ------------------                ------------------
R
R    TITLE: @@@@@@@@@@@@@@@
R
R ADDRESS1: @@@@@@@@@@@@@@@@@@@@@@@@@@
R ADDRESS2: @@@@@@@@@@@@@@@@@@@@@@@@@@
R ADDRESS3: @@@@@@@@@@@@@@@@@@@@@@@@@@
R     TOWN: @@@@@@@@@@@@@@@@
R   COUNTY: @@@@@@@@@@@@@@@
R POSTCODE: @@@@@@@@                    BIRTHDAY: @@@@@@@
R
R
R    PHONE: @@@@@@@@@@@@@@@@
R
R
R OTHER INFORMATION: @@@@@@@@@@@@@@@@@@@@@@@@@@@@@@   #
R
R   -----------------------------------------------------------------
R
P 70
```

```
L Space 251  Indexed by entry
                          Report format definition
List of fields to be output


.................................................................


"SURNAME","FORENAME"


"TITLE"

"ADDRESS1"
"ADDRESS2"
"ADDRESS3"
"TOWN"
"COUNTY"
"POSTCODE","BIRTHDAY"


"PHONE"


"OTHER INFO?"
```

Figure 11.8 Report Format for the Address file, and Field List

database. If you kept a record of these on paper at the time, it will save you having to look them up now by loading the ADDRESS file. Normal text on the H and R lines will be printed as it stands, and notice that it is possible to mix text and record information on a single line. There is more to the Record format than is immediately visible: there are four columns in all. The first is the Type column, holding the single characters already mentioned. Moving the cursor to the right you will come across Half1, where all the text details are entered in this example. Next comes Half2, which is not used here, but can hold more text and record information if a) you are working in an 80 column screen mode and need to define a printed report of up to 160 characters, or b) you are working in a 40 column mode, in which case you need two screen widths to define the standard printer width of 80 characters. The final column in the Report file is called a Field List, and this is where you should enter the names of all the fields to be inserted in place of the @ characters. This section can also hold details of mathematical expressions, page and record numbers, total and subtotal registers. (For a full account of these features, see the ViewStore User Guide section on Reports.)

In the ADDRESS example, the field names are entered in the field list as shown in Figure 11.8. Notice that they are all contained within double quote marks. Entering them like this is a good habit to get into, because if there are any spaces in a Field name, it may not be properly recognised by the Report file when the time comes to look through the database to assemble the report. Once you have completed the Report file you should press **ESCAPE** (which will make the software save all the details on disc in the R.ADDRESS file) then you can reload the database and run the Utility REPORT option, this time using the Report Format file.

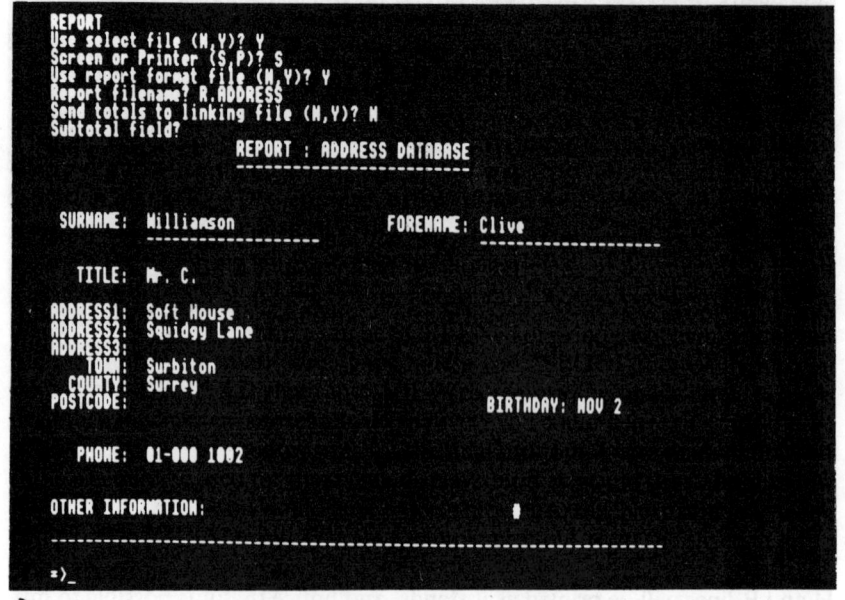

```
REPORT
Use select file (N,Y)? Y
Screen or Printer (S,P)? S
Use report format file (N,Y)? Y
Report filename? R.ADDRESS
Send totals to linking file (N,Y)? N
Subtotal field?
                    REPORT : ADDRESS DATABASE
                    ----------------------------


      SURNAME: Williamson              FORENAME: Clive
               ----------------                  ----------------------

        TITLE: Mr. C.

     ADDRESS1: Soft House
     ADDRESS2: Squidgy Lane
     ADDRESS3:
         TOWN: Surbiton
       COUNTY: Surrey
     POSTCODE:                          BIRTHDAY: NOV 2

        PHONE: 01-000 1002

  OTHER INFORMATION:                             #

  ---------------------------------------------------------------
  *)_
```

Figure 11.9 Answers to Utility REPORT, and the results on screen

One difference between this and an ordinary report is that you can obtain a subtotal from a number of specified fields at this stage if needs be, and also specify that any subtotals and totals calculated in the report be sent to a linking file, where they can be read by ViewSheet or ViewPlot. As this is not applicable to the ADDRESS file you should enter N or just press **RETURN** in response to the prompt.

The final result from the Report, whether you have chosen the screen or printer for the output, will be a series of records with full details in each case. Once again, you can halt the stream of records on screen by pressing both the **CTRL** and **SHIFT** keys down at once. Designing and using these Report formats does take some getting used to, and it is as well to get some practice in early on, to give you a better idea of just how useful they can make ViewStore.

Generating Mailing List Labels

Once you have a sizeable body of data in store, you will probably want to do something substantial with it! The most likely application for this database is to use it in the preparation of a set of sticky address labels, for example at Christmas, or for invitations. The **LABEL** Utility provided with ViewStore works very well, enabling professional-looking results to be obtained – as it strips out the unwanted spaces and blank lines in the database records from the final printout. Here is a typical set of responses when running this utility:

```
Use select file (N,Y)?              Y (Selected for Christmas cards?)

Screen or Printer (S,P)?            P
Label height (lines)?               8 (depends on label size)
Lines between each label?           4 (depends on label 'pitch' on sheet)

Width of label?                     30
Characters between each label?      0
Number of labels across the
page?                               0
Line 1?                             TITLE,SURNAME
Line 2?                             ADDRESS1
Line 3?                             ADDRESS2
Line 4?                             ADDRESS3
Line 5?                             TOWN
Line 6?                             COUNTY,POSTCODE
Line 7?                             <RETURN>
                                    (terminates the Line routine)

Alignment Print (N,Y)?              Y
```

The questions enable you to adjust the printout for any size of label, and number of labels across the page. Several different fields can be printed on one line by separating them with commas (as in Lines 1 and 6 in the example). Here the **LABEL** Utility prints the contents of each field one after another, with a single space between each. The resulting printout will look something like Figure 11.10.

```
Mr. C. Williamson
Soft House
Squidgy Lane
Surbiton
Surrey
```

Figure 11.10 A printed label produced by the LABEL Utility (printed on a daisywheel printer)

CHAPTER TWELVE

ViewStore Examples

Mailshot and Standard Letters Database

This database is closely based on the ADDRESS example, except that the address fields are not specified in the same way. Because there are no gaps in the fields it is possible to use the information both for mailing labels using the **LABEL** Utility, and in a standard letter designed using a Report file. The information in this form would also be suitable for producing standard letters on VIEW using its Macro facility, and the MACRO Utility. (Remember that ViewStore includes a Utility called **CONVERT** to enable you to take the contents of one database file and reconfigure them into another. The process of designing and redesigning your databases can be considerably eased by using this facility.)

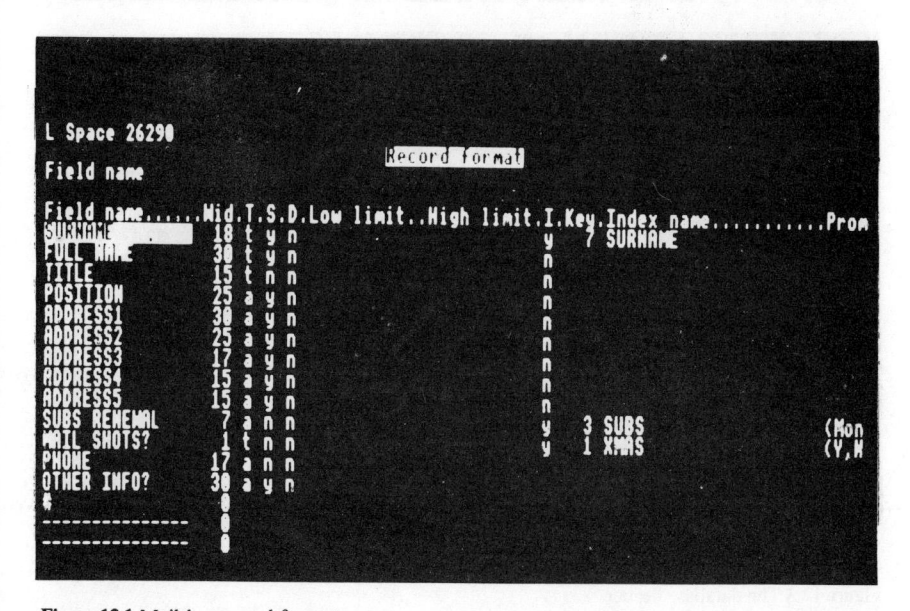

Figure 12.1 Mailshot record format

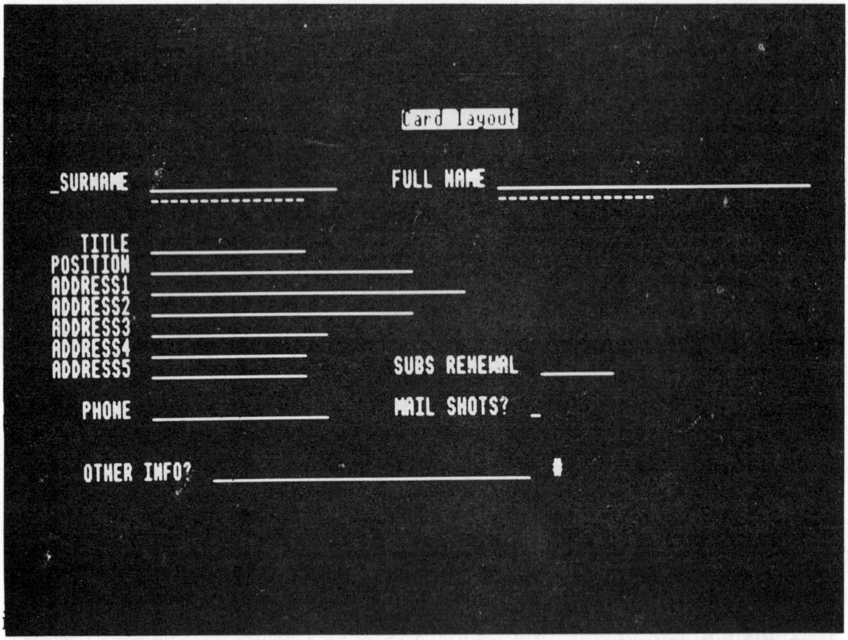

Figure 12.2 Card layout

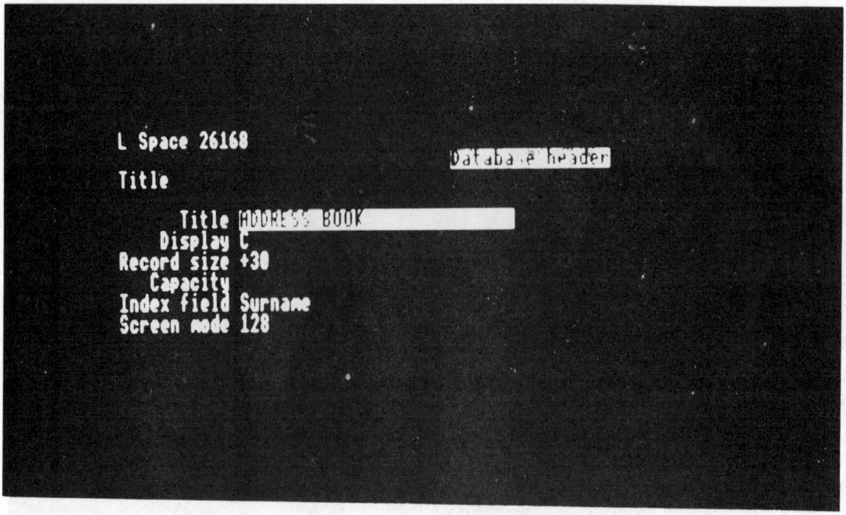

Figure 12.3 The database header

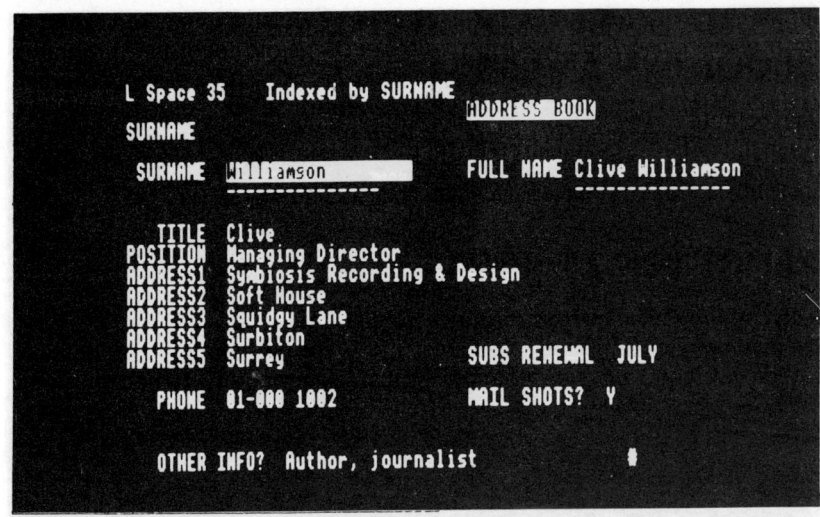

```
L Space 35    Indexed by SURNAME
                              ADDRESS BOOK
SURNAME
SURNAME   Williamson              FULL NAME  Clive Williamson
          ---------               ---------------

    TITLE    Clive
    POSITION Managing Director
    ADDRESS1 Symbiosis Recording & Design
    ADDRESS2 Soft House
    ADDRESS3 Squidgy Lane
    ADDRESS4 Surbiton
    ADDRESS5 Surrey             SUBS RENEWAL  JULY

    PHONE    01-000 1002        MAIL SHOTS?  Y

    OTHER INFO?  Author, journalist            #
```

Figure 12.4 A typical printout from the database

Business Software Monthly

Clive Williamson
Symbiosis Recording & Design
Soft House
Squidgy Lane
Surbiton
Surrey

23.7.86

Dear Clive

Many thanks for your recent enquiry about Business Software Monthly. The rate for subscriptions until the end of July is £12.00. If you wish to take advantage of this, please send a cheque or postal order as soon as possible.

Yours sincerely,

E. Softley (Editor)

Figure 12.5 Printout obtained from the Mailshot Report

```
L Space 213   Indexed by entry
                        Report format definition
List of fields to be output
Field List...............................................................




"FULL NAME"
ADDRESS1
ADDRESS2
ADDRESS3
ADDRESS4
ADDRESS5
^C1


TITLE

^C2
```

Figure 12.6 The Report Format definition

```
L Space 26    Indexed by DATE
                        ACCOUNTS - 1985/86
Description of item:

DATE......ITEM............................TAXCODE.OUTGOING.TYPE.INCOMING.7
28.03.86  Repairs to Frame                                  I      50.00
28.03.86  Supply Coins (I Ching)                            I      75.00
28.03.86  Sale of Towel                                     I      10.00
28.03.86  Sale of Tea Chests                                I      65.00
28.03.86  Computer                            500.00 C
28.03.86  Disc Drives                         400.00 C
28.03.86  TV Monitor                          300.00 C
28.03.86  Discs                                65.00 E
29.03.86  Flash Gun                           200.00 C
29.03.86  Journalism Course Fees              200.00 E
29.03.86  Coffee Maker                         30.00 E
29.03.86  Repairs to Trolley                   15.00 E
29.03.86  Microwave Oven                      200.00 C
30.03.86  Stationary                           30.00 E
01.04.86  Photograph of Stately Home                        I     300.00
01.04.86  Boxed Butterfly Set                               I      45.00
01.04.86  Mugs x 30                            45.00 E
```

Figure 12.7 A typical record from the database.

```
L Space 215   Indexed by entry
                       Report format definition
Type (C=comment,H=header,M=margin,P=page length,R=record,S=subtotal,T=total)
: Halfl.........................................\........................
P 70
M 3
C Today's Date?
C Subscription Rate?
H                       Business Software Monthly
H
R @@@@@@@@@@@@@@@@@@@@@@@@@@@@@@@@@@@@@@@@@
R @@@@@@@@@@@@@@@@@@@@@@@@@@@@@@@@@@@@
R @@@@@@@@@@@@@@@@@@@@@@@@@@@@@@@@@
R @@@@@@@@@@@@@@@@@@@@@@@@@@@
R @@@@@@@@@@@@@@@@@@@@@@@@@@
R @@@@@@@@@@@@@@@@@@@@@@@
R                                               @@@@@@@@
R
R Dear @@@@@@@@@ @@@@@@@@@@@@@@@@@@@@@@
R
R Many thanks for your recent enquiry about Business Software Monthly. The rate
R for subscriptions until the end of July is @@@@@@. If you wish to take
R advantage of this, please send a cheque or postal order as soon as possible.
R
R Yours sincerely,
R
R
R
R E. Softley  (Editor)
```

(continued)

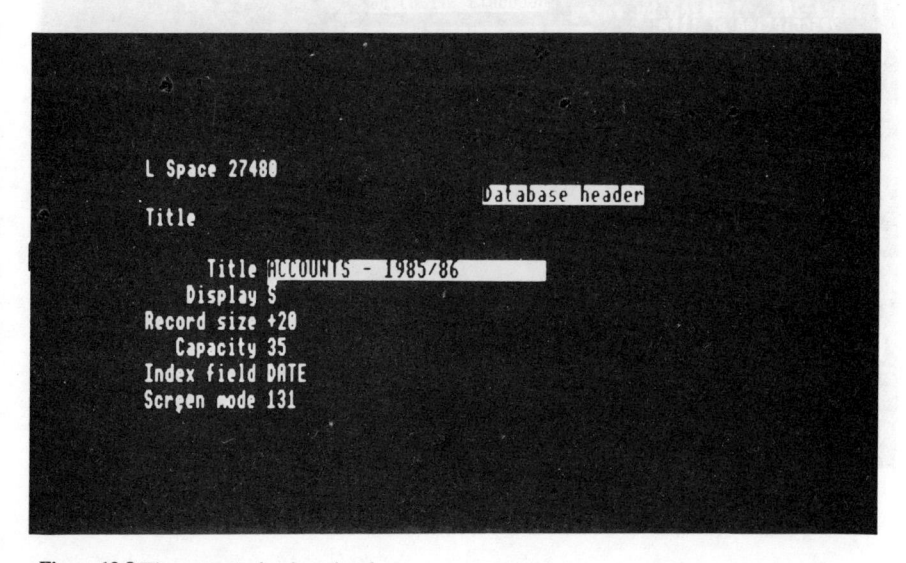

```
L Space 27480
                                     Database header
    Title

        Title ACCOUNTS - 1985/86
      Display S
  Record size +20
     Capacity 35
  Index field DATE
   Screen mode 131
```

Figure 12.8 The acounts database header

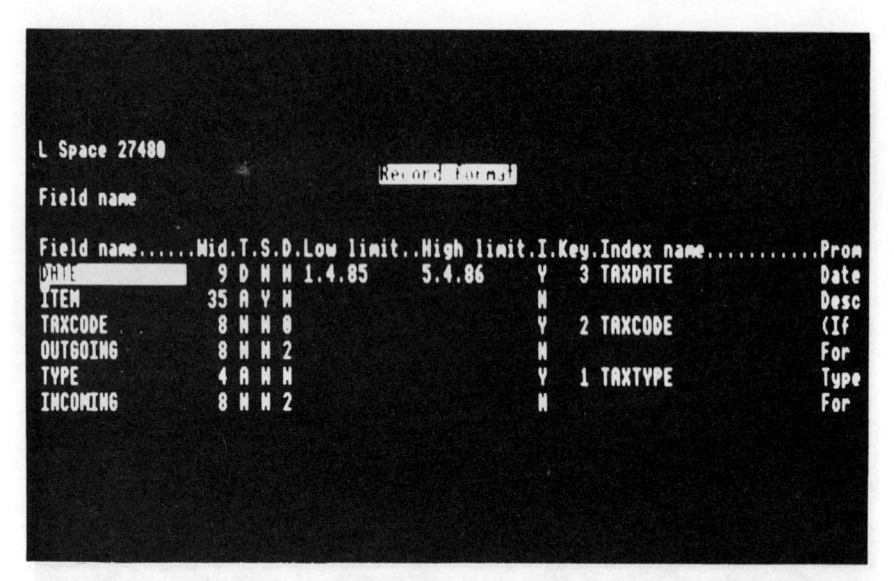

```
L Space 27480
                            Record format
Field name

Field name......Wid.T.S.D.Low limit..High limit.I.Key.Index name..........Prom
DATE             9 D M M 1.4.85    5.4.86   Y  3 TAXDATE           Date
ITEM            35 A Y M                    N                      Desc
TAXCODE          8 M M 0                    Y  2 TAXCODE           (If
OUTGOING         8 M M 2                    N                      For
TYPE             4 A M M                    Y  1 TAXTYPE           Type
INCOMING         8 M M 2                    N                      For
```

Figure 12.9 The record format

```
L Space 209   Indexed by entry
                         Report format definition
List of fields to be output

Field List....................................................
^C1


"DATE","ITEM","TAXCODE","OUTGOING","INCOMING",O:OUTGOING,I:INCOMING

!SO,!SI
```

Figure 12.10 The accounts Report Format

```
L Space 27480
                        Record format
Prompt

Prompt..........................................................
Date (D.M.Y)?  (April 85-March 86)
Description of item:
(If any)
For Expenses only
Type of entry  (Capital Expense, Expense, Income
For Income only
```

Figure 12.9 (continued)

```
L Space 279    Indexed by entry
                      Report format definition
Type (C=comment,H=header,M=margin,P=page length,R=record,S=subtotal,T=total)

T.Half1..........................................................
H  eeeeeeeeeeee
M
M Date       Item                          Code    Outgoings    Incomin
M
R eeeeeeee   eeeeeeeeeeeeeeeeeeeeeeeeeeeeee  eb      ebbb.bb      ebbb.
S
S                                         Subtotals  eeeee.ee    eeeee.
S
T                                         Totals     eeeee.ee    eeeee.
C Today's Date?
```

Figure 12.10 (continued)

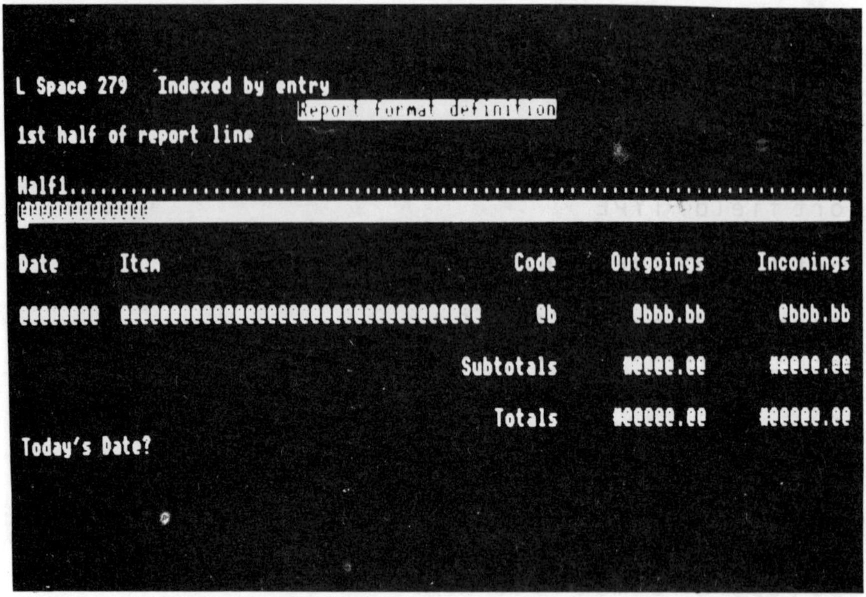

```
L Space 279   Indexed by entry
                          Report format definition
1st half of report line

Half1.........................................................
[gggggggggggg]

Date      Item                          Code    Outgoings   Incomings

eeeeeee   eeeeeeeeeeeeeeeeeeeeeeeeeeee   eb      ebbb.bb     ebbb.bb

                                Subtotals      #eeee.ee    #eeee.ee

                                Totals        #eeeee.ee   #eeeee.ee
Today's Date?
```

Figure 12.11 Half1 in full

Accounting

This database is of the spreadsheet style layout, and uses the advanced system of reporting to generate sets of accounts for Income, Expenses, and Capital Expenditure on one report. The function key definition used to obtain a copy of the accounts data is:

*KEY Ø U SELECT | M F | M | M TYPE | M DATE | M | M A | M U REPORT | M Y | M S | M Y | M ACCOUNT | M | M TYPE | M | M

A printout from the accounts data is shown in Figure 12.12. By amending the function key slightly, it is possible to set up linking files of the results in the reports, to be read into a spreadsheet showing the current balance for the business. Details of this integrated approach are given in Chapter Fourteen. This database could easily be expanded to include a section for VAT returns, and could then be sorted quarterly to produce the necessary figures.

Pressing function key *f0* produces the following set of answers automatically:

```
=> UTILITY SELECT
SELECT
List or create select file (L,F)? F
Select criteria? <RETURN>
Sort field? TYPE
Sort field? DATE
Sort field? <RETURN>
Key width: 4
Ascend or Descend (A,D)? A
Selecting................
17 records selected out of 17
SORT
Sorting....
=> UTILITY REPORT
REPORT
Use select file (N,Y)? Y
Screen or Printer (S,P)? S
Use report format file (N,Y)? Y
Report filename? ACCOUNT
Send totals to linking file (N,Y)?
Subtotal field? TYPE
Subtotal field? <RETURN>
Today's Date?05.08.86
```

Date	Item	Code	Outgoings	Incomings
28.03.86	Disc Drives		400.00	
28.03.86	TV Monitor		300.00	
28.03.86	Computer		500.00	
29.03.86	Microwave Oven		200.00	
29.03.86	Flash Gun		200.00	
		Subtotals	£1600.00	£ 0.00
28.03.86	Discs		65.00	
29.03.86	Repairs to Trolley		15.00	
29.03.86	Journalism Course Fees		200.00	
29.03.86	Coffee Maker		30.00	
30.03.86	Stationary		30.00	
01.04.86	Mugs x 30		45.00	
		Subtotals	£ 385.00	£ 0.00
28.03.86	Repairs to Frame			50.00
28.03.86	Sale of Towel			10.00
28.03.86	Sale of Tea Chests			65.00
28.03.86	Supply Coins (I Ching)			75.00
01.04.86	Boxed Butterfly Set			45.00
01.04.86	Photograph of Stately Home			300.00
		Subtotals	£ 0.00	£ 545.00
		Totals	£ 1985.00	£ 545.00

Figure 12.12 A typical printout from the database

Office Administration

A more advanced use of the ADDRESS format, this application includes details of each employee's bank account number, salary, National Insurance number, Tax Code and Next of Kin. More careful use has been made of the Card format, with dummy fields inserted to provide some underlines for the principal data. Two Report files have been built to act on the data in store: the first produces a list of cheques to be made out for monthly salaries; the second generates a report of all the pay slips, which can then be distributed to the employees. The system could be expanded to include details of annual leave.

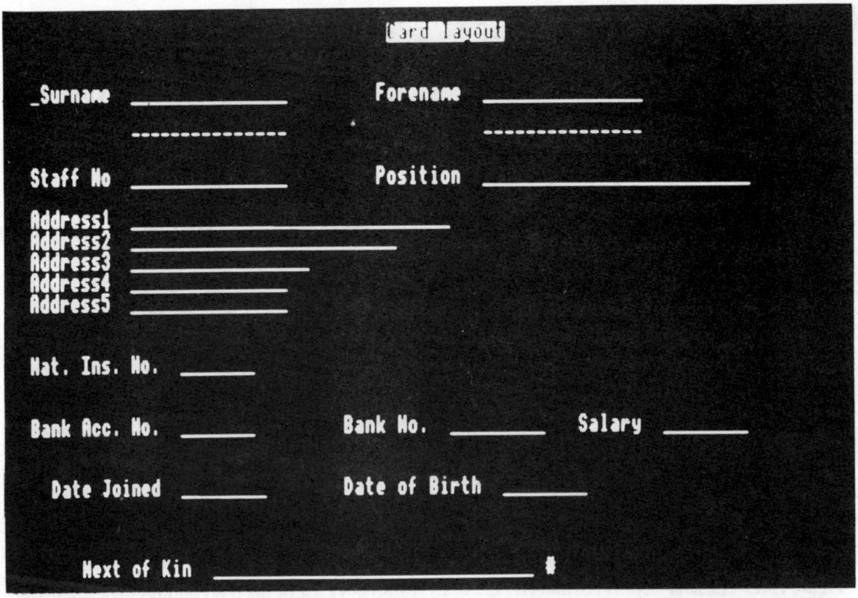

Figure 12.13 Card layout for the office database

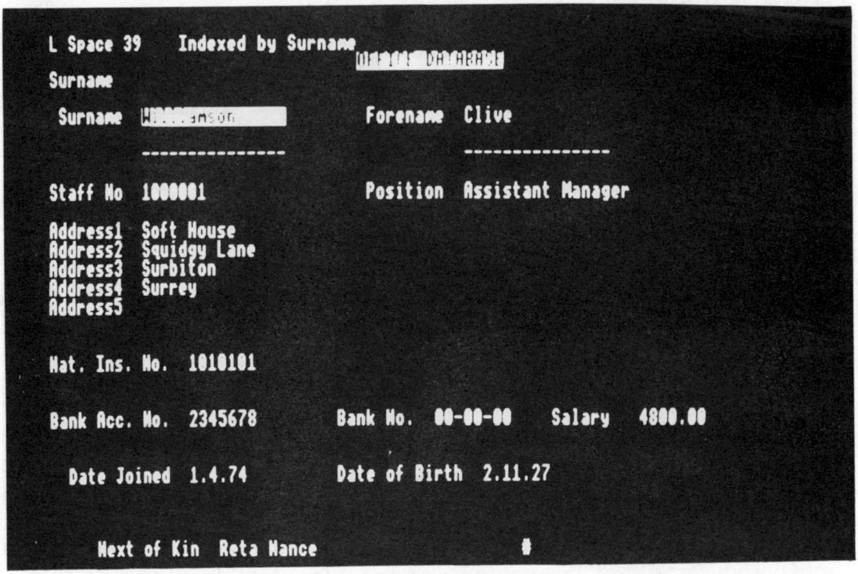

Figure 12.14 Data held in the office database

```
L Space 295   Indexed by entry
                              Report format definition
Type (C=comment,H=header,M=margin,P=page length,R=record,S=subtotal,T=total)
T.Half1..........................................................................
W 70
M 3
C Today's Date?
R
R Vandenberg Antiques Inc.          PAYMENT NOTIFICATION                  @@@@@@
R -----------------------                                                 ------
R
R Name: @@@@@@@@@@@@@@@@    @@@@@@@@@@@@@@@@
R
R Staff Number: @@@@@@@    National Insurance Number: @@@@@@@
R
R Salary: #@@@@@.@@        Bank Account Number: @@@@@@@@    Bank Number: @@@@@@
R                                                               Payment: #@@@.
S
S
S
S ---------------------------------------------------------------------------
```

Figure 12.15 The first Report Format (R.OFFICE1) produces a list of the pay cheques to be made out

```
L Space 213   Indexed by entry
List of fields to be output
Field List.........................................................................




"ON LOAN TO?"
DEPARTMENT
"ROOM NO."



TITLE
AUTHOR

^C2
```

Figure 12.16 Half 1 in full

```
L Space 213    Indexed by entry
List of fields to be output
Field List.........................................




"ON LOAN TO?"
DEPARTMENT
"ROOM NO."




TITLE
AUTHOR

^C2
```

Figure 12.15 (continued)

```
=)*KEY O L OFFICE:M U REPORT:M N:M P:M Y:MOFFICE  :M N:MSURNAME:M :M N:M
=)L OFFICE
=) U REPORT
REPORT
Use select file (N,Y)?  N
Screen or Printer (S,P)?  P
Use report format file (N,Y)?  Y
Report filename? OFFICE
Send totals to linking file (N,Y)?  N
Subtotal field? SURNAME
Subtotal field?
Single sheets (N,Y)?  N
Today's Date? 05.08.86

Vandenberg Antiques Inc.      ****  CHEQUES TO BE PAID  ****        05.08.86
-----------------------                                             --------

NAME                                     A/C. NO.   BANK NO.
----------------------------------------------------------------------------

Williamson          Clive                2345678    00-00-00    Payment: $400.00
Young               Sally                2020202    00-00-00    Payment: $450.00
Simpkins            Nigel                1231231    00-00-00    Payment: $500.00
                                                             Total Payments: $1350.00
                                                                             ========


----------------------------------------------------------------------------
=)_
```

Figure 12.17 Entering the key definition, then running the Report utility

The function key definition to produce the results automatically from R.OFFICE1 is:

```
*KEY 0 L OFFICE|M U REPORT|M N|M P|M Y|MOFFICE1 |M N|MSURNAME|M |M N|M
```

```
Vandenberg Antiques Inc.          ****  CHEQUES TO BE PAID  ****      05.08.86
------------------------          -------------------------------     --------

NAME                                    A/C. NO.   BANK NO.
------------------------------------------------------------------------------

Williamson         Clive                2345678    00-00-00    Payment: £400.00
Young              Sally                2020202    00-00-00    Payment: £450.00
Simpkins           Nigel                1231231    00-00-00    Payment: £500.00

                                                         Total Payments: £1350.00
                                                                        ========
------------------------------------------------------------------------------
```

Figure 12.18 Printed results from the first report

```
L Space 295   Indexed by entry
                      Report format definition
Type (C=comment,H=header,M=margin,P=page length,R=record,S=subtotal,T=total)
T.Halfl.................................................................
M 70
M 3
C Today's Date?
R Vandenberg Antiques Inc.            PAYMENT NOTIFICATION            eeeeee
R ---------------------
R Name: eeeeeeeeeeeeeeee   eeeeeeeeeeeeee
R Staff Number: eeeeee     National Insurance Number: eeeeeee
R Salary: eeeee.ee         Bank Account Number: eeeeeee    Bank Number: eeeeee
S                                                             Payment: eeee.
S
S
S ---------------------------------------------------------------------
S
```

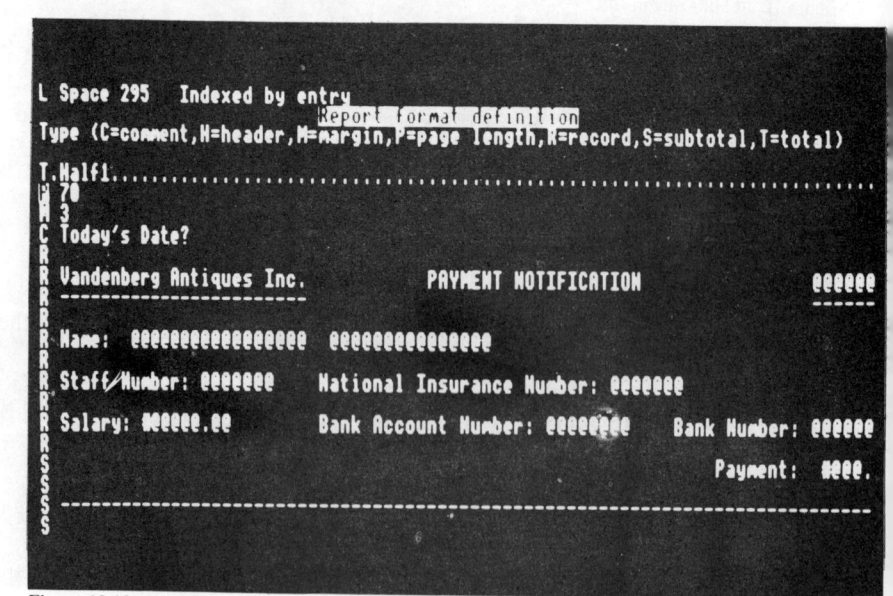

Figure 12.19 The Report format for the second report (R.OFFICE2) which produces the payment slips for each employee.

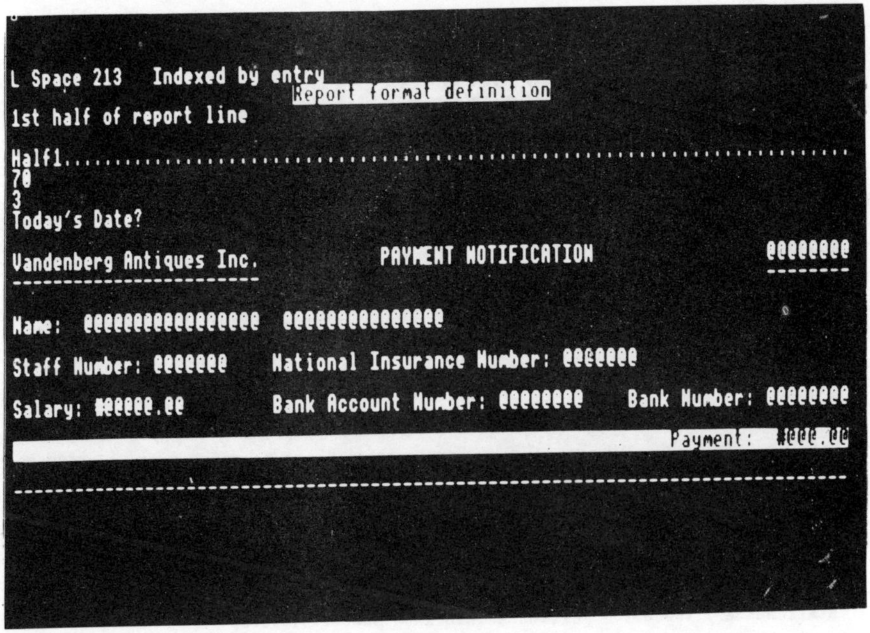

```
L Space 213    Indexed by entry
                             Report format definition
1st half of report line

Half1.............................................
70
3
Today's Date?

Vandenberg Antiques Inc.         PAYMENT NOTIFICATION              eeeeeeee
---------------------                                              --------
Name: eeeeeeeeeeeeeeeee  eeeeeeeeeeeeeee
Staff Number: eeeeeee    National Insurance Number: eeeeeee
Salary: #eeeee.ee        Bank Account Number: eeeeeeee   Bank Number: eeeeeeee
                                                          Payment: #eee.ee
```

Figure 12.20 Half one in full

The function key definition needed to produce a set of payslips using the R.OFFICE2 report format file is:

*KEY 0 L OFFICE|M U REPORT|M N|M P|M Y|M OFFICE2 |M N|M SURNAME|M |M N|M

When ƒ0 is pressed, the following sequence happens automatically:

```
U REPORT
REPORT
Use select file (N,Y)? N
Screen or Printer (S,P)? P
Use report format file (N,Y)? Y
Report filename? OFFICE2
Send totals to linking file (N,Y)? N
Subtotal field? SURNAME
Subtotal field? <RETURN>
Single sheets (N,Y)? N
Today's Date? 05.08.86
```

The resulting printout is shown in Figure 12.21.

```
Vandenberg Antiques Inc.              PAYMENT NOTIFICATION                          05.08.86
------------------------                                                            --------
Name:    Williamson           Clive
Staff Number: 1000001         National Insurance Number: 1010101
Salary: £ 4800.00             Bank Account Number:  2345678      Bank Number: 00-00-00
                                                                 Payment:     £400.00
-------------------------------------------------------------------------------------------


Vandenberg Antiques Inc.              PAYMENT NOTIFICATION                          05.08.86
------------------------                                                            --------
Name:    Young                Sally
Staff Number: 1000002         National Insurance Number: 3456789
Salary: £ 5400.00             Bank Account Number:  2020202      Bank Number: 00-00-00
                                                                 Payment:     £450.00
-------------------------------------------------------------------------------------------


Vandenberg Antiques Inc.              PAYMENT NOTIFICATION                          05.08.86
------------------------                                                            --------
Name:    Simpkins             Nigel
Staff Number: 1000003         National Insurance Number: 4567890
Salary: £ 6000.00             Bank Account Number:  1231231      Bank Number: 00-00-00
                                                                 Payment:     £500.00
-------------------------------------------------------------------------------------------
```

Figure 12.21 A set of pay slips produced by R. OFFICE2

Library (Stock and Issues)

The principle feature here is that there are two levels of record access, provided by setting up the database with the full details visible under a Format file called F.ADMIN, while limited access is through a second Format file called F.INFO. The first Format includes full details of the purchase of each book, who it is loaned to, the date due back, and so on, while the INFO format only gives details of the books themselves. The different formats are created using the SF (Save Format) command, each being edited to reveal different amounts of information, and then placed on different types of use. The different formats are loaded using the LF command, e.g :

`LF ADMIN`

will load the full access Format file into the database. Note that ViewStore does not contain any security features, and so would not be suitable for storing confidential information in this way.

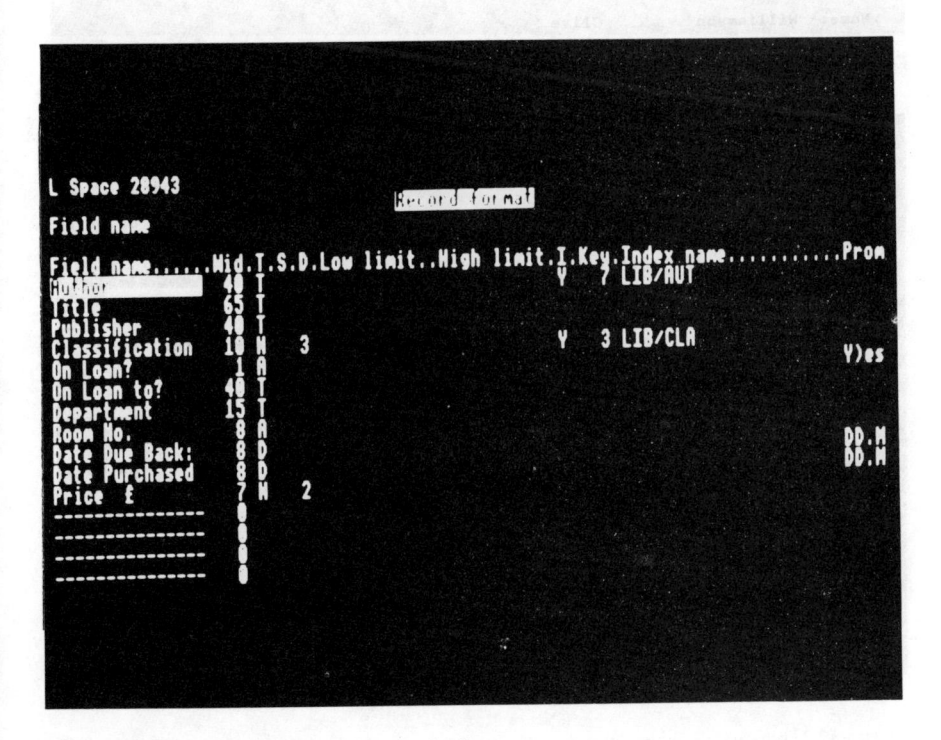

```
L Space 28943                  Record format
Field name
Field name......Wid.T.S.D.Low limit..High limit.I.Key.Index name..........Prom
Author           40 T                            Y   7 LIB/AUT
Title            65 T
Publisher        40 T
Classification   10 M  3                         Y   3 LIB/CLA                Y)es
On Loan?          1 A
On Loan to?      40 T
Department       15 T
Room No.          8 A
Date Due Back:    8 D                                                         DD.M
Date Purchased    8 D                                                         DD.M
Price £           7 N  2
--------------    0
--------------    0
--------------    0
```

Figure 12.22 Record format for the Library database

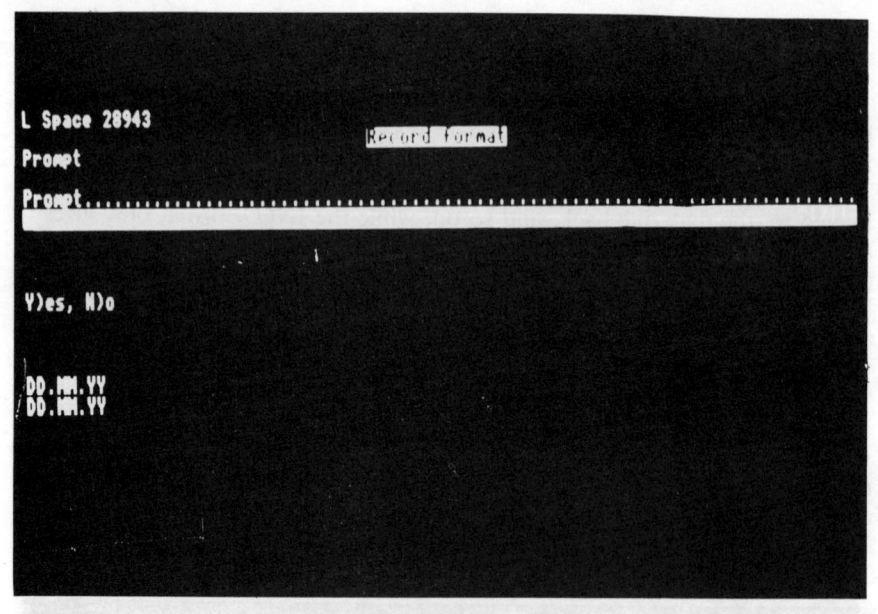

```
L Space 28943
Prompt                    Record format
Prompt........................................................




        '
Y)es, N)o


DD.MM.YY
DD.MM.YY
```

Figure 12.22 Record format for the Library database

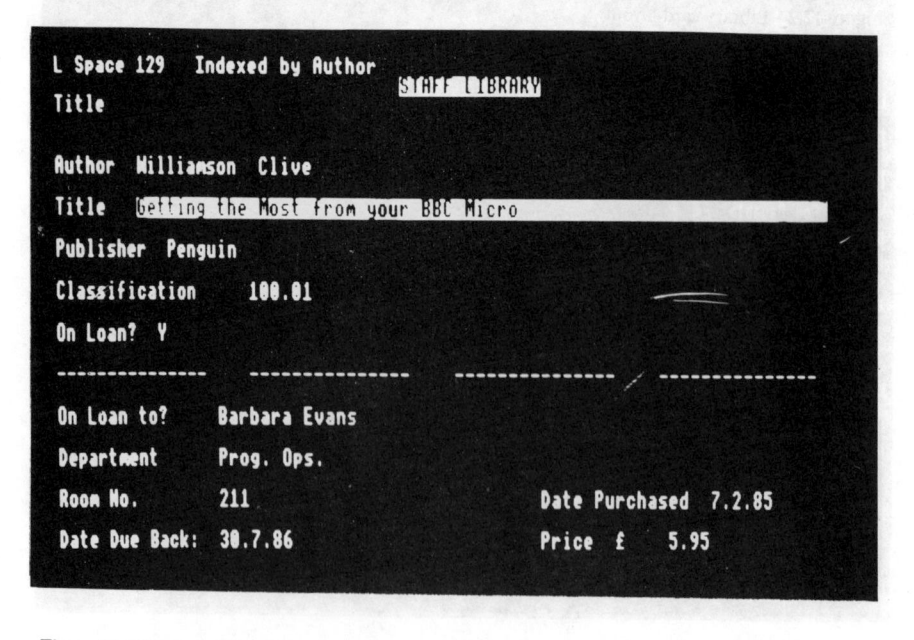

```
L Space 129    Indexed by Author
                                  STAFF LIBRARY
Title

Author   Williamson Clive
Title    Getting the Most from your BBC Micro
Publisher  Penguin
Classification    100.01
On Loan?  Y
-----------------    ---------------    ----------------  /  ----------------
On Loan to?     Barbara Evans
Department      Prog. Ops.
Room No.        211                       Date Purchased  7.2.85
Date Due Back:  30.7.86                   Price  £   5.95
```

Figure 12.23 Typical data in the database

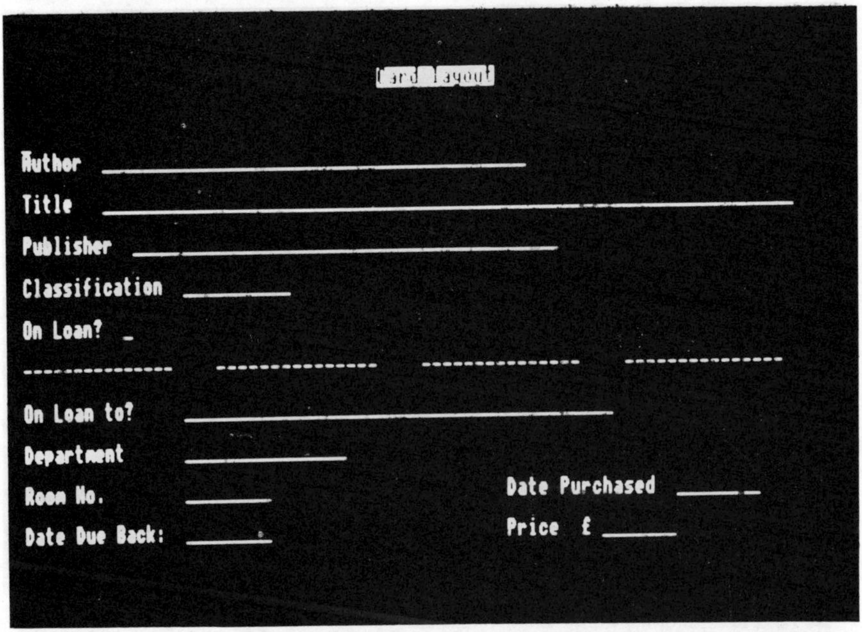

Figure 12.24 Library card layout

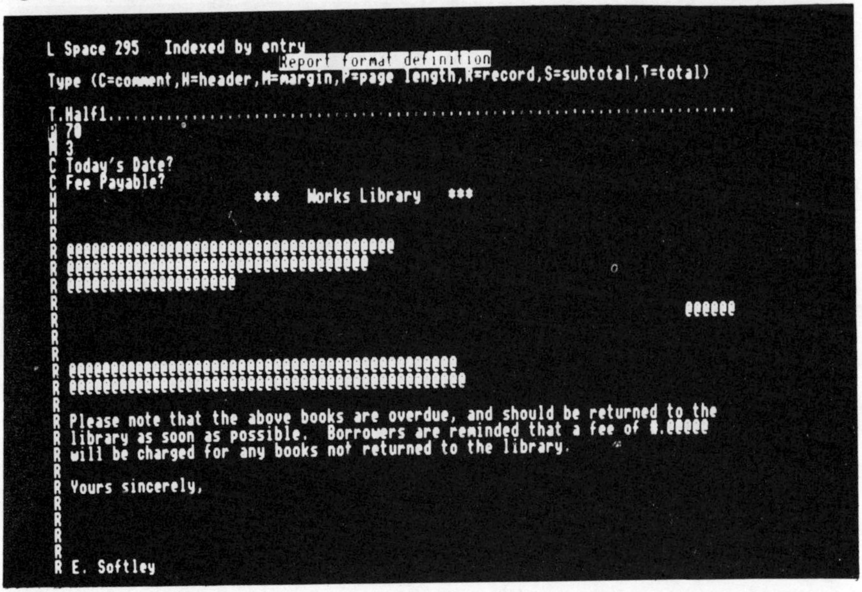

Figure 12.25 Report Format to obtain a reminder letter. A Select file should be made to find all the overdue books before using it

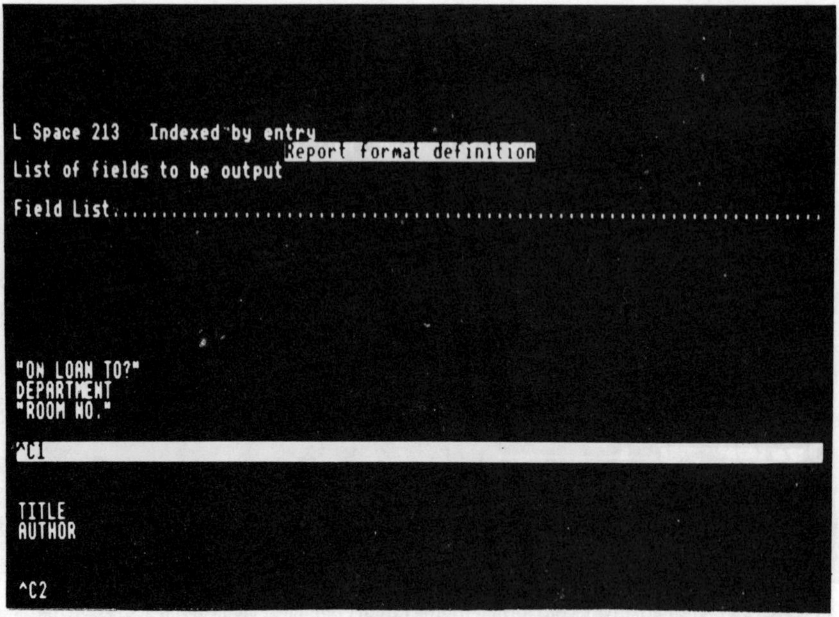

```
L Space 213   Indexed by entry
                         Report format definition
List of fields to be output
Field List:.................................................................




"ON LOAN TO?"
DEPARTMENT
"ROOM NO."

^C1


TITLE
AUTHOR

^C2
```

                        *** Works Library ***

Clive Williamson
Computers
402

                                                              4.9.86

Edgar Cayce's Story of the Origin and Destiny of Man
Robinson Lytle W.

Please note that the above book is overdue, and should be returned to the
library as soon as possible. Borrowers are reminded that a fee of £2.00
will be charged for any books not returned to the library.

Yours sincerely,

E. Softley (Librarian)

Figure 12.26 A reminder produced using the Report Format in Figure 12.25

```
L Space 29137
                          Record format
Field name

Field name......Wid.T.S.D.Low limit..High limit.I.Key.Index name..........Pron
Author            40 T                              Y    7 LIB/AUT
Title             65 T
Publisher         40 T
Classification    10 M  3                           Y    3 LIB/CLA
On Loan?           1 A
                   0 T
                   0 T
                   0 A
                   0 D
                   0 D
                   0 M  2
                   0
                   0
                   0
                   0
```

Figure 12.27 An alternative record format for the Library database, giving limited access to the data. Library staff can show details of the books, but not the people who have borrowed them. This format is produced by saving the full format under a new name, loading it back in using the LF command, then deleting the unwanted field names and reducing their field widths to zero.

```
                          Card layout


Author        _____

Title         _____


Publisher     _____

Classification  _____

On Loan?  _

■
```

Figure 12.28 A card layout for the reduced display

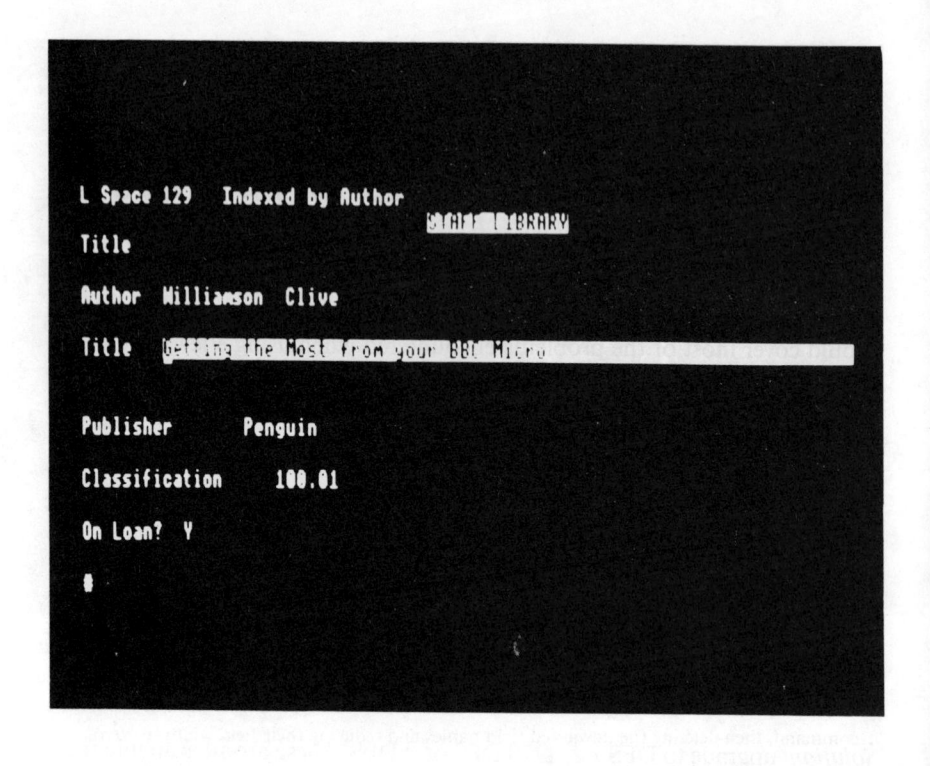

```
L Space 129    Indexed by Author
                              STAFF LIBRARY
Title

Author  Williamson  Clive

Title   Getting the Most from your BBC Micro


Publisher      Penguin

Classification    100.01

On Loan?  Y

■
```

Figure 12.29 Data as diplayed by the alternative record format. Note that the full data is still held on disc, and can be viewed by loading the original format once again.

CHAPTER THIRTEEN

ViewStore Hints and Tips

The following hints and tips are based on information supplied by Acorn, and should cover most of the problems encountered when using ViewStore which do not have ready answers supplied in the ViewStore manual.

DFS 0.90

Acorn cannot recommend the use of ViewStore with DFS 0.90.

When using multiple surfaces, the disc catalogue can be written to an incorrect surface. This is manifested by the 'Disc changed' error message on returning to the Command screen, followed by drive 0 apparently being overwritten with the files from drive 2. In addition, some problems can occur when building indexes.

Solution: upgrade to DFS 1.2, 1770 DFS or ADFS. These are all available from Vector Services, London Road, Wellingborough, Northants (0933 79300).

Running Out of Room using the Report Utility

Report Format files can grow very large, and this can cause memory problems when using them in Utility Report. Their size can be significantly reduced by running them through Utility Convert after editing them. In Convert reply as follows:

```
Use select file (N,Y)? N
Field 1? * <RETURN>
Field 2? <RETURN>
New record size (+20)? <RETURN>
New filename? r.newfilename
```

Rebuilding Indexes after using Convert

If you use the Convert Utility to build a new database from an existing one, be sure to rebuild all the indexes using the Index Utility.

Indexes on Entering Data

Remember to index by entry when entering new data. This gives faster response times and reduces the likelihood of index corruption if an unexpected error like a Disc fault occurs. In general, the more Indexes you have for your database, the slower the response time of the system, so try to use as few as possible.

Scrolling Fields

ViewStore can scroll text within its fields, so the data held in each record can be much greater than is visible on the screen at any one time.

Database Drive

Remember not to leave any files after the data file on the data drive. This reduces 'Can't extend' problems when using the DFS. The easiest, but most expensive way to do this is to use a fresh disc surface for each database. There are no such problems with the ADFS, and this is the better system to use with ViewStore.

Backing up Your Work

At the end of each ViewStore session be sure to make a backup copy of your files using ***COPY** or ***BACKUP**. This will help prevent the loss of vast quantities of your hard work in the event of a disc fault. It is best to mark the backup copy clearly, so that you always update the master copy first. Then if you forget to make a backup you will know which disc has the most recent data on it.

The Difference between Alphanumeric and Textual Field Types

When the Select Utility is run, the whole field has to match the select criteria in the alphanumeric type, while a textual field is checked word by word for the correct match. Hence it would be important to opt for a textual field if you needed the maximum versatility in retrieving data quickly.

F.Report

Remember to copy the special Format file F.Report from the Utilities disc onto your Format file disc before editing Report Format files.

Selecting on Blank Fields

When using Select you can match a blank field by giving the criterion:

    FIELD=""

Select Syntax

Remember to use brackets and delimiters in select criteria. For example:

    TITLE = Pride and prejudice OR AUTHOR = Jane
    Austin

is unlikely to have the desired effect. You should enter:

    (TITLE = "Pride and prejudice") OR (AUTHOR =
    "Jane Austin")

to be completely unambiguous.

Using Wildcard Characters

The single (?) and multiple (*) wildcard characters can be used to facilitate searching the database. For example:

    Select? *=Vandenberg

would find that name in any field, while:

    Select? ADDRESS?="Palmerston North"

would search through ADDRESS1, ADDRESS2, ADDRESS3 and so on.

Sort memory

Before running Utility Select to sort a file on the BBC Model B remember to enter Mode 6 or Mode 7 to give the greatest available memory for the sort, and the fastest sorting speed.

Printer Drivers

Printer Drivers created using the Acornsoft Printer Driver Generator use Highlight characters 1 and 2 in the VIEW word processor, with Highlight 2 reset to correspond to ASCII 130. In ViewStore there are nine Highlight characters corresponding to ASCII characters 128 to 136. 1 and 3 correspond to characters 128 and 130 and so these two characters should be used in the extended highlight sequences. For example, bold is represented by ^3,^3,^3, superscript by ^3,^3, subscript by ^3,^1, and so on. (These Highlights are available when preparing complex reports on ViewStore.) ViewStore's Highlight 2 corresponds to the default VIEW Highlight 2 (ASCII code 129) and should be used with normal Printer Drivers other than the Epson.

BASIC Utilities

The simple format of ViewStore database files enables the relatively easy manipulation of ViewStore data by programs written in BBC BASIC. For example, the following program appends one database file to another. Note that the field order within records of both databases should be the same for sensible results.

```
10 INPUT "File 1 ";file1$
20 INPUT "File 2 ";file2$
30 one=OPENUP(file1$)    :REM BASIC I
users should use OPENIN
40 two=OPENIN(file2$)
50 REPEAT UNTIL BGET#one=1
60 PTR#one=PTR#one-1
70 REPEAT
80 byte=BGET#two
90 BPUT#one,byte
100 UNTIL byte=1
110 CLOSE#one
120 CLOSE#two
```

Figure 13.1

Editing Report Format Files

Report Format files can be edited in the VIEW word processor. READ the Report Format file into VIEW and insert a ruler at the top of the file which has no right margin, and has tab stops set wide enough to align the fields in columns (e.g. after 3, 83 and 85 characters on the ruler). Now edit the file. Be careful to keep the fields separated by the correct number of tabs and make sure that the lines do not exceed 132 characters. Before saving the file delete the ruler at the top. Finally Import the file back as a database (the field separator being 9 and the record separator being 13).

Importing Corrupt Databases

If a database is corrupted for any reason, for example if you lose the end marker or get 'Bad file' you can generally recover all or almost all of your data by importing the database into another file. This is often much quicker than retyping, (although you will hopefully have a backup copy).

Final Report Editing

Reports can be edited by spooling the report to disc, READing into the VIEW word processor, editing and printing from VIEW (see Chapter Fourteen).

Case Sensitivity in Non-standard DFS

Some versions of DFS supplied by other manufacturers (incorrectly) do not allow a mixture of cases in directory names. It is necessary to ensure all filename specifications are in the correct case. In particular Utilities should be renamed from directory 'u' to 'U'.

File Sizes and Utilities

The ViewStore Utilities all assume maximum file sizes of 65536 when performing calculations on file sizes. You should not therefore give a value greater than 65535. This does not limit the size that either your database files or Index files may grow to.

Bytes to Reserve - Load Time Tradeoff

On loading a database, ViewStore quickly loads the Format file, opens up the Data file and reads it from the end of file backwards to the end of data marker. If there is a lot of space reserved at the end of the file this may take a little time. Consequently, unless you need space reserved at the end of the data file (if you are using a single DFS surface) it is best to reserve 0 bytes when setting the database up.

Writing Utilities

It is possible to write extra Utilities for use with ViewStore and information on doing this is available from Acorn. However, this should only be attempted by experienced 6502 programmers who either require a utility for special use or who are planning to exploit their utilities commercially. Acorn have no copyright restrictions on others selling their own ViewStore Utilities.

The following Hints and Tips apply to ViewStore version 1.0 only:

Label Utility

On ViewStore 1.0 Utility Label does not prompt for use of the select file.

Solution: prepare a patch file as follows. Type:

```
*BASIC
?&2800 = &FF
*save patch 2800 + 1
```

Then immediately before using Utility Label enter:

```
*load patch 50
```

Utility Label will now give the 'Use select file (N,Y)' prompt.

Entering Records

On ViewStore 1.0, it is good practice when entering records to frequently force ViewStore to write the records to disc. This can be done by pressing CTRL and the down arrow. This will write all the new records safely to disc and remove any of risk of data corruption.

Report Format File Prefix

On ViewStore 1.0, different prefixes are required at different times when using Report Format files. When editing Report Format files the Format file is treated as a database and uses the Data prefix. However when using the Report Format file in the Report Utility it is treated as a Format file and so uses the Format prefix.

There are two solutions to this. If you are using the Acorn DFS you can specify the full filename when using Utility Report. So if the Report Format file is in directory R on the data drive 0, answer the question 'Report filename?' with :O.r.filename. Alternatively, before using the Report Utility, copy the file from the data drive to the format drive.

Minimal space after using the Setup Utility

In ViewStore 1.0 it is occasionally possible for the Space field at the top of the database display to be a small number, e.g. 11, rather the several thousand bytes which it should be. This can be rectified by making an entry, e.g. +30, in the record size field in the database header.

SECTION FOUR

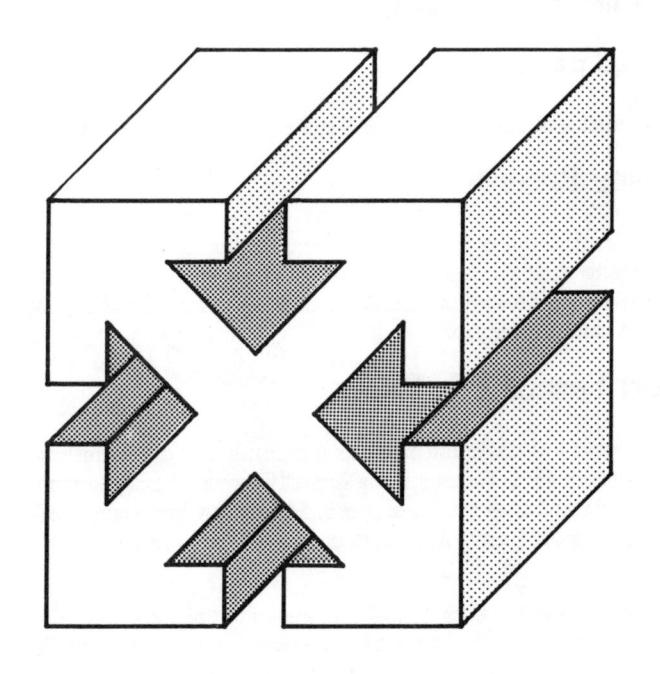

INTEGRATION

CHAPTER FOURTEEN

Integration

Linking the VIEW Products

While each of the major VIEW products – ViewSheet, ViewStore or the VIEW word processor itself – functions perfectly well individually, the software really comes into its own once data from two or more sources can be combined or linked. For example, you may want to include the contents of a ViewSheet spreadsheet as a table within a report written on the VIEW word processor, or add details of accounts held on ViewStore to a letter to your accountant. This process of exchanging data from one program to another is known as integration. You can easily achieve quite complex results like the example in Figure 14.1 by using a little forethought, and the BBC Micro's *SPOOL command.

Using textual output from ViewSheet and ViewStore in VIEW is relatively easy, but you can take integration still further using a number of other commands available in the VIEW software family. The ViewStore database has an **IMPORT** function which can be used to pull data from other database files, or files sent on electronic mail, or held in word processed files. And if you are using the OverView upgrade for the Master Series 128, there are *READ and *RC commands which can extend the use of ViewSheet. Numerous other links can be forged between the VIEW range, especially involving ViewStore, which has extra Utilities to create Macros (for use in VIEW) and Linking files to tie in with ViewSheet.

Special commands are needed to achieve the integration between the different VIEW family members because, for the most part, the data files are not compatible from one program to another. Each stores information in different ways. For example, VIEW cannot successfully LOAD or READ a ViewSheet file, and although VIEW can READ ViewStore data files, the same is not true in reverse.

```
                        ACCOUNTS   1985-86
                        ==================

Enclosed please find full details of our accounts for the year ending April
1986.  An analysis of the year's figures is followed by a breakdown of the
year's expenses and income.


                        Total Expenses    =      1985.00
                        General Expenses  =       385.00
                        Capital Expenses  =      1600.00
                        Writing Down %    =          100
                        Capital Allnce.   =      1600.00
                        Carried Forward   =         0.00
                        -----------------------------
                        Total Allowances  =      1985.00
                        Total Income      =       545.00
                        -----------------------------
                        Taxable Earnings  =     -1440.00
                        ===============================


Date       Item                        Code    Outgoings      Incomings
-----------------------------------------------------------------------
28.03.86   Disc Drives                           400.00
28.03.86   TV Monitor                            300.00
28.03.86   Computer                              500.00
29.03.86   Microwave Oven                        200.00
29.03.86   Flash Gun                             200.00

                                  Subtotals   £1600.00      £    0.00


28.03.86   Discs                                  65.00
29.03.86   Repairs to Trolley                     15.00
29.03.86   Journalism Course Fees                200.00
29.03.86   Coffee Maker                           30.00
30.03.86   Stationary                             30.00
01.04.86   Mugs x 30                              45.00

                                  Subtotals   £  385.00     £    0.00


28.03.86   Repairs to Frame                                      50.00
28.03.86   Sale of Towel                                         10.00
28.03.86   Sale of Tea Chests                                    65.00
28.03.86   Supply Coins (I Ching)                                75.00
01.04.86   Boxed Butterfly Set                                   45.00
01.04.86   Photograph of Stately Home                           300.00

                                  Subtotals   £    0.00     £  545.00
-----------------------------------------------------------------------
                                  Totals      £ 1985.00     £  545.00
-----------------------------------------------------------------------
```

Figure 14.1 A complex report using VIEW, ViewSheet and ViewStore

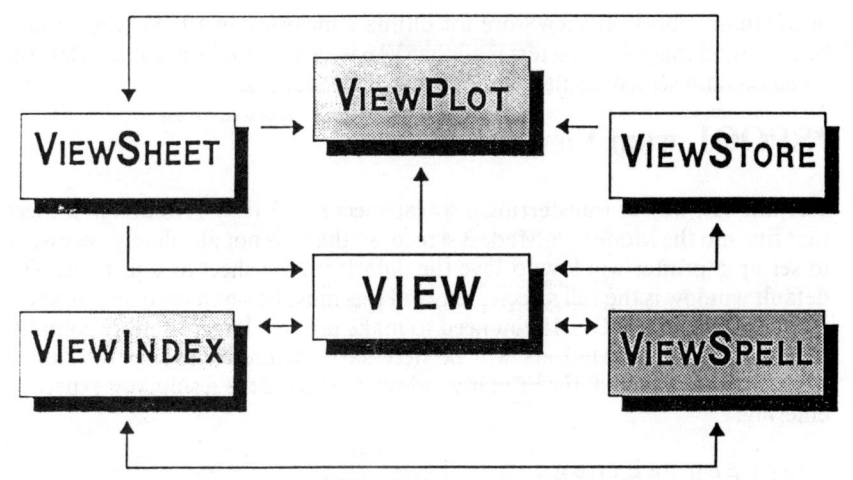

Figure 14.2 Integration between the VIEW products

Simple Exchange Using *SPOOL

The following is a useful universal routine that can be used to prepare files from ViewSheet and ViewStore for inclusion in VIEW, and can also be used when editing files on the word processor to go into ViewStore (using the IMPORT Utility), or to be sent on electronic mail, or even (as described in Chapter Seven) to make 'boot' files for the micro. The routine can also be used to edit output from ViewStore in tabular form so that it can be included in ViewSheet using the *READ Utility supplied with the OverView upgrade.

The technique when using *SPOOL is to set the software up as if it were to produce printed output, but only to SCREEN the results, not actually PRINT them. The *SPOOL command opens a disc file and saves everything that appears on the micro's screen. Hence it can only contain 'pure' ASCII characters—there are no hidden control codes which can cause incompatibility between the normal files associated with the different forms of VIEW software—the resulting file is thus suitable for incorporation in lots of other programs. When the results have been SCREENed, the new file is closed using the *SPOOL command once more, but this time without a specified filename. This has the effect of closing all the *SPOOL files that are currently open.

The thing to bear in mind when using *SPOOL is that you should prepare output from ViewSheet and ViewStore in a form that will be suitable for your finished document. If, for example, you are limited to an 80 column printout, then text from either the spreadsheet or database should ideally be restricted in width to fit into VIEW without any editing. Thus when you are laying out the data in ViewSheet, defining printer windows, or designing a database or database report on ViewStore for ultimate inclusion in VIEW, you should bear in mind that 74 characters is all that VIEW can normally accommodate on an 80 column screen display without scrolling sideways.

*SPOOL from ViewSheet

The simplest way of transferring a spreadsheet into VIEW is to design a sheet that fits into the Mode 0 or Mode 3 screen, so that it is not absolutely necessary to set up a printer window to save the data from the sheet as a text file. The default window is the full screen area, and this must be saved onto disc as a text only file using *SPOOL. If you need to make use of a larger or more complex screen area, screen windows will be necessary. Before following this simple routine, check first that the printer windows are giving the results you expect by entering:

    `SCREEN <RETURN>`

Once you are satisfied with the printer window layout, and the contents of the sheet itself, choose a name for the file to hold the ViewSheet material in ASCII form. Something in the 'A' directory would be sensible, standing for 'ASCII only' (or you may find 'T' for Text easier to remember). If you were *SPOOLing a table of results, the file could be called '`A.TABLE`', and you can open the file by entering:

    `*SPOOL A.TABLE <RETURN>`

Then **SCREEN** the data again, using:

    `SCREEN <RETURN>`

and finally enter:

    `*SPOOL <RETURN>`

to close the file. You will find that the file 'A.TABLE' is present on the disc, and that it can now be brought into VIEW using the **READ** command, or split into sections and incorporated into a database file using the ViewStore **IMPORT** Utility. (You may find it useful to put TAB characters between the different parts of the SPOOLed sheet once it is in VIEW, so that its layout can be altered using a VIEW ruler. If the results are tightly packed, you may be able to do this using the **REPLACE** command, substituting TABs for spaces where necessary. If you do not do this, make sure that you never **FORMAT** the table by mistake, as this will ruin the layout completely.)

The report shown in Figure 14.3 includes the table produced by *SPOOLing a file from the class examination results spreadsheet example in Chapter Nine.

```
CLASS OF 86 EXAM REPORT
=======================

   Pupil's           Question Number  (Marks out of 10)
   Name                  1       2        3        4      TOTAL     %age
   ----------        ---------------------------------    -----    -----
    1 Nicki              8       9        8        8        33     82.50
    2 SaraJane           8       6        9        9        32     80.00
    3 Dave               4       8        7        8        27     67.50
    4 Barbara            7      10        8        7        32     80.00
    5 Robin              6       8        9        6        29     72.50
    6 Elizabeth          7       7        9        7        30     75.00
    7 Fenella            5      10        7        8        30     75.00
    8 Barry              7       6        9        8        30     75.00
    9 Ian                6       8        6        7        27     67.50
   10 Ellen              8       5        9        8        30     75.00
   11 Merrill            5       7        8        8        28     70.00

   Highest mark         8      10        9        9        33     82.50
   Average mark       6.45    7.64     8.09     7.64     29.82     74.55

Teacher's Comments:

In general the class did very well, scoring well above average in the test.
Even the lowest marks were comfortably above the minimum standard.  Several
pupils have done extremely well, and should go on to do the school proud in
the final exams next term.  Perhaps we should consider making the test more
difficult in future if we continue to see results like these.         CDW.
```

Figure 14.3 Class exam results produced using VIEW and ViewSheet

*SPOOL from ViewStore

In the case of ViewStore, a similar routine is followed to that for ViewSheet, except that here you should run the chosen method of reporting (e.g. the **REPORT, SELECT** or **LABEL** Utility) on screen as a trial first, and when you are happy with the results, open the *SPOOL file e.g :

    *SPOOL A.DATA <RETURN>

Then run the Utility again as normal. When the reporting on screen is over, enter:

    *SPOOL <RETURN>

on its own to close the file. You will find that the file contains all the Utility questions, and also your responses, but these can easily be edited out after reading the file into VIEW.

*SPOOL from VIEW 1.4 and 2.1

First **LOAD** the text file you wish to *SPOOL, and prepare a version of the text using a suitable width ruler. This can be anything up to 132 characters for **IMPORT** or *READ, but would probably need to be 80 characters or less if the file was to be sent on electronic mail. Then set **LM, HM, TM, FM** and **BM** all to 0, and delete any headers and footers. When using VIEW 1.4 you will have to save a copy of this new file onto disc in order to SCREEN it. If you are using VIEW 2.1 you could save a copy anyway, for safety, but either way be sure to give the file a new name. We will call the file TEXT for sake of argument. The TEXT file has to be re-saved to disc using *SPOOL, to create the necessary ASCII file as follows...

```
*SPOOL A.NEWFILE
SCREEN TEXT
*SPOOL
```

We could send A.NEWFILE on electronic mail through terminal software at this stage, but unfortunately files spooled from early versions of VIEW contain a lot of unwanted material – carriage returns, the VIEW command screen header, all your instructions, and two blank lines where every page break would be – so the best thing is to tidy up the file as follows. Type NEW to empty the memory, then use the command READ A.NEWFILE to load the new version of the text. Use the Delete Line function key to delete any unwanted material, then use the SAVE command to save the file under same name (i.e. A.NEWFILE). The file is then ready for transmission or inclusion in other work.

*SPOOL from VIEW 3

One important improvement in VIEW 3 is the addition of a new PB (Page Break) stored command. This eases the problems of generating *SPOOL files considerably, as it can be used to turn off all the page formatting effects, thus producing all the contents of the file in memory as an uninterrupted stream. To use it, you should enter the command in the left-hand margin on a spare line at the top of the file, and place either a '0' or 'OFF' on the same line in the text area. All the headers, footers and margins at the top and bottom of the page are disabled (but not the effects of the LS or LM commands, which are probably best set to zero) so that when you **SCREEN** the text, the whole file is displayed in one long sequence. You can turn the Page Break effects back on again by entering '1' or 'ON' on the **PB** line, or by deleting the line completely.

Reading Files into VIEW

Any ASCII file, such as one *SPOOLed from electronic mail, or from ViewSheet, or a ViewStore Report, Label or Select Utility, can be imported into the current VIEW file using the **READ** command. The file can either be added at the end of the file, e.g :

        READ TEXT <RETURN>

or at a point in the text specified by a marker, e.g :

        READ TEXT 1 <RETURN>

which **READ**s a file to Marker 1's position. This can be a very powerful feature, because it allows data from sources other than the VIEW family of software to be included in your work, such as that from other databases or spreadsheets, from electronic mail via 'terminal' software on the BBC Micro, or from another micro via the RS423 interface.

If you try to read a *SPOOL file into VIEW 1.4 or 2.1 that uses line lengths over 132 characters long, the software may 'lock up' and refuse to give you control of the cursor, first in Text mode, then in Command mode. In this case the only thing to do is press the **BREAK** key and begin again. You can either reformat the file at its source, or re-read it, this time entering the **FORMAT** command to format the text in memory BEFORE pressing **ESCAPE** to get into Text mode! Note that if any of the text is in tabular form, the layout will almost certainly be reformatted, and hence completely ruined by this procedure.

From ViewStore to VIEW : Alternative Methods

Macros

In addition to using the *SPOOL command before running a **SELECT**, **REPORT** or **LABEL** Utility, there are two other ways of using ViewStore information in the VIEW word processor. The first involves the **MACRO** Utility, which can generate selected information from a data file in the correct Macro form needed by VIEW to make standard letters. For example, you might want to produce a set of names and addresses from the Club Secretary example given in Chapter Twelve, and use them with the letter at the end of Chapter Seven. If you are running ViewStore, you should enter:

        UTILITY MACRO <RETURN>

You will be presented with a series a questions to find which fields from the database should be included in the Macro data, i.e :

```
Use Select File(N,Y)? (answer N or Y as appropriate)
Field 1? AD1
Field 2? AD2
Field 3? AD3
Field 4? AD4
Field 5? AD5
Field 6? NAME
Field 7? <RETURN>
Two letter macro? AA
Output filename? M.CLUB
```

Once the questions have been answered, the Utility runs and produces a file called M.CLUB. This can then be **READ** into VIEW on the end of the file containing the standard letter asking for subscription renewals.

Reading Entire Database Files

An additional way of transferring data from ViewStore into VIEW is to use the **READ** command directly on a ViewStore data file. Using this approach there is no need to go through the intermediate stage of preparing an ASCII file. Thus if your ViewStore data is held in a suitable field layout to start with, it can be used without any further editing. To read a ViewStore file in from the Accounting example in Chapter Twelve, you would enter:

```
READ D.ACCOUNT <RETURN>
```

Each record in the data file will appear on a single line. A nice aspect of this feature is that TAB characters are used to separate the fields, so once ViewStore data has been **READ** into VIEW, the different fields can be laid out to taste by adjusting the TAB stops (*) on a ruler positioned immediately above the data. If you fail to adjust the TABs the data may appear in a rather odd form, the fields all bunched together in a generally illegible fashion.

Knowing that you can **READ** ViewStore files into VIEW like this, you can usefully impose restrictions at the outset on the way you design your databases. It is sensible to plan each database carefully at the initial stages. For example, the most significant fields should be placed in the first 70 or so characters, and should be formatted in such a way that the fields are in the desired order across the screen when read into VIEW. Also, it is better to put an Indexed field such as the date or surname first in a ViewStore definition, so that a list will appear in the correct sorted order, reading the fields from left to right!

(Having said that, the records will be unsorted when read into VIEW in this way, and can only appear in order of entry. This can be a little frustrating, but you can easily rectify the problem by creating a new, sorted version of the same data using the **CONVERT** Utility.)

```
F/I......*.......*......*.......*......*.......*.......*.......*.......*.(
..  ......*......*......*......*......*......*......*......*.(

Paxman   Nicola    Miss M.   Dunroamin      14, Acacia Avenue     Hornsey  Londo
Williamson Clive   Mr. C.    Soft House     Squidgy Lane                   Surbi
Allen    David     Mr. D.    36 Railway Gardens  Richmond         Surrey
Young    Sally     Miss S.   Temperate House Kew Gardens   Richmond        Surre
Simpkins           Nigel     Mr. N.    11 Tokyo Street Fulham   London
```

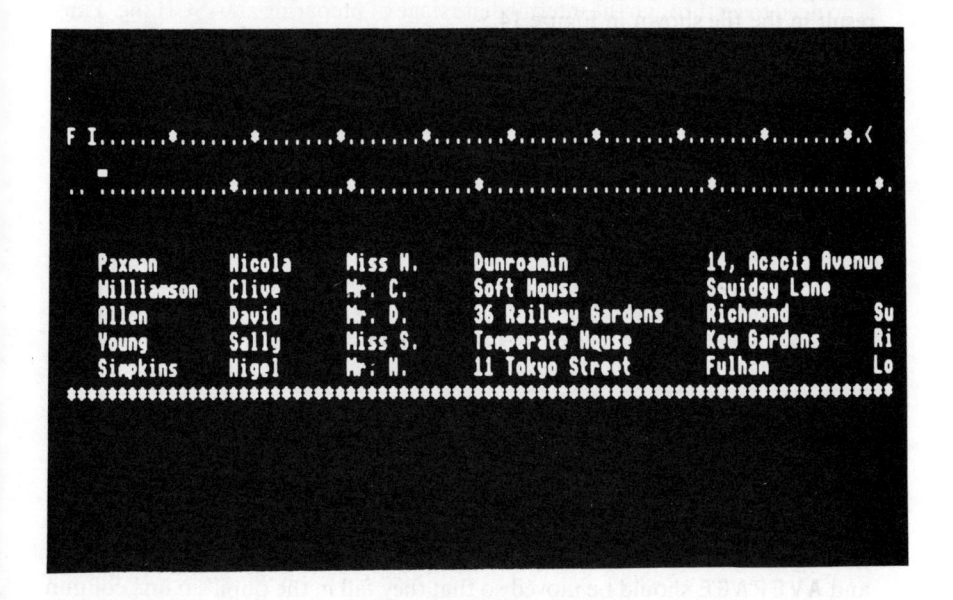

```
F I......*......*......*......*......*......*......*......*......*.(
..  ......*......*......*......*.

Paxman       Nicola    Miss M.   Dunroamin         14, Acacia Avenue
Williamson   Clive     Mr. C.    Soft House        Squidgy Lane
Allen        David     Mr. D.    36 Railway Gardens  Richmond       Su
Young        Sally     Miss S.   Temperate House   Kew Gardens      Ri
Simpkins     Nigel     Mr. N.    11 Tokyo Street   Fulham           Lo
```

Figure 14.4 ViewStore file in VIEW before and after TAB adjustment

From ViewSheet to ViewStore

You may well want to use a table of data from ViewSheet as the starting point for a database, or you may wish to translate the ViewSheet information into 'raw data' so that you can search or sort it in some way, or even analyse it using the **SELECT** Utility. ViewStore's **IMPORT** Utility and VIEW can be used to transfer ViewSheet files to these ends. The way to go about it is to prepare the sheet using printer windows as in the '*SPOOL from ViewSheet' example above. You should **READ** this file into VIEW and remove any unwanted lines from the file, at the same time noting the exact make-up of the data. In the example shown in Figure 14.5 (also taken from the 'Class of 86' spreadsheet in Chapter Nine), the printer window has been amended slightly to give columns of equal width:

```
Wi  TopL  BotR  Pos  Cw  Bw  Fmt  Opt
P0  A4    H19        9   0   FRM  TS
```

so that each column in the spooled file will be made up of one separating space followed by nine characters containing the data. This makes life a little easier when running the **IMPORT** Utility. Going through the usual *SPOOL (file name); **SCREEN**; *SPOOL routine with a file name such as A.CLASS will result in the file shown in Figure 14.5:

```
=>SCREEN
         Name       Question1     2         3         4       TOTAL     %age
         ----       ---------  --------- --------- ---------  -------  --------
      1  Nicki          8          9         8         8        33      82.50
      2  SaraJane       8          6         9         9        32      80.00
      3  Dave           4          8         7         8        27      67.50
      4  Barbara        7         10         8         7        32      80.00
      5  Robin          6          8         9         6        29      72.50
      6  Elizabeth      7          7         9         7        30      75.00
      7  Fenella        5         10         7         8        30      75.00
      8  Barry          7          6         9         8        30      75.00
      9  Ian            6          8         6         7        27      67.50
     10  Ellen          8          5         9         8        30      75.00
     11  Merrill        5          7         8         8        28      70.00

  HIGHEST MARK          8         10         9         9        33      82.50
  AVERAGE MARK       6.45       7.64      8.09      7.64     29.82      74.55
=>*SPOOL
```

Figure 14.5 A spooled file containing the ViewSheet output

The file should then be edited slightly in the VIEW word processor, so that the format is suitable for reading into the database. First, **READ** the file A.CLASS into VIEW. All unnecessary lines should be removed, i.e. the leading and trailing lines, and the underline and blank lines. Then the words **HIGHEST** and **AVERAGE** should be moved so that they fall in the pupil's name column (by deleting the word 'mark' in each case). The finished file should look like that shown in Figure 14.6.

1	Nicki	8	9	8	8	33	82.50
2	SaraJane	8	6	9	9	32	80.00
3	Dave	4	8	7	8	27	67.50
4	Barbara	7	10	8	7	32	80.00
5	Robin	6	8	9	6	29	72.50
6	Elizabeth	7	7	9	7	30	75.00
7	Fenella	5	10	7	8	30	75.00
8	Barry	7	6	9	8	30	75.00
9	Ian	6	8	6	7	27	67.50
10	Ellen	8	5	9	8	30	75.00
11	Merrill	5	7	8	8	28	70.00
	HIGHEST	8	10	9	9	33	82.50
	AVERAGE	6.45	7.64	8.09	7.64	29.82	74.55

Figure 14.6 An edited version of the ViewSheet data

SAVE a copy of this altered file (under a new file name – you may need to amend the file and try again!). The new file is the one to use with the **IMPORT** routine. Now is a good time to decide on the sort of Field names you will need for the Format file in the new database. Each column in the spreadsheet will be a new field. A suitable set for this example would be:

```
Field 1: Pupil No.
Field 2: Name
Field 3: Question 1
Field 4: Question 2
Field 5: Question 3
Field 6: Question 4
Field 7: Total
Field 8: Marks%
```

so jot these down on a piece of paper for reference before moving on to the next stage: actually running the Utility. It is important to note that IMPORT is a BASIC program, and does not run from ViewStore. After saving the final version of the file to be 'Imported', you have to enter the BASIC language first by typing:

```
*BASIC <RETURN>
```

then:

```
CHAIN"IMPORT" <RETURN>
```

to make it run. The Utility asks a set of questions designed to enable the software to split the contents of any disc file in a suitable format into its constituent parts, so that the data can be saved in a new file in the ViewStore format. The questions and answers for the example are:

```
Source File? A.CLASS2
Destination file? D.CLASS
Position in file where data starts? <RETURN>
Record separator? &D (this is a carriage return)
Appears before the first record? N
Appears after the last record? N
Field separator? <RETURN>
End of file marker? <RETURN>
Number of fields? 8
Length of field 1? 9
Length of field 2? 9
Length of field 3? 9
Length of field 4? 9
Length of field 5? 9
Length of field 6? 9
Length of field 7? 9
Length of field 8? 9
Is the data reversed? N
Leading character to skip? " "   (takes front space off each field)
Trailing character to skip? <RETURN>
ViewStore record size? +200   (leaves extra 200 characters per
                               record for comments by teacher)
```

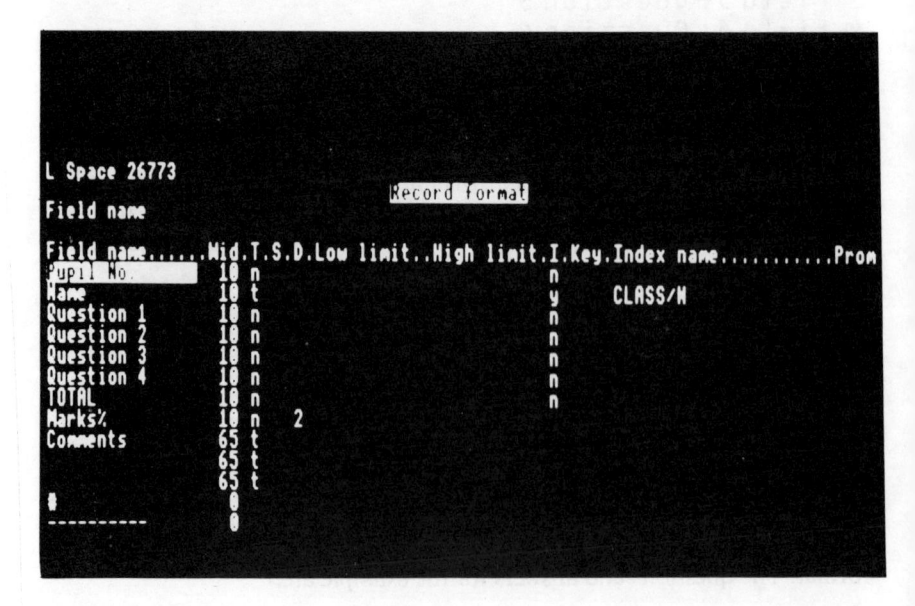

```
L Space 26773
                          Record format
Field name

Field name......Wid.T.S.D.Low limit..High limit.I.Key.Index name..........Prom
Pupil No.        10  n                            n
Name             10  t                            y    CLASS/N
Question 1       10  n                            n
Question 2       10  n                            n
Question 3       10  n                            n
Question 4       10  n                            n
TOTAL            10  n                            n
Marks%           10  n  2
Comments         65  t
                 65  t
                 65  t
#                 0
---------         0
```

Figure 14.7 Format file for the Class database

After answering all these questions, you will see the display change as the program begins reading in data from A.CLASS2 and depositing it in D.CLASS. When the sequence is complete (the display should report 13 records of eight fields each) you must then create a format file to go with the new database. The quickest way to do this is to go into ViewStore, load a database with a similar format, save its format file under a new name (SF F.CLASS), then re-load F.CLASS using the Load Format (LF) command. Edit this format file for use with the new data (with the help of the written notes from earlier) until it looks something like Figure 14.7.

Once done, you can LOAD the complete file using:

```
LOAD CLASS
```

whereupon the data will be visible in the correct fields, and can be added to and analysed as you wish. You can now edit the Header and Card displays as necessary:

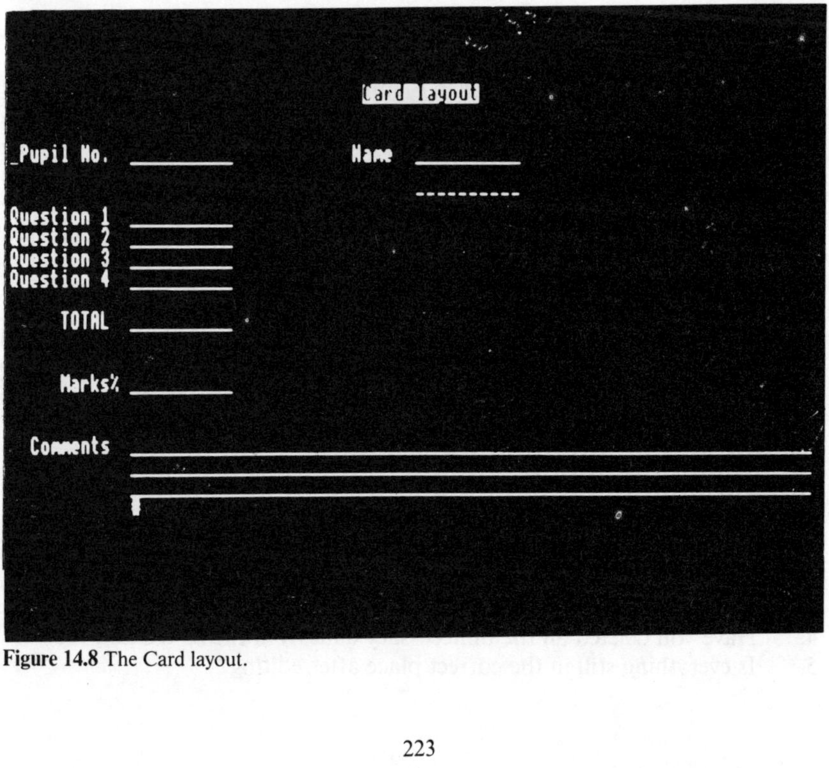

Figure 14.8 The Card layout.

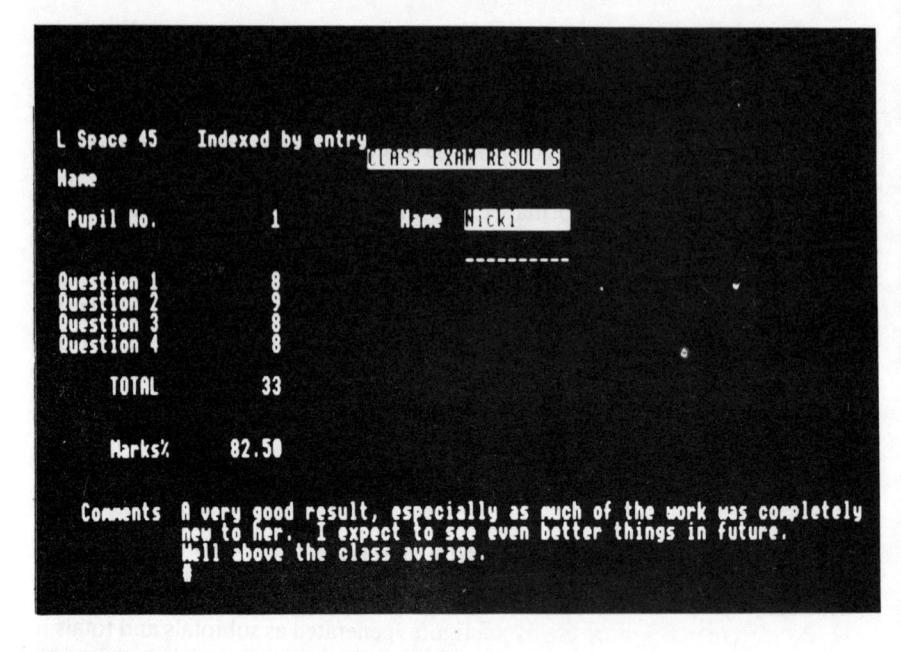

```
L Space 45    Indexed by entry
                            CLASS EXAM RESULTS
 Name
  Pupil No.            1           Name  Nicki
                                         ----------
  Question 1           8
  Question 2           9
  Question 3           8
  Question 4           8

     TOTAL            33

     Marks%         82.50

   Comments  A very good result, especially as much of the work was completely
             new to her.  I expect to see even better things in future.
             Well above the class average.
```

Figure 14.9 Sample record from 'Class' database

The final records should appear as in Figure 14.9. The last stage is to build any necessary indexes (such as pupil's name or number). The index in the example is for the Name field, and is called CLASS/N. It is built by entering a Y in the Index column of the Record Format, adding the Index name (i.e. CLASS/N) then running the **INDEX** Utility. This creates a new Index which sorts the Name fields into alphabetical order so that the Locate function key (*f7*) can be used as required to find individual pupil's results when writing their reports.

If the data is not correct throughout the database (it is a good idea to check all the way through!) then you may have to repeat the **IMPORT** Utility, having made the necessary adjustments to the intermediate VIEW file. Things to bear in mind are:

1. There is a single space at the start of each ViewSheet field.
2. There is an extra space before each new window.
3. There is a carriage return character at the end of each line.
4. Have you deleted all the unnecessary data from the SPOOLed file?
5. Is everything still in the correct place after editing?

If you do not have the VIEW word processor in your micro, you can achieve this editing by preparing a second version of the database with rows 1, 2, 3, 5 and 17 removed (see Chapter Nine). Then answer '**9**' for the '**Position?**' prompt so that the database ignores the '**=>SCREEN**' part at the beginning of the file. (Nine, not eight, because there is a carriage return character to miss at the end of the line.)

From ViewStore to ViewSheet

The standard ViewSheet program does not have an equivalent to VIEW's **READ** command, so it is not normally possible to read both textual and numerical data into a sheet unless you have the OverView upgrade for the Master Series 128 (which includes the extra command *READ described later in this chapter). What you can do, though, is use the 'linking file' feature of ViewSheet to take in numerical data previously saved in a file, and place the values in the necessary places on the sheet.

Links from the REPORT Utility

If you wish to make more use of the figures generated as subtotals and totals in the ViewStore Accounts example in Chapter Twelve, you can place them in a linking file when the **REPORT** Utility is run, then incorporate them into a spreadsheet that works out a balance for your accounts. Before doing so, decide on a name for the linking file to be set up. As already mentioned in Chapter Ten, these files should normally be in the form V.VSn (where 'n' is any number between 1 and 255), e.g. V.VS100. Amend the function key definition that produces the accounts results to read as follows:

```
*key0 U SELECT¦M F¦M ¦M TYPE ¦M DATE¦M ¦M A¦M U
REPORT¦M Y¦M S¦M Y¦MACCOUNT¦M Y¦M 2¦MV.VS100 ¦M
TYPE ¦M ¦M
```

Then when you press function key *f0*, the full select and sort routines are carried out as before, but this time the **REPORT** Utility generates the linking file containing first the two totals, then three pairs of subtotals (for the three different entries in the Type field, i.e. C)apital Expenditure, E)xpenses and I)ncome). Remember to enter the *SPOOL command followed by a filename if you wish the results to be saved for inclusion in VIEW, and a *SPOOL command once more after the Utility has been run.

The report produces a two by four linking file (V.VS100), and its contents are as follows:

```
1,1 Total Expenses         2,1 Total Income
1,2 Subtotal Capital Exps. 2,2 (blank)
1,3 Subtotal General Exps. 2,3 (blank)
1,4 (blank)                2,4 Subtotal Income
```

It is now a simple matter to set up the following spreadsheet to **READ** the relevant figures from the linking file and display the current balance of your accounts. The column width is 11 characters, and a general format of D2FM is in operation, hence Window 0 is:

```
Wi TopL BotR Pos Cw Bw Fmt Opt
 0  A1   C26     11  7 D2RM
```

```
.........A..........B...........C
......1     ACCOUNTS * 1985-86 *
......2     ======== ===========
......3
......4     Total Expenses  =      1985.00
......5
......6     General Expenses =      385.00
......7
......8     Capital Expenses =     1600.00
......9
.....10     Writing Down %  =          100
.....11
.....12     Capital Allnce. =     1600.00
.....13
.....14     Carried Forward =        0.00
.....15
.....16     TOTAL ALLOWANCE=      1985.00
.....17                          -----------
.....18
.....19     TOTAL INCOME    =      545.00
.....20                          -----------
.....21
.....22
.....23     TAXABLE EARNINGS =   -1440.00
.....24                          ===========
.....25
```

Figure 14.10 A spreadsheet to use linked files from the Accounts database in Chapter 12

The formulae on the sheet are as follows:

C4: READ(100,1,1)   (takes the Total Expenses figure from linking file)

C6: READ(100,1,3)   (takes General Expenses Sub-total from file)
C8: READ(100,1,2)   (takes Capital Expenses Sub-total from file)
C10:   Contains the rate of writing down allowance on capital expenditure for the year in question.
C12: C8*C10/100   (calculates amount of Capital allowances to be claimed in this tax year)
C14: C8-C12   (this is the remainder of Capital allowances to be carried forward to the next tax year – in this case zero, but normally a sizable sum if allowance on capital expenditure is around 25%)
C16: C6+C12   (the sum of actual allowances for the year)
C19: READ(100,2,1)   (this takes the Income Total from the linking file)
C23: C19-C16   (the taxable income for the year)

The linked spreadsheet can also be *SPOOLed to create a file for use in VIEW, so a complete report can be prepared for your accountant, or for the tax office, using all three VIEW products.

Using the Linking Utility from ViewStore to ViewSheet

A more direct way of integrating data held in ViewStore files with a ViewSheet spreadsheet is to set up linking files by running the ViewStore LINK Utility. This takes numerical data from up to 255 records and passes it to a spreadsheet via a linking file on disc. At least 42 different fields can be linked in this way, depending on whether or not you are using the maximum 255 records. To establish a linking file you should first load the required database. (You could enter 'LIST' at this stage to remind yourself of the field names.) Then enter:

    UTILITY LINK

The software prompts for the names of the fields from which data is to be taken, rejecting any attempt to use a field that contains textual data. Remember that only numerical data can be held in linking files. ViewStore then asks for a name to give to the linking file, and this should be in the form V.VSn as before. The linking file will then be created, and you can either transfer it to a disc containing the necessary ViewSheet spreadsheet, or (if the disc has enough spare space) set the sheet up on the same disc. You will need to go through this procedure each time the data in the database is changed, since ViewStore does not update the linking files automatically, and it may be worth setting up the instruction sequence as a function key definition so that the routine can easily be repeated.

Numbers stored in the linking file are read into the spreadsheet as before using **READ(x,y,z)** where x is the number of the linking file, y is the column and z the row number inside the file itself. An example that makes good use of this facility is that of a store of weather observations, where the value of the information is greatly increased by the ability to perform complex calculations on the data to obtain averages, and maximum and minimum values. The data could be collected as a classroom project, and could equally be a set of measurements from any scientific or statistical observations!

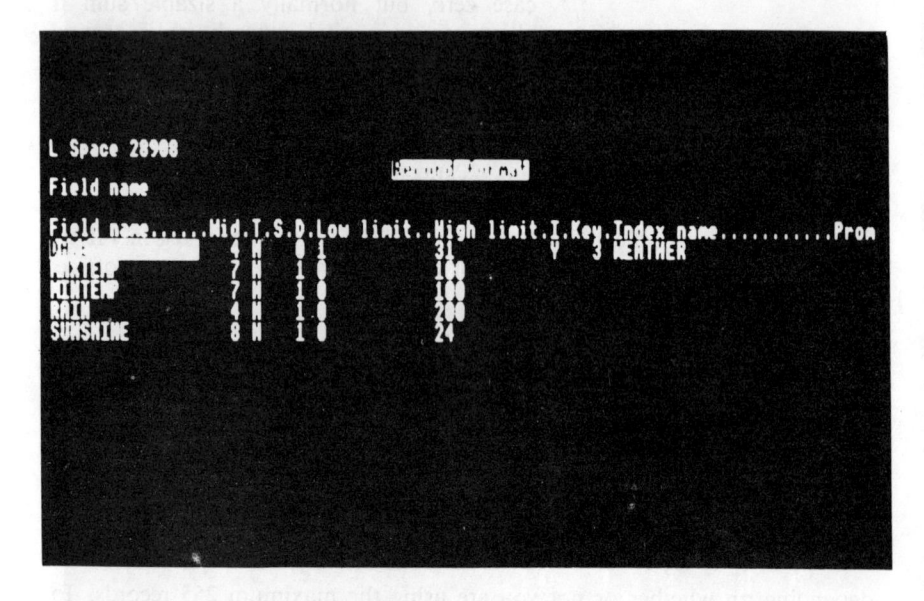

Figure 14.11 A Record format to display weather data in ViewStore

The dialogue required to set up a linking file to contain the maximum and minimum temperatures, total rainfall and number of hours sunshine is:

```
=>LIST
1 DATE          2 MAXTEMP       3 MINTEMP       4 RAIN
5 SUNSHINE
=>UTILITY LINK
LINK
Use select file (N,Y)? N
Field 1? DATE
Field 2? MAXTEMP
Field 3? RAIN
Field 4? SUNSHINE
```

```
Field 5? <RETURN>
4 Fields
Output file name? V.VS200
Creating File.........................
File is 4 by 30
```

A spreadsheet that uses these figures is shown in Figure 14.13.

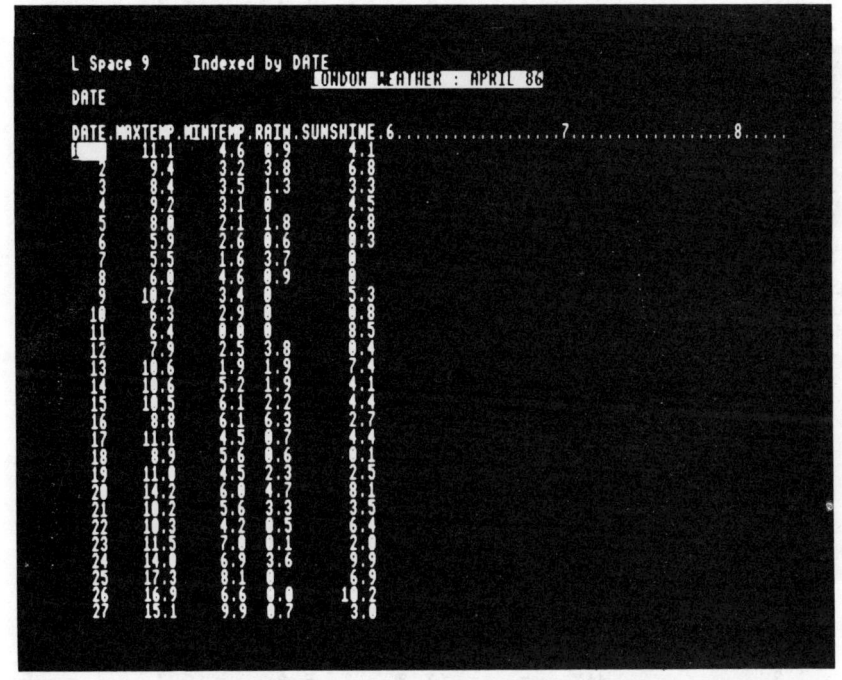

Figure 14.12 The ViewStore version of the weather data (spreadsheet style display) *(Data reproduced by permission of the Meteorological Office,.)*

Rows 42 and 44 contain the formulae which produce totals from the sets of values for the month's rainfall and sunshine figures, while Row 40 gives the average value for the month, and rows 38 and 39 give the maximum and minimum values. The sheet has an overall format of D1RM (although column B is altered to FRM), and the column width is eight characters. The formulae required to set up the sheet and read the data from the linking files are:

229

```
........A........B........C........D........E........F
......1        LONDON'S WEATHER    APR 86
......2        ========  ========  ========
......3
......4        DATE      MAXTEMP   RAINFALL  SUNSHINE
......5                  deg. C    mm        hrs
......6        --------  --------  --------  --------
......7              1     11.1      0.9       4.1
......8              2      9.4      3.8       6.8
......9              3      8.4      1.3       3.3
.....10              4      9.2      0.0       4.5
.....11              5      8.0      1.8       6.8
.....12              6      5.9      0.6       0.3
.....13              7      5.5      3.7       0.0
.....14              8      6.0      0.9       0.0
.....15              9     10.7      0.0       5.3
.....16             10      6.3      0.0       0.8
.....17             11      6.4      0.0       8.5
.....18             12      7.9      3.8       0.4
.....19             13     10.6      1.9       7.4
.....20             14     10.6      1.9       4.1
.....21             15     10.5      2.2       4.4
.....22             16      8.8      6.3       2.7
.....23             17     11.1      0.7       4.4
.....24             18      8.9      0.6       0.1
.....25             19     11.0      2.3       2.5
.....26             20     14.2      4.7       8.1
.....27             21     10.2      3.3       3.5
.....28             22     10.3      0.5       6.4
.....29             23     11.5      0.1       2.0
.....30             24     14.0      3.6       9.9
.....31             25     17.3      0.0       6.9
.....32             26     16.9      0.0      10.2
.....33             27     15.1      0.7       3.0
.....34             28     16.2      0.0      10.2
.....35             29     15.3      0.0      10.7
.....36             30     16.0      0.0       5.8
.....37
.....38        MAX  =    17.3        6.3      10.7
.....39        MIN  =     5.5        0.0       0.0
.....40        AVGE =    10.8        1.5       4.8
.....41
.....42        TOTAL RAINFALL      45.6 mm
.....43
.....44        TOTAL SUNSHINE     143.1 hrs
```

Figure 14.13 Weather details as displayed in ViewSheet via the linking files. *(Data reproduced by permission of the Meteorological Office.)*

```
B7: READ(200,COL-1,ROW-6)
then replicate B7 from C7 to E7
Replicate range to range from B7E7 to B8B36
C38: MAX(C7C36)        then replicate C38 from D38 to E38 (relatively)
C39: MIN(C7C36)        then replicate C39 from D39 to E39 (relatively)
```

```
C40: AVERAGE(C7C36)   then replicate C40 from D40 to E40 (relatively)
D42: D7D36            (gives total rainfall)
D44: E7E36            (gives total sunshine)
```

To tidy up the DATE column use *f6* (Edit Slot Format) for slot B7 (change to FRM) and then re-replicate B7 from B8 to B36.

The screen window is:

```
Wi  TopL  BotR  Pos  Cw  Bw  Fmt   Opt
0   A1    F26        8   7   D1RM
```

while the windows to print out the sheet are:

```
Wi  TopL  BotR  Pos  Cw  Bw  Fmt   Opt
P0  A1    B44        8   0   FRM   ST
```

```
Wi  TopL  BotR  Pos  Cw  Bw  Fmt   Opt
P1  C1    E44   R0   8   0   D1RM  ST
```

The *READ command gets round the problem of only being able to pass numerical data in linking files, since it can take data from any ASCII or ViewStore file, and read it into a sheet, starting at a specified slot. This feature is described in more detail in the section on OverView at the end of this chapter.

VIEWPLOT

ViewPlot can be used to obtain graphical output from the VIEW family, either through ASCII files obtained using the ***SPOOL** command, or through linking files from ViewSheet or ViewStore. In the former case, data is prepared in ASCII form complete with labels, and read into ViewPlot by a special ***PREPARE** Utility supplied on the ViewPlot disc. A new SPOOL file must be created each time a graph is required from fresh data on the sheet. In the case of a linking file, data is constantly amended in the file itself, but here (once again) only numerical data can be passed in the file, so labels have to be added afterwards using ViewPlot's editing facilities.

Graphs can be obtained in three forms: pie charts, bar graphs (also known as 'histograms') and line graphs, and the results can either be delivered on hard copy using a screen dump routine (one is supplied for Epson FX compatible dot matrix printers), shown on screen as part of a report or presentation, or photographed and used as necessary in slide or print form.

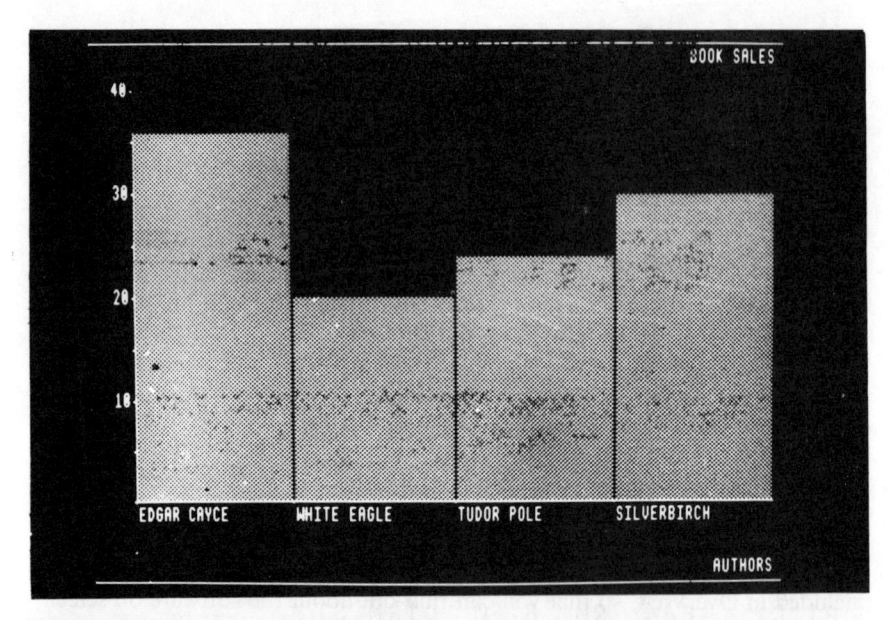

Figure 14.14 A bar graph produced on ViewPlot

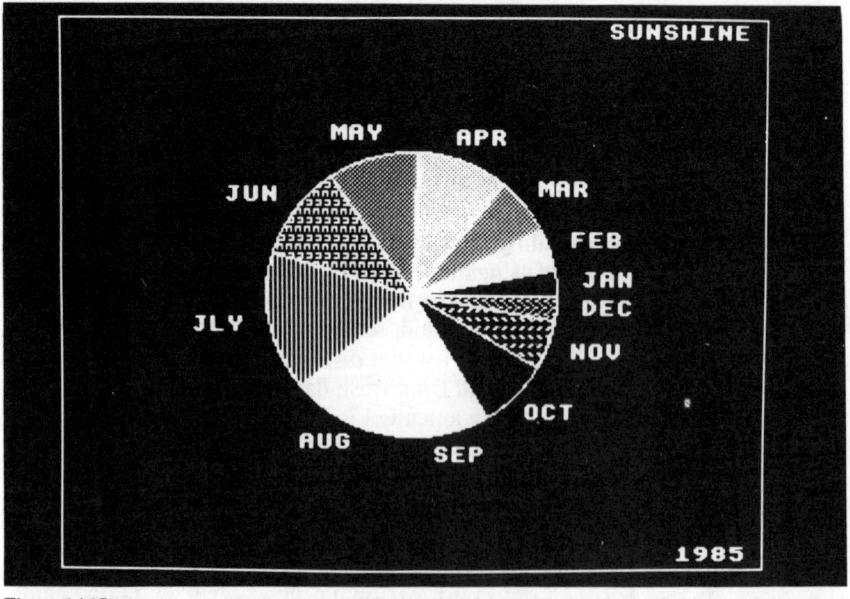

Figure 14.15 Pie chart showing annual weather conditions.

ViewPlot can also display figures and labels that have been entered directly (i.e. without the use of files from ViewSheet or ViewStore). A wide variety of displays is possible by virtue of changing the screen colours used, and by incorporating patterned effects as well as solid colour. Several sets of data can be shown on one chart if required.

OVERVIEW

One way of obtaining all the VIEW family of software for the Master Series 128 is to buy an upgrade called 'OverView', which consists of all the disc-based programs (ViewPlot, ViewIndex and the View Printer Drivers), documentation, and a plug-in ROM cartridge. The cartridge holds ViewSpell and ViewStore, as well as a number of useful new Utilities in the form of 'star' commands for the micro. Once the cartridge is in place, the following are available:

*HELP

A comprehensive set of 'Help' information about all four VIEW languages is included in OverView, so that you can find out about the software on screen without the need to refer to manuals so often.

*WIDE

Enables more characters to be shown on the standard BBC Micro screen display modes. It works in any of the two-colour modes (0,3,4,6 and their shadow equivalents) and gives 106 characters instead of 80, or 53 characters instead of 40. The 106 column display is very difficult to read on normal TV sets and low resolution monitors, but perfectly legible on high resolution monitors, and is very useful when you need to see large parts of a ViewSheet spreadsheet in one go. The 53 column display is a good size for medium and low resolution monitors, once again giving a bigger window onto your work. The effect is activated by entering *WIDE ON, and de-activated by typing *WIDE OFF.

*KEEP

This is an interesting new command geared to better integration of the VIEW range. The 'Keeper' can set up a large file – either on disc or in the Master's sideways RAM area – to hold the entire state and memory of the computer when you change from one VIEW language to another. For example, if you were writing a document on the VIEW word processor but needed to refer to ViewSheet to *SPOOL a table of information for inclusion in your document, you would normally SAVE your text from the word processor, enter ViewSheet and do the work there, then restart VIEW, having to reload the text file you were working on and any special set up instructions. If the Keeper is active when you do this however, the text, marker positions, state of justification and formatting, and so on – in fact the entire contents of memory – are saved in the disc file, or in the spare sideways RAM area in the Master. You can then do what you like using another language: on returning to VIEW you will find everything there just as you left it. The format for the *KEEP command is *KEEP ON and *KEEP OFF, and the command can be followed by the optional specification of a disc drive to hold the *KEEP file, so this does not have to be held on the current drive if you have a multi-drive system. If several languages are 'kept' on disc, they will all be stored separately so that you can retrieve them all, either during the current session, or later (having switched the micro off completely!).

*READ

*READ is another useful command in an integrated system, allowing the contents of ASCII files to be read into ViewSheet at a specified location, so that data in the form of numbers or words can be incorporated into spreadsheets from other sources, including the other VIEW programs. For example, **READ TABLE A1** would read in the contents of a SPOOLed file called TABLE, placing each separate item in a new slot starting at A1, and moving down to a new line whenever it sees a carriage return. The command interprets spaces or TAB characters as the signal to move on to a new slot, so any text that contains spaces should be deleted and added to the sheet later. Alternatively the spaces could be replaced with another character such as an underline before running the command.

*RC

This command (Read Contents) enables ViewSheet to read a list of slot contents from one sheet into another, as if they had been typed in, and effectively allows the merging of two or more spreadsheets. If you have a spreadsheet (or part of a sheet) that you wish to incorporate in a second sheet, you can prepare a version of the source spreadsheet so that its slot references correspond to gaps on the second. A list of the desired slot contents can be obtained from this source sheet by turning off the printer (using the command *FX 5,0), opening a *SPOOL file to hold the information, then using the **PC** command to 'print the contents' of the first sheet. The *SPOOL file is then closed, and the second sheet loaded in. The *RC command can then read the contents of the file and enter them on the sheet slot by slot. (The Printer is turned back on at some stage using *FX 5,1 for a parallel printer, or *FX 5,2 for a serial one.)

INDEX

!BOOT 94
*ACCESS 91
*CDIR 149, 164
*COMPACT 24
*FX 11 82
*FX 12 82
*HELP 234
*KEEP 233
*KEY 90
*OPT 4,3 94
*PREPARE 231
*RC 234
*READ 225, 234
*SPOOL 146, 211, 213
*TV 42
*WIDE 233
80 character display 43
Abbreviations (of commands) 81
Accounting (spreadsheet application) ... 142
Address labels 100
ADFS 22, 25
Administration database 190
Advanced Disc Filing System 23
Altering text 34
AND 174
ASCII 92
Auto-entry (ViewSheet) 113
AVERAGE 122

BACKUP 74
Bad file 207
Bar graphs 232
BASIC, returning to 11
BBC Micro 9
Beginning of field 166
BM 68
Bold 61
Books, printing 94
Border width 139
Bottom margin 54
BREAK key 40
Bw 139

Calculation, order of 141
Can't Extend 73, 74, 204
Card layout 168
Cassettes 22
Cat Full 74
CE 52, 58

Centronics interface 13
Change display 168
Change 87
Chapters 57
CLOSE 75
Colours, screen 12
Column width 112, 139
Command mode 35
COMPACT 72, 74
Conditional operators 134, 172
Continuous processing 70
CONVERT 181
COPY 74
Copying text 90
Corrupt databases 207
CREATE 149
CTRL key 37
Cursor keys 35
Cursor, speeding up 81
Cw 139

Database format 164
Database 6
Databases 157
Define Macro 96
Delete character 166
Delete command 51
Delete end of field 166
DELETE 36, 51
Delimiters 55
DFS 22, 203
Disc drives 22
Disc Full 74
DM 97
Dot Matrix 13

Edit command 50
EDIT 71
Editing report format files 206
Electron 10
Electronic mail 216
EM 96
End Macro 96
EP 95
Epson 63
Error Messages 74
ESCAPE key 35, 46
Even Page 95
Extended highlights 63

235

F.Report 204
Facit 63
Field list 178
Fields 157
File Open 75
Files 157
Finding words 85
FINISH 73
FM 54, 68
FOLD 89
Footer margin 54
Footers 47, 55, 57
Format Block 39
FORMAT 214
Function key strip 111

Graphs 231

Half1 and Half2 178
Hard discs 21
Header margin 54
Headers 47, 55, 57
Help pages 59
HI-VIEW 69
Highlight 140
Highlights, extended 63
Highlights 63
Histograms 231
HM 68

IMPORT 211, 214, 220
Index field 170
INDEX 224
Indexes, rebuilding 203
Indexes 103
Insert character 166
Integration 7, 211
Interfaces 13
Interlace effect 42

Juki 63
Justification 33, 35, 39

LABEL utility 179
LABEL 171, 181
Labels 100
Left margin 52
Library database 197
Line layout 58
Line Spacing 53
Linking files 147
LJ 52, 58
LM 52
LOAD 25, 44
Loading files 24

Locate 171
Locked 75
LS 53

Macros 96, 217
Mailing lists 179
Mailshots 181
Margin, left 52
Margins 48
Markers 83
Masks 147
Master series 166
Mathematical functions 134
Mathematical operators 132
Mathematics (ViewSheet) 115
MAX 122
Memory driver 67
Memory Printer Driver 45
Memory, available 44
Memory, running out of 69
Microspacing 64
Mode 7 42
Monitors 11, 12

NAME 24, 111
Near letter quality 14
New page, forcing a 53
Next Window 145, 146
NLQ 14, 32
No Text 75
Number registers 56

Odd Page 95
OLD 41
OP 95
OR 174
OverView upgrade 211
OVERVIEW 233

Page Break 101
Page break 68, 216
Page eject 53
Page layout 46, 47
Page length 52
Page numbering 47
PB 68, 101, 216
PE 53
Pie charts 231
PLUS 1 10
PLUS 3 10
Portions of text, saving and loading 84
Pound sign 65
PREFIX 163
Price-lists 124
PRINT 45

236

Printer buffer	17
Printer driver, making your own	64
Printer drivers	16, 61, 140, 205
Printer functions, switching	17
Printer menu	17
Printer windows	122, 140
Printers	13
Printing (from the VIEW family)	61
Printing (from ViewSheet)	119
Printing from VIEW	45
PROTECT	141
Protecting spreadsheets	117
QUIT	73
READ	73, 146
Records	157
Reformatting	39
Release margins	49
REPLACE	214
Replace	33, 87
Replication	115, 126
Report formats	176
REPORT utility	174, 225
Report utility	203
Reports	175
Ricoh	63
RJ	52, 58
RS232 interface	13
RS423 interface	13, 15
Ruler, default	47
Ruler	47
SAVE	44
Saving files	24
Scratch pad	83
Screen colours, changing	12
Screen display	43
Screen dumps	231
Screen modes	41
Screen windows	144
Screen, types of	11
SCREEN	44, 55, 120, 213
Scrolling fields	204
Search	33
SEARCH	85
Searching (database)	171
Second Processor	9
Select utlity	204
SELECT	171
Setting registers	56
SETUP	94, 163, 176
Shadow RAM	9
SHEETS	45, 46, 95
Spreadsheet design	141

Spreadsheet	5
Spreadsheets as databases	129
Spreadsheets	107
SR	56
Standard letters	96, 181
Start file	57
Stored Commands	50
Stored commands	68
TAB stops	47
TAB	49, 88, 160
Text colour	12
Text mode	35
TM	54, 68
Top margin	54
Turbo co-processor	10
Turbo	17
Underline	61
Upper and lower case	89
VDU 19	12
VIEW 1.4, problems with	75
VIEW 1.4	216
VIEW 2.1, problems with	76
VIEW macros	96
VIEW	29
ViewIndex	103
VIEWPLOT	232
ViewSheet and ViewStore	220
ViewSheet, problems with	142
ViewSheet	107
ViewSpell	102
ViewStore, running	162
ViewStore	157
Wild characters	166, 172
Wild Search	88
WILD	88
Wildcard characters	205
Winchester discs	23
Window parameters	138
Windows, in ViewSheet	137
Windows	112
Word Processor	4
Word-wrap	32
Words, finding	85
WRITE	84
WYSIWYG	33
XWORD program	77

An Invitation

Sigma Press is still expanding—and not just in computing, for which we are best known. Our marketing is handled by John Wiley and Sons Ltd, the UK subsidiary of a major American publisher. With our speed of publication and Wiley's marketing skills, we can make a great success of your book on both sides of the Atlantic.

Currently, we are looking for new authors to help us to expand into many exciting areas, including:

> Laboratory Automation
> Communications
> Electronics
> Professional Computing
> New Technology
> Personal computing
> Artificial Intelligence
> General Science
> Engineering Applications

If you have a practical turn of mind, combined with a flair for writing, why not put your talents to good use? For further information on how to make a success of your book, write to:

Graham Beech, Editor-in-Chief, Sigma Press,
98a Water Lane, Wilmslow, Cheshire SK9 5BB
or, phone 0625-531035